MONSTERS AND MIRACLES

HORROR, HEROES AND THE HOLOCAUST

IRA WESLEY KITMACHER

CONTENTS

Introduction	ix

PART I
A SIMPLE LIFE

Bustling, Simple Life before the Torches and Pitchforks	3
Jewish, Polish, and German Folklore, Monsters, and Miracles	15
Early Christian and German Views of Jews. Dr. Jekyll and Mr. Hyde (Good or Evil)	29
The Kitmachers	48
The Harris Family	68

PART II
EVIL AT THE GATE

Nazis Invade and the Holocaust Begins	87
America, the Allies, the Holocaust, and Superheroes	109
America before World War II	120
Hope, Miracles, and Extraordinary Interventions	124
America Enters the War	129
Nightmare	134
In the Navy	140
In Hell	150
Dreams and More Miracles	159

PART III
GOOD PREVAILS

Back to Civilian Life	171
Freedom	175
Al and Pearl Together—Hope Realized	185
Stepping Back in Time—a Return to Germany and End of Life	194
Why It Happened: Grim Reality, Black Holes, and Hope Survives	203

About the Author	219
Kind Request	221
Bibliography and Filmography	223
Notes	237
Amsterdam Publishers Holocaust Library	245

ISBN 9789493276239 (ebook)

ISBN 9789493276215 (paperback)

ISBN 9789493276222 (hardcover)

Publisher: Amsterdam Publishers, The Netherlands

info@amsterdampublishers.com

This book is part of the series Holocaust Survivor True Stories WWII

Copyright © Ira Wesley Kitmacher, 2022

Cover image: Angel wings, 2020. Courtesy of sergeitokmakov, Pixabay.

All rights reserved. No part of this book may be reproduced or transmitted in any form or by any means, electronic or mechanical, including photocopying and recording, or by any information storage and retrieval system, without permission in writing from the publisher, except for brief quotations in critical reviews and articles.

I dedicate this book to my beloved family: my wife, Wendy; son, David; daughter Gabi; sisters Lois and Miriam; and brother Gary.
I also dedicate this book to my parents, Al and Pearl Kitmacher, who were the best parents I could have asked for. Any errors, omissions, and personal opinions are entirely my own. Thank you to Gabi for lending her editing skills to this project.

INTRODUCTION

There have been many books and movies written and made about the Holocaust. Why then am I writing this book? Mainly it is to honor my father and mother, Al Kitmacher and Pearl Harris, both of whom were heroes: I lost my father in 2000 and my mother in 2016. My father, through his intelligence, resourcefulness, and use of prescient dreams and other extraordinary interventions, survived the Warsaw Ghetto, Nazi death, concentration, and slave labor camps, and overcame the horrors of the Holocaust. He later successfully emigrated to the United States and created a family and career despite knowing no one and speaking no English. My mother overcame the norms for women and her parents' objections by serving in the U.S. Navy WAVES (Women Accepted for Volunteer Emergency Service) during World War II. Through her military service, she helped fellow Jews suffering at the hands of the Nazis.

Secondly, it is to breathe life into the times and the spirits of those lost to this nightmare, including virtually all my father's European family. I seek to give these family members, and others who were lost, a voice. I tell their stories, invoking the senses of seeing, smelling, hearing, and feeling.

In attempting to make the story "stick," I have taken a cinematic view of the Holocaust. The cinematic construct of the Holocaust is one-part horror and the other hero and superhero story, and it is through this lens by which I tell the story. The forces of good, right, and benevolence overcome those of evil, wrongdoing, and wickedness. I firmly believe that by reexamining the Holocaust, and through our joint humanity and hope, we can stop a similar nightmare from occurring.

As a second-generation Holocaust survivor, I strongly believe we each must bear witness to this horror and help people to never forget. We the Jewish people must tell and write about the Holocaust effectively. If not, our voices may be replaced by antisemitic views that discount what we know is true.

Lastly, I seek to provide a cautionary tale of the similarities between the 1920s–1940s and the 2020s, the conditions of which gave and are giving rise to forces of Nazism, fascism, White nationalism, and intolerance.

The transfer of memory into writing is especially urgent for children of survivors, who often feel the need to fulfill their task of imploring the world not to forget the horror and lesson of the Holocaust. Many members of the second generation of Holocaust survivors have felt the call to write about their experience, their parents' experience, or both—myself included. Some felt it their duty to bear witness to these horrors, while others have come to it more gradually.

In writing this book, I combined my interests in Jewish history, my family's story, folklore, the supernatural, horror, hero and superhero stories, and movies. This is truly a story that starts "in the light," enters and stays in a long period of dark and reenters the light after World War II. One-third of Jews alive before the Holocaust were killed; two-thirds, or six million, European Jews were killed, leaving three million alive. Six million is the minimum number murdered, as thousands of babies were killed before their births were recorded.

I believe there is no way to fully understand the Holocaust and why we are experiencing a resurgence of Nazism, fascism, and White nationalism without first understanding the underlying Jewish, Polish, and German tenets surrounding good and evil, angels and demons, folklore, miracles, the supernatural, monsters, heroes, and superheroes. Of course, the Holocaust is far more terrifying than any imaginary horror story because it really happened. Through the lenses of a horror, hero, and superhero story, I do my best to give color and dimension to the times, lives, and spirits affected by the Holocaust while ensuring the voices of those involved are not lost or diluted by the thematic elements I introduce in this narrative.

As I researched and wrote this book, I found myself greatly affected by the brutality, outright inhumanity, raw courage, and prevailing hope that was present. If the Holocaust weren't true, it would almost be impossible to imagine such horror. Further, it has caused me to examine my own "Jewishness," along with the stark reminder that I am only one generation away from suffering these terrors. Throughout my life, I have been keenly aware of and taken great pride in my Jewish background. At the same time, I have been purposely guarded in my relationships, viewing my religion as a personal matter and one that I do not ordinarily share—except for with those with whom I am close. I am sure I have learned from my father the need to demonstrate minimal trust. I have also been sensitive to my first name Ira, which is a Jewish name. No doubt this is at least partly based on my inherited fear of how strangers and acquaintances may react to my background. I discuss this in more detail, as well as the whims of history and nature that caused my father and his family to suffer, while I enjoy the comforts of growing up and living in late 20th- and early-21st-century America.

I also tell the story of the United States from the 1920s through the 1940s, with America as one of the protagonists that opposed the evil Nazis. The imaginary superheroes Captain America, Superman, Rosie the Riveter, and others were Jewish creations who argued and pushed for America's entry into the war against the Nazis. The superhero Wonder Woman also has strong connections to a Jewish author and an Israeli Jewish actress. A superhero is a protagonist with superhuman capabilities. I tell my mother's story, as she joined those opposed to the monsters by way of the WAVES. The stakes and costs could not have been higher as victims and allies alike sought to survive and protect their loved ones. The lives of millions were hanging in the balance.[1][2][3][4][5]

I explore what each protagonist and family member was or may have been thinking as well as their courage, compassion, and other emotions. I would love to sit down with my parents and ask them specific questions that didn't occur to me while they were living. Where person-specific information is unavailable, primarily with my father's European family, I describe what others who were similarly situated experienced and what I believe these family members may have been feeling and thinking. My goal is not to fictionalize their story but to give them a voice that the Holocaust did not allow them to have.

I reflect on the millions of people who lived and died during World War II and the Holocaust and who are not remembered. Though I focus on the six million Jewish victims of the Holocaust, there were many other people murdered by the Nazis. They included the physically and mentally disabled, Roma (Gypsies), Poles, Jehovah's Witnesses, homosexuals, courageous resisters, priests and pastors, and others. It is estimated that 40 million individuals died at the hands of the Nazis during the war.

Some may argue that human history is full of hatred and atrocities committed by humans against their fellow humans, and therefore the Holocaust is not unique. No doubt it is true that hatred and atrocities have occurred throughout history. However, many factors make the Holocaust unique. The Nazis' "Final Solution" was created to exterminate every Jewish man, woman, and child; being of Jewish birth was considered sufficient reason to murder; the extermination of the Jews had no reasonable political or economic justification; and the Holocaust was carried out primarily by average citizens who were members of a society that had, in previous generations, been active and engaged citizens. Prior generations of this society had significant positive impacts on writing, music, and culture in the region. Jewish children were targeted as they posed the risk of growing up and parenting future generations of Jews.

Concentration and slave labor camps, and other locations of Nazi terror, represent tears in history's moral and ethical fabric, black holes from which little escaped. They are seemingly straight out of the 1950s–1960s American paranormal and supernatural television series *The Twilight Zone*. The atrocities committed may be beyond understanding. The horrors inflicted on the innocent Jewish and non-Jewish victims at these locations scream out for silent prayer.[678]

Love and pain transcend generations. We cannot lose sight of or forget the people who lived, loved, hoped, demonstrated strength and resilience, experienced triumphs, and losses, prayed, dreamed, worried, and lost their lives in this nightmare. It is not possible to know each person who was murdered by the Nazis. But for those we know of who suffered, we can try to give them a voice and a name.

European Antisemitism, Folklore, and Superstition Fed the Holocaust

Europe has long been a bastion of wild, outrageous antisemitism. Antisemitism is the baseless hatred of Jews that has stretched across the centuries and all lands. It is also a political movement and ideology that arose in Central Europe in the late 1800s and reached its zenith during the Holocaust. It is an irrational hatred of Jews originating in Christianity's conflict with its Jewish roots. Antisemitism ranges from prejudices to a paranoid hatred of Jews as a race out to destroy civilization. When many Jews declined to follow Christianity's breakaway, hostility was inevitable.

Scorned as outsiders and strangers, labeled as criminals, and blamed for everything from poverty to disease, Jews suffered millennia of persecution, intolerance, and horrific violence. Antisemitism continues in many areas of today's world, including through folklore, stereotypes, conspiracy theories, violence, and other means. These tragedies raise the question of why hatred of Judaism runs so deeply, in so many disparate cultures. To eliminate this hatred, we must first understand it. Few methods of examining the roots of antisemitism are more revealing than studying folktales and local stereotypes concerning the Jewish people. We must then fight against this hatred, as ignoring it or "turning the other cheek" is ineffective, as proven by the attempted appeasement of Hitler by British Prime Minister Neville Chamberlain before World War II.

I also explore the superstitions, folklore, beliefs in the

supernatural, and Eastern European horror and other stories underpinning Polish, German, and Jewish points of view. However, folklore and stories pale in comparison to the very real, non-supernatural threat of human hatred that has served as the true Jewish horror genre. This hatred reached its zenith with the Holocaust.

While some folklore can be benign or entertaining, other types can be dangerous and give rise to conspiracy theories and antisemitism, resulting in violence and persecution.

Horror, Hero, and Superhero Construct

Horror stories have been described as stories or allegories that contain moral meaning in the guise of monsters and other supernatural beings. They may reflect the anxieties of the time or warn and predict anxieties yet to come. These stories are used to deliver a broader message about real-world issues. While allegories are often imagined stories, the Holocaust was a very real tale. Why a horror story construct? The Nazis viewed the Jews and other "subhuman" peoples as outsiders, strangers, and backstabbing vampires draining the blood of the Fatherland by way of its wealth and resources. German history unfolded similarly as Robert Louis Stevenson's 1886 novella *Dr. Jekyll and Mr. Hyde*, and the 1941 movie starring Fredric March based on it. It was a battle to see if the cultured Germans or the bloodthirsty Nazis would rule the culture. In the story, March's character is a doctor who invents a formula that releases his inner demon. The Nazis saw themselves as honorable werewolves, members of a pack protecting the blood and soil of the homeland against invading vampires sucking the lifeblood out of the homeland.[9,10]

The Jews and other persecuted peoples saw and felt themselves living through a nightmare, where their only offense was being a member of a group. Some, like my father, attempted to be "invisible" to the monsters, to fade into the background and not call attention to themselves. These attempts were in line with science fiction stories and movies like *The Invisible Man*, the H.G. Wells 1897 character, featured in subsequent movies, who perfected a way to go unseen by others.[11][12]

The Allies who fought the Nazis saw them as marauding monsters, intent on taking control of the world. "Peaceful" Polish and other villagers who at first lived side by side with the Jews as neighbors later became pitchfork- and torch-bearing pursuers like in *Dracula* and *Frankenstein*.[13][14]

The core emotions elicited in horror stories are fear and terror, and the overall arch of horror stories tends to be similar: the protagonists (heroic main figures) who live a relatively simple existence, working to get by in their day-to-day lives; antagonists (in the form of monsters and evil beings) who attack and claim initial victory; and finally, protagonists who attempt to overcome evil.

In telling this tale, I refer to numerous horror stories and movies. The two earliest movies are Germany's 1915 *The Golem*, and 1922 *Nosferatu*, both of which have antisemitic overtones, foretelling the Holocaust. Many of the other movies I reference were created in the 1930s and 1940s and reflect the anxiety spurred by the approaching World War II. These include 1931's *Dracula* (based on Bram Stoker's 1897 novel) starring Hungarian Bela Lugosi as an ancient, bloodthirsty vampire; 1931's *Frankenstein* (based on Mary Shelley's 1818 novel) starring Boris Karloff, in which a scientist plays god by creating a living being from dead flesh; 1933's *The Invisible Man* starring Claude Rains, in which a secret experiment to become invisible goes awry; and 1941's *The Wolf Man* starring Lon Chaney Jr. (based on the screenplay by Curt Siodmak, a Jewish refugee from Nazi Germany), about a man who is bitten by a werewolf and becomes one. Two horror movies, 1941's *King of the Zombies* and the 1943 sequel *Revenge of the Zombies*, featured sinister Nazis as the main antagonists and monsters. I believe these and other horror movies and stories foreshadow and provide insight into the ultimate horror story, the Holocaust. I also refer to a few nonhorror, but World War II-related films.[15][16][17][18][19][20][21][22][23][24]

The horror that was the Holocaust was steeped in European folklore, antisemitism, monsters, and miracles. German folklore and monsters reflected their belief in their own militaristic superiority, fear of encroaching outsiders, and the lack of worthiness of "lesser" people, including the Jews. Poles' beliefs reflected their history of being at the "crossroad" of Europe through which countless Russian, Prussian, Austrian, and other armies traveled, conquered, and laid waste to the countryside and people. The old Polish proverb *"Nieszczescia chodza parami,"* or "Misery loves company," and *"Z deszczu pod rynne,"* or "Out of the frying pan and into the fire," reflect these experiences. The Jews' folklore and belief in monsters, angels, and other supernatural phenomena reflected their history of being scapegoated and persecuted for everything from supposedly killing Jesus, spreading the plague, to causing financial collapse. The Holocaust was, in and of itself, a horror story of epic and unheard-of proportions. Based on their histories and folklore, it is easy to see how many Germans became brutal bullies, Poland was overrun, and European Jews were victimized.

I start this book by examining the protagonists—Jews and other persecuted people—living their day-to-day lives, doing normal things. I begin with the bustling, simple life in Lublin and Warsaw, Poland, with the villagers struggling to survive and unaware of the evils that lay ahead. The early-20th-century technology-fueled mood was hopeful, despite the lack of work, food, medical care, and other necessities, and with dark storm clouds gathering over the horizon. I foreshadow and reflect on these dangers and warning signs through thoughts and recollections of my father, Al, and mother, Pearl. We in the 21st century know, with the benefit of twenty-twenty hindsight, what the danger signs meant and wish we could have shouted: "get out of there." However, many of those living at the time understandably did not or could not fully grasp the meaning of these dangers.

The Nazis used stories and images of vampires, like in *Dracula*, to represent Jews and other "subhuman" people from Eastern Europe who drained the superior and virtuous Germanic people of their lives, happiness, and prosperity. The Germans felt encroached upon and longed for "breathing space." Not coincidentally, *The Golem* and *Nosferatu* saw vampires as the "bad" monsters. The Nazis saw themselves as represented by brave and true werewolves, Nordic gods, and other "good" supernatural beings. They communicated and reinforced this fantastical belief in their superiority by way of propaganda and other means. The Germans believed Jews and other minorities "stabbed them in the back," resulting in Germany's defeat in World War I. Germans represented the innocence of the light and Jews the dark, malevolent corruption of the innocent. This belief allowed the Germans to undertake atrocities that others would not have undertaken.[25][26][27]

The Jews, throughout their history, knew and understood the need to protect themselves. This resulted in their search for, and employment of, super weapons such as the Ark of the Covenant (containing the Ten Commandments), the trumpets of Joshua (Joshua succeeded Moses as leader of the Israelites), and the inanimate clay figure the golem, which served as a form of superhero brought to life by rabbis to protect the Jewish community. Movies have been made, including *Raiders of the Lost Ark*, *Inglourious Bastards*, and others, telling the story of the search and use of these super weapons. Further, American Jewish cartoonists and composers created Captain America, Superman, Rosie the Riveter, and others to spur the United States to confront and go to war with Nazi Germany.[28][29]

The middle part of our story occurs with the rise of the evil antagonist Adolf Hitler, his henchmen, and the hatred they spawned. They were possessed by evil and intent on devastation and annihilation. Interestingly, Hitler saw himself as a cinematic hero, an idol who played to adoring crowds awestruck by his strength of personality. He practiced his heroic poses and rhetoric in front of mirrors and cameras, helping him perfect his cinematic style. He fed his audience antisemitic folklore and conspiracy theories, seducing the German people with stories of their superiority and others' inferiority. Hitler worked with Propaganda Minister Josef Goebbels to weave tales that supported the Nazis' horrific aspirations of world conquest. They even made movies to further their evil objectives.

The reality and the scale to which the monstrous Nazis attacked the innocent, invaded Poland, and other countries, and tortured and committed atrocities, is almost unfathomable. We wonder how humans could create the factory-like killing centers and concentration camps the Nazis and their allies used to destroy humanity. The Nazis considered their victims to be subhuman, minimizing any introspection or guilt they may have practiced or felt. It seemed to be a world absorbed by the malignant growth of ideas, justifying the killing and displacement of entire nations, cultures, and peoples. Hateful ideas led to hateful actions. The German people, many well educated and sophisticated, had a choice like the main character in *Dr. Jekyll and Mr. Hyde*, between evil and good. They all too often followed the easier path of evil.[30]

Interestingly, the Germans' long militaristic past resulted in their being viewed as brutal and monstrous several times in their history before World War II. For example, a German Hessian mercenary who fought for the British in the American Revolutionary War served as the inspiration for American author Washington Irving's Headless Horseman in his 1820 horror story *The Legend of Sleepy Hollow*. In another example, Great Britain, America, and others referred to the German military in World War I as "Huns" for their brutish and monstrous ways. The Germans were depicted as marauding gorilla-like figures, carrying the innocent to their deaths.[31]

As is often the case, evil at first appears insurmountable and undefeatable; all appears lost. The Nazi antagonists, appearing to be a race of supermen, seemingly had all the power, with the Jews, Roma, homosexuals, disabled, political dissidents, and other innocent mortals having none. Some who should have been allies, including fellow Jews, prove otherwise, in mandated service to the Nazis as *Judenrat*, or ghetto police, and other capacities. This disappointment may have been because they had few other choices to survive, but their negative impact remains. Our protagonists were unable to escape their dark, isolated, fear-inducing nightmare. However, time and time again, good proves itself stronger and wins out, often after great loss. This proved to be the case with World War II and the Nazis' defeat.

Holocaust victims were treated by the Nazis as Mary Shelley's Frankenstein monster was—misunderstood, villainized, ostracized, and deemed less than human. In fact, the real Frankenstein Castle, built in 948 CE, is in Germany, south of Frankfurt. Konrad Dipple von Frankenstein resided at the castle and may have been the real-life inspiration for Dr. Victor Frankenstein of Mary Shelley's novel and the movies. He was an alchemist (medieval chemist), scientist, and grave robber. He purportedly experimented on dead bodies, and the castle is said to be haunted either by one of his creations or by the doctor himself.[32]

Despite the depravity, many individuals—Poles, Germans, and others—demonstrated heroism and virtue at great risk to themselves by hiding and saving the persecuted. For the persecuted, they fought hard to exist, survive, and prevail against overwhelming odds. For many who perished, they form a great army of unknown and unrecorded. The Holocaust was a searing story of human rights abuses and genocide, on a scale never seen before.

I end with the belief in God, miracles, and angels that repeatedly gave my father hope and ultimately saved his life, resulting in his liberation, emigration to America, and meeting with a force of good—my mother. As with many horror stories, good overcomes evil and hope wins out. However, victory may be fleeting, and the protagonists must remain vigilant, working to ensure a similar horror does not reoccur. Even though the Nazis were vanquished, evil and potential monsters still lurk and could reappear at any time, especially if we fail to learn the lessons of the Holocaust and let our guard down. Eternal vigilance is needed to continue to live in peace.

Heroes and Protagonists

My father serves as the primary hero in this story. He was the smartest and strongest person I ever knew. He believed in hope and miracles, persevered in the Warsaw Ghetto and captivity in Nazi concentration and slave labor camps, and overcame the horrors of the Holocaust. He also knew and understood the underlying folklore, Nazis' supernatural bent, and used horror-related themes, such as becoming an "invisible man" to survive. He was the sole survivor of his immediate family, losing his parents, Gershon and Miriam, sisters Frieda and Sarah, and brother Yitzhak. My father also lost almost all his extended family (perhaps as many as 30 separate families with the same surname). My father faced pure evil and won, surviving the worst human calamity we have ever known. He successfully immigrated to America, not knowing a word of English or anyone there. He made his way from Ellis Island in New York to Erie, Pennsylvania, worked several jobs at once, learned English, helped raise a family, and thrived.

While I have fond memories of my father and was close to him, it is important to not underestimate the damage the Holocaust did. He was traumatized (subject to lasting shock due to the emotionally devastating events he experienced) and fully trusted few people after the war. He was plagued with nightmares, insomnia, and anxiety. Further, his ability to demonstrate love to some of his children (especially to his daughters) and others was negatively impacted. Although outwardly he could seem to be a gregarious type, appearing hearty, friendly, and congenial, he was guarded, limited my mother's and our contacts with others, and demonstrated negativity (verbally and through his actions) toward his daughters. Also, his thinking was shaped by the early 20th-century European norms that at times placed men in a higher societal position than women. To a certain degree, my father passed on the trauma he experienced to his children, especially his daughters, who have battled to overcome the drama and negativities of their childhoods. He was very human, and I have no doubt he would have been a different person but for the nightmares he went through.

My mother was a "living angel," with infinite patience, kindness, and never a cross word—truly a practitioner of the "Golden Rule." She challenged the gender norms of her time by joining and serving in World War II with the WAVES despite the objections of her parents, Louis and Rose. She heard of the monstrous crimes and atrocities the Nazis perpetrated against fellow Jews and had to act. I believe my mother, in part, was the pure good for which my father survived and to whom he was drawn. In many ways, my mother saved my father from what a post-Holocaust life might have been. Like my father, my mother was also very human, including some of the flaws many of us have. She was, to a degree, a creation of her times, playing a secondary role to my father in decision-making and in raising a family. Her essential goodness was often tested by my father's demons. To a degree, she sacrificed her sense of self and her relationships and connections with her own family to help ensure my father's happiness. No doubt she could and should have done more to shield her daughters from the trauma passed on from my father.

History and Unique Views

Throughout this book, I try to recreate the ambiance, atmosphere, and horrors of pre-World War II, wartime, and postwar Poland, Germany, and America.

I always wished I had a chance to meet and get to know my father's and mother's families. I was one year old when my mother's mom, Rose, died. I never met any of my other grandparents, Gershon, Miriam, or Louis. I knew and was close with my mother's sister Celia, but I never met any of my father's siblings. I long to know the family members who perished. I explore what the psychology of the individuals' minds may have been, their courage, compassion, and other emotions. Unfortunately, I'm separated by the 50 to 80 years that have passed since they were alive.

I am so sorry for what my father's family and others had to go through. No human being should suffer the way they did. I know each was a real person, with unique and individual identities. Each was irreplaceable. I want to make sure their lives don't disappear. I view it as my obligation, as a second-generation survivor, to be a witness on behalf of my relatives who perished in the Holocaust.

The stories of my parents and their families provide unique views of a comparatively innocent world lost, turned into a nightmare by way of the Holocaust, Warsaw Ghetto, the Depression, and World War II. This is their story, told in their words—where possible—with the history of the times interwoven.

My father was interviewed and told his story in April 1994 as part of the San Francisco Bay Area Holocaust Oral History Project (inspired by Steven Spielberg's Shoah Foundation, which was started one year after his Academy Award-winning Holocaust movie

Schindler's List). His recorded interview is now housed in the United States Holocaust Memorial Museum in Washington and is available online. My mother relayed her story through writings, conversations, and interviews with the U.S. Women's War Memorial, located adjacent to Arlington National Cemetery in Virginia. I have expanded on those interviews (and separate conversations), including drawing, and enhancing connections to the supernatural, horror, superhero, and other elements of the story to tell their stories and shine a light on the times more fully.[33]

The story of my parents coming together is a miracle in and of itself: a story of love, resilience, and hope transcending two different worlds despite the horrors of the Holocaust through strong underpinnings of faith. Theirs is a story of good overcoming evil. Despite his unfathomable losses and horrors, my father was able to love again and build a family and a legacy with my mother. My parents reflect the unwavering human spirit. If I were to sum up this story in a few words, it would be this: hope prevails.

I view myself as a historian, researcher, very interested taleteller, and proud son. I have conducted extensive research in writing this book and this story is of utmost importance to me. We must never forget.

PART I
A SIMPLE LIFE

BUSTLING, SIMPLE LIFE BEFORE THE TORCHES AND PITCHFORKS

"I bribed, tricked, and escaped the Nazis' attention."
—Al Kitmacher

My father, 1948, age 28, in Germany.

My father, Al Kitmacher, was born on February 23, 1920, in Lublin, Poland. I was born on his birthday 41 years later. He and his father, Gershon, his mother, Miriam, older sisters Frieda (five years older) and Sarah (three years older), and younger (by two years) brother Yitzhak lived in Lublin from 1920 to 1933. From 1933 to 1940, my father (from ages 13 to 20) and his family lived in Warsaw before being forced into the Warsaw Ghetto in November 1940. My father described his family as happy, although they endured struggles:

"Despite not having enough food, work, comforts, or belongings, we didn't realize how good we had it, ahead of the oncoming nightmare. We worked, we lived, we loved each other. We enjoyed living in the warmth and light of each other's company. It was a fairly simple life, not too different than our ancestors' *shtetl* way of life. Although there had always been antisemitism, it didn't rule our lives. It was truly the 'calm before the storm.' As the old Polish proverb says: '*Nie dziel skóry na niedźwiedziu,*' or 'Don't count your chickens before they're hatched.' I used this proverb throughout my life, not believing good would occur until it actually did. After my experiences in the Holocaust, trust was hard to come by."

A shtetl was a small town with a large Jewish population that existed in Central and Eastern Europe before the Holocaust. A larger city was called a *shtot* and a village a *dorf*—although I use shtetl and village interchangeably. A ghetto is a part of a city in which minority group members live, usually due to social, legal, or economic pressure. It is often more impoverished than other parts of the city.

Like at the beginning of many horror stories and movies, such as *Dracula* and *Frankenstein*, Poland's pre-Holocaust Jewish life was village or shtetl-like; bustling, rich, varied, yet simple. Early 1930s Poland was tranquil. The Nazi monsters, their collaborators, and World War II destroyed that peace, the community, and millions of lives.

The intensity of Jewish life was astonishing. Polish Jews created impressive religious institutions, political movements, secular literature, and a distinctive way of life.

There was a multitude of Jews: pious Jews in black gabardine—a smooth, durable twill-woven cloth looking like priests in medieval garb—and those dressed in more modern clothing. While many younger Jews in bigger towns adopted modern ways and dress, older people often dressed traditionally, with men wearing hats or caps, and women modestly covering their hair with wigs or kerchiefs. My father's family was more like today's Reform Jews, exhibiting relaxed, secular, nontraditional attributes, not directly related to religion. They honored Judaism's many traditions, such as having bar mitzvahs and celebrating major holidays, but did not abide strictly by dietary rules.

Judaism is a religion, a nationality, and a culture. As a religion, Judaism has specific beliefs in God, kosher dietary rules, and a calendar of holidays. Throughout history, Judaism has been recognized as a distinct group of people with its own nation (being a nation does not require territory or government), unique culture, and language (Hebrew). Although Judaism arose out of a single ethnicity in the Middle East, people have converted in and out of the religion throughout history, and it no longer constitutes a separate ethnicity.

It was the early 20th century, but many clung to the ways and customs carried forward from the distant past. In short, it was a very different world. Although to us in the 21st century, it may feel "quaint" and simple, shtetl living provided as many challenges, joys, disappointments, and emotions as we experience. However, it's important not to get too nostalgic for these "good old days." Jews and other downtrodden people faced crippling poverty, a daily shortage of food, medicine, and other necessities. They faced persecution, whether through government pogroms (massacres), riots, or day-to-day antisemitism and discrimination. They were forced to live in less desirable locations, whether shtetls or ghettos, and faced disease and a lack of medical care. Jews were rarely at ease in their lives. But these struggles had a positive impact, forcing them to turn to their faith, traditions, and family values. Although Jews had known hardships and antisemitism throughout history, there seemed to be little inkling of the horrors that lay ahead. Prewar and pre-Shoah (the Hebrew word for Holocaust) Poland had an atmosphere, an ambiance, that may never be experienced again.

To truly understand the horrific impact of the Holocaust, it is important to understand the world in which pre-Holocaust Jews in Poland existed, including my father's family.[1]

Poland Before World War II: Peaceful Villagers

Pre-World War II Poland, including the Kitmacher hometowns of Lublin and Warsaw, was bustling yet simple. Jewish daily and religious life flourished. The Jews enjoyed a long and mostly peaceful existence. As is often the case in horror stories and movies like *Dracula* and *Frankenstein*, the Polish villagers who lived side by side with Jews were generally peaceful. It wouldn't be too long before some of these villagers took up pitchforks and torches, helping the monsters. Storm clouds gathered ahead of the Nazi invasion.

Lublin was described by locals as a pleasant, large town, rich in Jewish history. The Jewish Public Library opened in 1917, and the renowned Yeshiva Chachmel, built in 1930, became a rabbinical high school. In the 1930s, approximately one-third, or 43,000, of Lublin's 122,000 residents were Jewish. Fewer than 300 survived the Holocaust. Many of them lived in a bustling network of small streets around and between the ancient Grodzka Gate, built in 1342, and a 12th-century castle. There were houses, shops, and synagogues. Everywhere, you could hear people speaking Yiddish—a mix of German, Hebrew, and Slavic.[2]

Lublin's old town, 2017. Courtesy of Mexxicana, Pixabay.

In contrast to Lublin, Warsaw was a large, bustling city full of life, a mix of old and new. It was made up of broad streets and stately buildings, including Poland's first skyscraper, and was home to an opera house. The old royal capital building served as the president's residence.[3]

The summers in both cities were warm and comfortable. The falls and springs were cool with some rain. The winters were cold, and the ground was often covered with snow from December to mid-March.

Old town Warsaw dates to the 12th century and was charming. The market square was the jewel of the old city, with narrow, winding streets and old houses with small windows. Each building had a unique stylized facade. Cracow House was beautiful, housing a 400-year-old wine cellar. In 1483, Jews were expelled from Warsaw. In the 18th century, Jews were permitted to return and settled around Jerusalem and Marszalkowska streets. They later moved to the Nalewki Street area and settled in northern Warsaw.

The Warsaw city hall's clock tower bells chimed with a lovely, reassuring, resonating sound at noon. In the early 20th century, Warsaw was the largest Jewish community in Europe and second largest in the world after New York City. The Jewish community ran more than 100 modern Jewish and trade schools, hospitals, synagogues, and social institutions.

Although desiring to be a modern city, Warsaw clung to its medieval past.

Daily Life Before World War II

Jewish life flourished in Poland. The Jewish streets were always crowded and bustling, with Jews traveling between their homes and places of work, worship, and other institutions. Thirty thousand Jews lived on Zamenhofa Street, and Warsaw's Nalewki Street was an especially busy commercial center, where every building housed workshops, factories, or stores. It hummed like a beehive; you could hear early 20th-century machinery at work, grinding, buzzing, and cutting. Trains, horses, and early motorized vehicles were at work, each making particular noises and giving off distinct scents. The air was, in some places, thick with smoke from machinery and vehicles, as well as the familiar smell of horse manure.

The streets and courtyards were filled with porters pushing carts, merchants, and tradesmen announcing their wares and services for sale. The busy indoor market housed hundreds of food shops, while rows of merchant wagons waited outside the market. You could bargain over a turkey or goose for the Sabbath or an apple or orange from the Holy Land. The street vendors did well here, their goods spread out on small stools. They sold anything and everything: fresh bagels and rolls were especially popular. The scent of these freshly baked goods wafted through the air and enticed customers. Tinsmiths called out their services, and signs like "Buy from Ginzberg, he has a wife and children at home" were common. My father and his family did tailor and seamstress work from their home. It was through these streets that my father and his family walked, shopped, and lived.

There were also some who were unemployed, and they stood and hoped to be chosen for a few hours' work. Their clothing was torn and especially dirty from the little hard work they could find. A few smelled of alcohol or a lack of bathing.

Jewish café life thrived, as people enjoyed regular tables and meeting times. Their chatter resonated through the ancient courts and streets. These people were the few gentry, middle class, professionals, and intellectuals. People engaged in political speeches and arguments.

Young people participated in YIVO, the Jewish Scientific Society, and researched Jewish folklore and linguistics. Older people clung to traditions and beliefs in folklore that seemed antiquated to the young. There were cultural, drama, and women's clubs. Sports became an important part of Jewish life, as the importance of cultivating the body as well as the spirit and mind were emphasized. During the period between World Wars I and II, Jewish children often played with non-Jewish children in school and community recreational activities and sports. Despite the ever-present specter of antisemitism, Jews often had close friendships with Christians, which made Jewish integration into Polish culture seem possible and even welcome.

Literary works, poetry, and novels were created by Jews and were popular, and the performing arts were cultivated. Jews could enjoy performances of Jewish orchestras, brass bands, and theatrical troupes. The Nowosci Theater was the home of Yiddish theater; there were permanent and traveling programs, such as The Habima Theater from Eretz Israel ["Land of Israel"], which toured Warsaw in 1939, just before the start of World War II.

Many newspapers were published in Warsaw: six Yiddish daily papers and two Polish dailies. The news was filled with war and troubles, but these problems seemed distant as Polish Jews felt safe and were, for the most part, integrated into their communities.

Life seemed "normal" and generally free of worry, although few Jews had enough money or food. In retrospect, knowing what would occur a short time later, I wish I could stand on a rooftop and warn the populace to wake up to the dangers that lay just beyond their borders.

Religious Life

The Shabbat eve meal awaited. Cholent (a traditional stew) and other soups (matzo ball and *kreplach*, or dumplings), fish (usually pike, whitefish, or carp, as well as gefilte fish—a poached mix of minced fish), and *kugel* (a baked noodle dish) were staples. Other popular foods included herring, goose, duck, *challah* (braided bread), *cebularz* (a wheat bun topped with onion), *knishes* (dumplings), red borscht (a beetroot drink), *tzimmes* (sweet desserts), and *babkas* (desserts stuffed with raisins, poppy seeds, almonds, and other ingredients). Preferred tastes and ingredients included sweet and sour, onion, vinegar, sugar, spices, and pepper. Cooking was forbidden on Sabbath, so all dishes were prepared ahead of time. The pre-Sabbath kitchen was a beehive of activity, with wonderful aromas and anxious voices wafting through the home.[4]

There were small prayer houses and larger synagogues, including the famous Nozhik Synagogue. Some boasted organs and choirs, performing music by German Jewish and Russian Jewish composers. Hasidic (an Orthodox revivalist movement that emerged in Eastern Europe in the 18th century) and other religious Jews sang loudly on the Sabbath, while some of those who did not sing closed their windows to block out the sound. The Sabbath brought peace, if not quiet, and serenity to the bustling Jewish streets. Even the merchant wagons stood idle. The older generation was religious and did not work, carry money, or ride in vehicles on the Sabbath. Younger people were typically less religious and were usually the first to leave religious services.

Krashinsky Park was full on the Sabbath; young children crowded the walking paths. The older boys played elsewhere, practicing being athletic champions, while the little girls encircled and danced around the "Sabbath Queen," a young girl chosen to be the mystical Sabbath bride who reflects the feminine aspects of God through music and psalms. Jewish mothers pushed baby carriages in the park, while old folks sat on park benches and read newspapers.

Polish Jews were relatively free to practice their religion as they wished. However, liberty would not last for long.

A Long History

Jews had lived in Poland since at least the Middle Ages. They had enjoyed legal protections that allowed them to practice their religion and live in relative peace since the year 1264. With these protections, Jewish communities in Poland thrived. By the 1500s, 80 percent of Jews worldwide lived in Poland, where they enjoyed relative autonomy, tolerance, and were able to develop a rich social and cultural life. For 800 years, Jews lived side by side with their Christian neighbors in Poland in a relatively tolerant, though not fully assimilated, world. As the old Polish proverb says: *"Kiedy wejdziesz miedzy wrony musisz krakac tak jak one,"* which is similar to the more well-known saying, "When in Rome, do as the Romans do." They lived in the same towns but didn't really know each other.

Poland is situated at the crossroads of Europe and historically been invaded and frequently partitioned. The relatively peaceful existence of Polish Jews was threatened toward the end of the 1700s when, in a series of political moves, Poland was partitioned among Russia, Prussia, and Austria.

With Russia controlling large segments of Poland, many Polish Jews found themselves under Russian rule. Russia restricted Jews to certain geographic locations and professions. Jews were permanent residents of and confined to an area in the west of the Russian empire called the Pale of Settlement, which existed from 1791 to 1917. Based on common religious observances, the Yiddish language, a kashrut diet following certain Jewish dietary laws, and common occupations, these Jews forged a shared existence. Many of these individuals were small trade and craftspeople. Their occupations did not require them to own land, something many of them were prohibited or restricted from doing. In response to Russia's rule, these Jews fought side by side with Polish fighters seeking independence during a series of uprisings throughout the 1800s.

Except for a small minority of middle-class Jewish merchants, bankers, and factory owners, most Jewish people were poor and became even more so under Russia's control. They worked as traders, semi-skilled craftsmen in old and emerging industries (e.g., textiles and tailoring), and as shopkeepers. A few were farmers; many were destitute.

In the late 1800s, many Jews lived in shtetls. They were generally isolated from many aspects of modern life, especially if the shtetl was not near a city or railway line. These were vibrant centers of Jewish culture and tradition while also representing mixed communities, including Christians and others. We believe the first Kitmacher ancestor in Poland lived in the shtetl of Czemierniki, outside of Lublin. This village had approximately 1,000 Jewish residents just before the Holocaust, but many of these residents were sent to the Treblinka concentration camp and few survived. Our ancestor's name was Hershl, and he was born in approximately 1760. His son's name was Leibush Hershl, or Leib (my father's, grandfather's, and great-grandfather's middle name).

Most shtetl Jews were poor and worked as peddlers, simple artisans, shopkeepers, teamsters (driving teams of draft animals), bricklayers, shoemakers, tailors, dairymen, and blacksmiths. They served the people of the shtetl and surrounding villages. Author Sholem Aleichem's *Tevye the Dairyman* focuses on a shtetl resident, Tevye, and his family, and is the basis for the modern-day Broadway show and movie *Fiddler on the Roof*. Tevye and other shtetl residents lived separate lives as a minority within the majority's culture. They spoke Yiddish and read Yiddish books, attended Yiddish theater and movies, and clung to old world beliefs, fears, and hopes.[5]

In the 1880s and 1890s, following the assassination of Russian Czar Alexander II, Russian-Polish Jews were the focus of a series of pogroms, which targeted Jewish communities. In response, approximately two million Jews emigrated from this region, with the vast majority going to the United States. This included my mother's father Louis Harris and members of his family. Some of those who remained in Europe tried to isolate themselves from hostility and outside forces, while others tried to assimilate.

In the late 19th and early-20th centuries, once industrialization and urbanization began, many Jews left the shtetls to live more secular and modern lives in cities like Warsaw, Vilna (Poland, and later Lithuania), Krakow, and Lodz, Poland. The Kitmacher family moved to Lublin. Some Jews tried to integrate themselves within a broader European society, while others continued strongly valued Jewish religious and cultural traditions. Others still lived somewhere in between tradition and modernity, and between the religious and the secular. By the early 1920s, Jews made up between one quarter and one half of the population in Poland's larger cities. In some smaller towns, they made up as much as 90 percent of the population. Those cities became the cultural, religious, and intellectual centers of Jews in Poland.

In 1918, following the end of World War I, Poland became a democratic independent state with significant minority populations, including Ukrainians, Jews, Belarusians, Lithuanians, and ethnic Germans. However, increasing Polish nationalism made Poland a hostile place for many Jews. A series of pogroms and discriminatory laws signaled growing antisemitism, while fewer and fewer opportunities to emigrate were available due to Poland isolating itself from other countries.

In Poland's major cities, Jews and Poles spoke each other's languages and interacted in markets and on the streets. Antisemitism still had some impact on the lives of Polish Jews, but Jews were part of Poland, and Polish culture was, in part, Jewish. Despite this partial assimilation, however, Jews still represented a culture other than Polish.

Between World Wars I and II, Jews lived and thrived in diverse communities, across eastern and western Europe, with varying cultures and ways of life. European Jews came from little towns as well as cities and participated in politics, the military, business, education, civic activities, theater, and music. They considered themselves citizens of the countries in which they lived, not as outsiders. Being Jewish was just one part of their identity.

There were some wealthy Jews across Europe around 1930, as well as middle-class and extremely poor Jews. There were Jewish bankers, shopkeepers, doctors, nurses, actors, professors, soldiers, typists, peddlers, factory owners and workers, and teachers. Jewish politics included liberals, conservatives, nationalists, feminists, anarchists, and communists.

Some Jews identified more closely with the countries in which they lived than with the Jewish religion and culture. Others lived apart from non-Jews and followed a more traditional and religious way of life.

European Jews, like European Christians, were a disparate group. By the early 1900s, many Jews were highly acculturated (learning and incorporating the values, beliefs, language, customs, diets, and mannerisms of the home country). There was little or nothing about their appearance, daily habits, or language that distinguished them from their non-Jewish French, German, Italian, Polish, Greek, and other neighbors. Some of these Jews regularly attended religious services, some only attended religious services on High Holidays, while others never attended. Many held a strong sense of their Jewish identity, while others maintained very little or none.

Storm Clouds Together

Throughout history, Jews have been a small minority in Europe that never made up more than 1 or 2 percent of the population. Throughout much of their history, Jews lived in territories ruled by others. They were often treated as "strangers and others," scapegoated for calamities and misfortunes taking place in the countries in which they lived. Individuals spread baseless rumors, lies, myths, and misinformation about their Jewish neighbors. Many of these persist in today's world.

An Austrian 1920s silent film, *The City Without Jews*, predicted and warned against the further scapegoating of Jews and the rise of greater antisemitism. The movie described a fictional city in the 1920s, beset with rising unemployment and poverty, where resentments against Jews mounted. Residents increasingly blamed Jews for the city's woes. After a law was passed forcing all Jews to leave, residents celebrated but soon realized they were worse off than before. The law was reversed. Even before the Nazis annexed Austria in 1938, it was one of the centers of antisemitism, blaming Jews for the unemployment and economic woes that occurred after Austria's defeat in World War I. Despite the warnings of the movie, Austria was the birthplace and "incubator" of the primary monster in this horror story: Adolf Hitler.[6][7]

JEWISH, POLISH, AND GERMAN FOLKLORE, MONSTERS, AND MIRACLES

"All of a sudden, a Polish girl screamed, 'Here's a Jew!'"
—Al Kitmacher

In this chapter I describe Jewish, Polish, and German folklore, monsters, and miracles in the past tense, as they shaped views leading up to (and including) the Holocaust. However, some have never stopped believing in these tales.

Jewish Folklore

Jews, especially those living in Poland, as well as the Poles themselves had a history of folklore, tales, and beliefs in the supernatural, monsters, and miracles. Some beliefs were benign, and others were not; they colored thinking and traditions. They helped shape how Jews and others felt and thought about the world in which they lived.

Jewish folklore was and continues to be an important way in which history and beliefs are passed from one generation to the next. Folklore was also important to grasping why people acted and reacted the way they did. Jews, especially those in Poland, had a history of traditions, tales, and beliefs in the supernatural that permeated their world. Their stories consisted of beliefs, doctrines, customs, ethical and moral standards, and cultural values and attitudes that had been transmitted orally or by example. They impacted how Jews acted and reacted in the lead-up and response to the Holocaust. My father described his upbringing with superstitions as follows:

"We were raised with Jewish and Polish superstitions, stories of monsters and supernatural creatures. Although we knew these were mostly made up, we didn't take any chances—avoiding the evil eye, putting salt in the corners of rooms, and quickly saying 'bless you' after a sneeze. I believed knowing these stories gave me unique abilities to survive. Little did I know I would meet monsters even worse than those in the stories.

I also experienced prescient dreams, miracles, and extraordinary interventions throughout the Holocaust; they saved my life. I knew God and his angels were watching over me. I could feel it. Repeatedly, some overwhelming force of good intervened on my behalf and saved me. I don't know why I experienced this while so many others didn't; I couldn't help but feel that I was meant to contribute to the forces of good in some way.

I was raised with stories of miracles like the Hebrews escaping from ancient Egypt and the parting of the Red Sea. We also heard of the 1920 'miracle of Vistula' in Warsaw when the Poles defended the city against the Soviets. When I was a small boy, I prayed to God to 'please help my beloved mother recover from this horrible illness': it was dysentery and she recovered soon after. I truly believe God watched over me and I had his angels with me throughout that horror; they gave me hope and helped me survive."

Officially, superstition has little or no presence or influence in Judaism. The Torah warns against believing in lucky numbers, superstitious signs, and listening to diviners (those who use special powers to predict the future). Rather, Jews are commanded to put their faith in God (Deuteronomy 18:9-13). Despite this, there were many *bubbe meise*, or old wives' tales, and related beliefs that fueled the perspective that evils and monsters lay just over the horizon.

The underlying supernatural tales served many purposes: for believers, they documented paranormal activity. For others, they attempted to explain that which wasn't easily explained. For others still, like telling ghost stories around the fire, they were an escape from reality or at least a distraction from it. The scientific view was and is that supernatural phenomena are caused by optical illusions, hallucinations, air pressure and environmental changes, underlying psychological reasons, misidentification of animals, sleep issues, geomagnetic fields, sound changes, carbon monoxide poisoning, or wishful thinking. For those who believe in these stories, they can be good, evil, or something in between. They can be regarded as an omen or portent of death. No matter the reason for their existence, Jews carried these beliefs into World War II and the Holocaust. These stories foreshadowed the arrival of the truly evil and monstrous Nazis, who in turn confirmed their existence.

My father strongly believed in God, angels, the value of dreams, and the power of miracles.

Jewish Superstitions

Briefly described below are a number of the more prominent early-20th-century Jewish superstitions. Any could be the subject of a book in and of itself! Some readers will recognize cross-cultural similarities with some of these superstitions.

An oft-cited Jewish folk superstition is that of the evil eye. Historically, from the second century CE and earlier, belief in the evil eye, *ayin ha'ra* in Hebrew, can be found in the Midrash (ancient commentary on the Hebrew scriptures) and Talmud (the book of Jewish law). It was the idea that a person or supernatural being can bewitch or harm a person merely by looking at them. Over the centuries, Jews have employed numerous superstitious practices to ward off the evil eye, such as ritually spitting three times after a vulnerable person's name is uttered, or saying, when discussing the future, *kinehora*, or "let it be without the evil eye." Ritually spitting three times has also been practiced in response to good news or events, bad magic, and demons. Further, some wear talismans or lucky charms to ward against the evil eye.

A talisman against the evil eye, 2019. Courtesy of Ri Ya, Pixabay.

Chewing on a piece of thread when sewing a garment was another superstition. It is thought this practice may have originated with burial shrouds being sewn around the remains of the deceased, and chewing is a sign that the chewer is alive. It may also relate to the Yiddish phrase *"mir zollen nit farnayen der saychel,"* meaning one should not sew up the brains (or common sense). My father regularly chewed on a piece of thread while sewing clothes as a tailor. I never knew why, assuming it was just a habit.

Midrash legend had it that a sneeze was a grave omen announcing an impending death, "a little explosion in the head." The legend says that the Biblical Jacob (of Genesis), an aged person, sneezed and died instantly. Others believed the sudden exhaling accompanying a sneeze might allow a demon to rush into the sneezer's body. Those around the sneezer are asked to respond with "long life," "good health," and "God bless you" to ward off evil and death.

The Hebrew Bible (Tanakh—but the word Bible is used interchangeably here), prayerbooks, and other sacred documents were kept closed when not in use, based on the medieval fear of devils and demons taking "holy knowledge" and using it for their own nefarious purposes. Similarly, it remains common practice to kiss a prayer book if it has been dropped to show no offense was intended.

Salt, believed to have potent powers against evil spirits residing in the home, was often placed in the corners of rooms. The same logic applied to new clothes, wherein salt was placed in pockets to ward off small goblins and elves hiding in them. Salt was also thought to block a ghost from entering or departing a particular space.

Safety or straight pins were often attached, out of sight, on a traveler's clothing before a journey. According to the renowned medieval German Ashkenazi leader Eleazer of Worms, metal was said to repel evil spirits. This belief was partly based on the Bible's description of the first plague, in which water stored in wood or stone would turn to blood; metal was not mentioned.[1]

Monsters, Demons, and Witches

Judaism officially opposes all forms of sorcery and supernatural magic. Exodus 22:18 reads "You shall not allow a witch to live," while Deuteronomy 18:10–11 is more elaborate, saying, "Let no one be found among you who consigns his son or daughter to the fire," serving as a prohibition against offering a child as a sacrifice, as some religions did, "or who is an augur, a soothsayer, a diviner, a sorcerer, one who casts spells, or one who consults ghosts or familiar spirits, or one who inquires of the dead."

These Biblical prohibitions pointed out there are correct ways to relate to God (prayer) and incorrect ways (to try to manipulate divine power through magic or call upon the supposed power of other gods). Despite these prohibitions, Jews did occasionally attempt such practices. The first king of Israel, Saul, illicitly contacted the soul of the dead prophet Samuel for advice with the help of the Witch of Endor.

The Latin root of the word *monstrum* (monsters) means "ominous" or "warning signs." Monsters are often reflective of cultural fears. Because they live at the edges of what we believe is possible, monsters always manage to get away when we hunt them and then return to haunt us. Franz Kafka (one of the major Jewish figures of 20th-century literature) wrote about monstrous animal figures to warn Jewish readers about gentiles (non-Jews).

A gargoyle, 2015. Courtesy of desertrose7, Pixabay.

In ancient times, there was little difference between religion, magic, and medicine, with the only distinction being which of the three were deemed legitimate. The rabbis of the Babylonian Talmud thought the world was full of invisible *mazikin*, or demons disrupting human activities, endangering lives, and throwing communities into disarray.

Jewish tradition and lore are full of monsters, demons, witches, and supernatural creatures with dark powers. One of them is Asmodeus, the prince of demons, who tormented a woman named Sarah by killing each of her seven husbands on their wedding night. The Dybbuks, or possessor demons, are thought to be the souls of dead people who temporarily possess the living to accomplish certain tasks. The golem, introduced earlier, is an inanimate creature made from clay and brought to life by a rabbi that protects the Jewish community from persecution but is difficult to control and dangerous (Frankenstein's monster may be based on this). There is also the Leviathan, a terrifying sea monster, and its land-based counterpart the Behemoth. In addition is Lilith, the first woman created (even before Eve) that was purported to be a demon that killed women in childbirth to steal their babies. Finally, there is the Nephilim, which were the offspring of angels and human women.[2][3]

Polish Monsters, Werewolves, and Vampires

In addition to the monsters in Judaism, Poles such as my father and his family were raised with stories of Polish monsters. As with Jewish superstitions, it is important to understand Poles' beliefs, because they impacted how these individuals acted and reacted in the leadup and, in response to, the Holocaust.

Poland experienced numerous battles and death; its ground was soaked in blood and its towns were built on top of those who died for Poland. Violent and premature deaths caused great anxiety and fear in people. It is no surprise supernatural tales abounded.

Many of the oldest vampire stories originated in the Slavic world, including Poland. The vampire had many names: Upior, Wapierz, Strzyga, and Wraith. Thought to be living corpses, it was believed that people who were red-headed, left-handed, or had overgrown eyebrows could become a Wraith. Also, being born with teeth, having an animal jump over the grave shortly after burial, suffering from kyphosis (a curvature of the spine), dying prematurely, or not being baptized could mean becoming a vampire after death. These monsters stalked their relatives and others after rising from the dead to suck their blood or devour their insides.

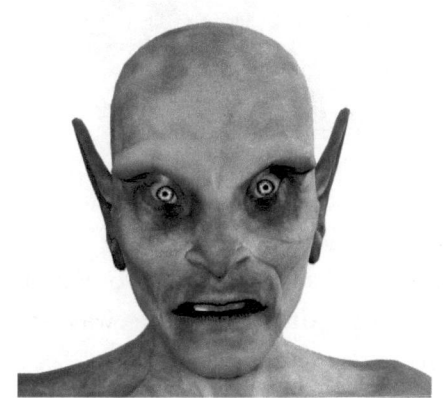

A vampire, 2016. Courtesy of Mysticsartdesign, Pixabay.

Some vampires, instead of having fangs, had a barb on the underside of their tongues. Those suspected of being a vampire were buried facing the ground, with their heads chopped off and placed between their legs, in a fetal position, with wooden or metal stakes piercing their bodies or hearts and placed under rocks. Stones were also placed into the corpse's mouth to stop them from biting anyone. Many of these graves have since been discovered, including under Krakow, Poland's main square.

Some Poles believed in werewolves; humans who transformed into wolves and murdered people. They were thought to be transformed after being bitten by a wolf or through a curse or charm.

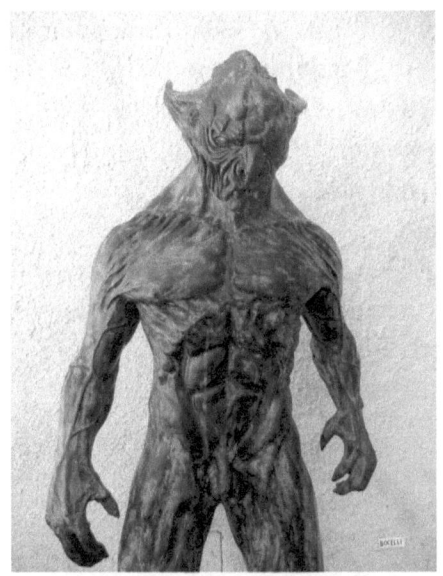

A werewolf statue, 2016. Courtesy of Efraimstochter, Pixabay

The Rusałka appeared as a beautiful woman but was the ghost of an unmarried girl who drowned. She was irresistible to men, seducing and trying to drown them.

The Południca, known as the Noon Witch, appeared amid whirling dust clouds during the hottest part of the day, carrying a scythe (a long, curved blade on a handle). She was known to quiz people and punish them if they answered incorrectly. Peasants blamed the Południca for heatstroke.

The Leshy was a giant woodland shapeshifting spirit, a mythical figure able to change form or identity at will, known to lead travelers astray. It was also believed to abduct children.

The Baba Yaga was an old witch who lived in a hut in the forest surrounded by a fence made of human bones. If she caught a human, she would kill and eat the person, adding the bones to her fence. Her favorite meal was small children.

The Nocnica, or night hag, was an evil spirit who visited people while they slept to draw their life force. Those who slept on their back were especially vulnerable, as she would sit on their chest while slowly sucking their life out. Her favorite victims were defenseless infants. In fact, she was thought to be the reason babies had trouble sleeping at night.

The Czernobog was the king of Polish monsters and was the source of evil in the world. It stole and devoured souls.

The Licho was an evil demon that appeared as a very skinny woman, with one big eye in the middle of her forehead, like a Cyclops. This demon would wander the countryside looking for places where people were happy. It would then send hunger, poverty, fires, and calamities upon the people.

The Poroniec were thought to be the souls of children who died in the womb or just after death, but before baptism. They were believed to be eternally damned and would transform into birds that attacked pregnant women and young children.

Poland also had its version of the devil, called the Devil Boruta, a creature that lived in the mountains, walked with a limp, and played evil jokes and games on unsuspecting Poles.[45]

Evidence of Polish Vampires?

In 2013, four skeletons were found buried in Gliwice, a town in southern Poland. The four individuals had been beheaded and buried with their heads between their legs to prevent them from rising from the dead. Decapitation was a common practice in the

Middle Ages for suspected vampires in Slavic areas. There is speculation these killings occurred in the 16th century. Similarly, under the streets of Krakow's historic market square, skeletons were found in 2010 in fetal positions, with hands tied and heads cut off and placed beneath their feet. These burials are thought to have taken place approximately 1,000 years ago to stop vampires from rising. The site is now the Rynek Underground, which opened in 2010 as a museum showcasing Krakow history. Included are displays of thousands of years of burial practices, including the vampire skeletons.

Although devoutly Roman Catholic, Poland is home to people who believe themselves exorcists, as well as those who believe in vampires. A weeklong exorcism conference entitled "the current fashion for vampirism in Europe and the world over, schizophrenia and other mental disorders as well as the devil's deceit during exorcism," was held in 2013 in Poland's Jasna Gora Monastery.

More than 100 "vampire graves" have been discovered in Eastern Europe since 2012.[6]

German Monsters

As with Jewish and Polish folklore, Germanic culture has its share of monsters. One such monster is the Mahr, whose name translates to nightmare. This goblin-like creature was connected to night terrors and would sit on its victim's chest while the individual slept, causing discomfort and even death.

The Nachzehrer was a terrifying, undead creature that made its home in Poland and northern Germany. Though believed to have some similarities to vampires, they did not suck the blood of the living but rather consumed already dead bodies or attacked the living. The Nachzehrer was said to rise from the dead after burial when someone died an unnatural or accidental death. Legend says you can only kill a Nachzehrer by placing a coin in its mouth and then cutting off its head.

The Erdhenne was a spooky house spirit that would occasionally appear as an old, shaggy, ash gray, hen-like creature with a shorter than normal neck. It was said to warn homeowners of dangers and death that would take place in the next 12 months. Other tales say the Erdhenne couldn't be seen, as they were spirit, but one could communicate with them.

A Drude was a German folklore demonic creature. It was said to attack people while they slept, invading their dreams to turn them into nightmares. It was like a malevolent nocturnal elf, hag, or a kobold (reptilian humanoids, lacking courage) that haunted people in their nightmares.

Knecht Ruprecht was first identified as a companion of Saint Nicholas (of Christmas fame). However, it has since become a more horrifying creature that is said to abduct disobedient children and punish them.

Finally, the Alps (not the mountains) were said to be demons that appeared in a victim's dream, giving them nightmares. People believed the Alps caused night terrors, sleep apnea, and sleep paralysis. They were also said to have the ability to transform into butterflies, pigs, cats, snakes, or dogs.[7]

Dreams and Nightmares

The Bible, in Numbers and Maimonides, states that dreams can contain divine revelations, like Jacob's, Joseph's, and the Pharaoh's in the book of Genesis.

We dream about hopes, fears, anxieties, and the people and events occurring during the day. But sometimes, our dreams catch us completely by surprise. Psychologists see dreams as a key to understanding the human subconscious.

In the Torah, Joseph is described as a dreamer. He had prophetic dreams, in which he saw the future and interpreted them for his family, and later, for the Egyptian Pharaoh. Joseph rose to be a senior adviser to the Pharaoh based on his ability to predict the future. The Talmud indicates dreams can come true in more than one way. As dreams show us our potential future, it is up to us to act on them. Joseph was informed through his dreams of the potential future and of what might be if he exercised his free will to effect it.

Joseph knew he had to act on his dreams to make real the potential future.

It is in each of our hands to try to make dreams come true or to avoid them.[8]

Miracles and Extraordinary Interventions

In the Bible, the word *nes* means "sign" of a miracle and is used to convey evidence of God's direct intervention. This intervention changes the normal course of events. My father experienced a series of 11 miracles and extraordinary interventions during the Holocaust that saved his life, including a prophetic dream.

The Hebrew Bible or Holy Scriptures (Tanakh) is Judaism's foundational text and is divided into three segments: the Torah (The Five Books of Moses—Genesis, Exodus, Leviticus, Numbers, and Deuteronomy), Nevi'im (21 Prophets), and Ketuvim (Writings). The Talmud is the compilation of the historic rabbis "discussing" or "debating" what the Torah means. The Midrash is the ancient rabbinic (rabbis' teaching of Jewish law) interpretation of scripture, while the Aggadah is the rabbinic narrative.

In the Bible, and other ancient and medieval Jewish writings, the existence of miracles is taken for granted. A miracle was viewed as an extraordinary event that, precisely because it was so different from the normal course of events, provided evidence of God's direct intervention (hence, the term *nes*). A miracle is a way in which God can manifest and alter world events. Before the rise of modern science, there was no need for the suspension of natural law to believe a miracle occurred.

Throughout rabbinic literature, the possibility of miracles occurring is accepted unreservedly while at the same time, the natural order is acknowledged as the manifestation of God's presence and will. As the great theologian Abraham Joshua Heschel said, "A few moments ago the most profound thing in all human history took place—the sun set."

The power of holy men to work miracles is recognized in the Bible. While a modern Jew is less likely to attribute extraordinary events to supernatural intervention, his belief in God's power allows for the possibility of miracles. A Hasidic proverb states that a Hasid who believes that all miracles performed by Hasidic masters happened is a fool, but one who believes they could not have happened is a nonbeliever.

The Haggadah describes God's intervention and the miracles that resulted in the Hebrews' exodus from Egypt, as commemorated by the celebration of Passover.[9]

Angels

Angelology is the study of angels and how they relate to humans and serve God's purpose. Angelology first became popular in 13th-century Germany. There are Biblical and non-Biblical views and accounts of angels; some present them as humans who have died and moved on to a higher place, while others see them as sources of divine-like power. In Judaism, angels are seen as supernatural beings and appear widely in folklore. *Mal'ach* is the Hebrew word for angel and means messenger, as Biblical angels deliver specific information and serve functions. In the Torah, an angel foretells the birth of Isaac and later stops Abraham from slaughtering him, gives direction to the Israelites during the desert journey following their liberation from Egypt, and wrestles with Jacob, who says: "I have seen a divine being face to face, yet my life has been preserved." Angels are also associated with visions and prophecies.

Stories of angels guiding people through conflict and trials are numerous. Similarly, in the Holocaust, there are stories of angels giving victims the strength to go on. My father experienced unseen voices urging him to keep moving when stopping would have resulted in death. He experienced dreams that foretold deadly circumstances and made decisions based on them. A divine or extraordinary intervention is one of the explanations for these circumstances.

In the Bible, angels speak, walk, fly, ride horses, use weapons, bring prophecies, speak with God, act as God's cabinet (as a sounding board and in advisory roles), worship God and sing in God's heavenly choir, do God's bidding, record humans' deeds in the Book of Life, carry divine messages, lift people's spirits, help people in times of need, and serve as God's escort service to heavenly realms and even to Sheol, the Jewish equivalent of a "dark place" after death. Angels are assigned different jobs and are presented as task-oriented.

The Midrash describes a debate between angels over whether human beings should be created. The angel of love favored creating humans, because of their capacity to love, while the angel of truth is against it, fearing humans will be prone to deceit. The angel of earth denies Gabriel the dust he needs to create people, fearing that humans would wreak devastation on the earth. The angel of Torah is against human creation, arguing people should not be created because they will suffer. Finally, God shows the angels how humans will have the capacity to be righteous. Angels in the Midrash and Talmud occasionally argue with God, and rabbis in the Talmud indicated the holiness of angels may be equaled or surpassed by righteous people.

According to Jewish texts, God chooses when the angels act and appear. Jews welcome the angels of Shabbat with the traditional song *Shalom Aleichem*.[10]

EARLY CHRISTIAN AND GERMAN VIEWS OF JEWS. DR. JEKYLL AND MR. HYDE (GOOD OR EVIL)

"The Nazis picked me out and left my parents and sister on the train. All was lost."
—Al Kitmacher

Folklore Leading to Conspiracy Theories, Antisemitism, and Worse

Folklore is often the starting ingredient in horror stories and movies. Folklore includes folktales and legends, ballads, jokes, and much more. They are embedded in society through oral history, books, and media. A conspiracy theory is described as a belief that some covert but influential organization or conspirators are responsible for a harmful or tragic circumstance or event. Believers reject the standard explanation for an event. Examples of well-known conspiracy theories include the assassination of President John F. Kennedy (conspiracy theorists say it wasn't just Lee Harvey Oswald· who committed the assassination but the CIA, Mafia, or others), the Apollo moon landings (some say they were fabricated and never happened), and the 9/11 terrorist attacks (some speculate the United States attacked itself, or maybe it was Israel), as well as numerous theories of alleged plots for world domination by various groups, including Jews.

Much of folklore is positive and seeks to communicate and celebrate traditions. Every group's folklore grows out of hopes, frustrations, fears, and joys that are shared by a substantial portion of the group's membership. Folklore provides comfort and stability, helping to build solidarity and cohesiveness among members of the group. Superheroes are often born from positive folklore.

However, some use folklore to denigrate and demonize other groups, such as by telling racist jokes or using derogatory stereotypes. An example is antisemitic stereotypes and cartoons shared by intolerant and unenlightened individuals that further solidify such views.

"Antisemitism was nothing new to us," my father said. "We grew up hearing horrible and untrue stories about Jews. Jews were blamed for everything, from the killing of Jesus to the medieval black death, to the economic deprivations of the Great Depression. German Jews even served loyally in the German Army in World War I but were still blamed for that loss. The Germans said Jews 'stabbed them in the back.' It didn't make any sense. I never realized these stories could be deadly until the Nazis invaded. These old, untrue stories seemed to fuel the hate and atrocities. Why can't people believe good about each other? Why do some people believe the worst?"

Historic European Antisemitism

Early Christian and German views of Jews included stories, rumors, and folklore that led to conspiracy theories, stereotypes, antisemitism, and worse. There has been a history of European antisemitism, including stereotyping and viewing Jews and others as subhuman. These beliefs permeated European societies.

Europe has served as the starting point for many monsters found in literature and movies: *Dracula*, *Frankenstein*, *The Wolf Man*, and *Dr. Jekyll and Mr. Hyde*. Interestingly, the man credited with creating *The Wolf Man* was Curt Siodmak, a Jewish refugee from Nazi Germany. Siodmak served as the screenwriter for the 1941 *Wolf Man* movie. He described *The Wolf Man* story as a man who has not sinned, but is bitten by a wolf with horrible results, and he searches for a way to escape his fate.

According to filmmaker John Landis, Siodmak was, in part, reflecting on Jews being marked with the sign of a star, which hastened their death. The movie's music composer was Hans Salter, a Jewish refugee from Austria. One line used in a modern remake of *The Wolf Man* was: "Never look back, the past is a wilderness of horrors." This aptly described Siodmak's view of the Holocaust.[1]

Europe has long been a stronghold of wild, outrageous antisemitism. Viewed as outsiders and labeled as criminals, Jews have been persecuted for more than 1,000 years, beset by intolerance and horrific violence. These actions raise the question of why hatred for Judaism runs so deeply in so many cultures. To eliminate this hatred, we must first understand it. Few methods of examining the roots of antisemitism are more revealing than studying folktales and local stereotypes concerning Jewish people. The Holocaust was spawned out of the long and vicious hatred of Jews by many European cultures.

Soon after the Kingdom of Poland's creation in 1025 and the expulsion of Jews from Germany and elsewhere in Europe, Polish noblemen favored Jewish immigration in part because of a desire for their expertise in commerce. Jews flourished in Poland, establishing an autonomous community, government, and educational institutions. This was a high point of Jewish European intellectual life. However, the era would fade with the increasing prevalence of antisemitic tales and legends.

Jews were blamed for many of the crises that befell societies. They were repeatedly blamed for cities' fires, outbreaks of disease, and other maladies. Many Christians believed Jews used sorcery or collaborated with evil to cause these events. They were repeatedly viewed as seeking to kill Christians with poisonous and hazardous substances. These accusations lacked evidence, were absurd, based on unreliable rumor, but still, they were used as excuses to persecute Jews.

Aspects of these unfounded beliefs originated with the "common people" of the Middle Ages, who were largely rural and illiterate. These beliefs helped them explain what otherwise was unexplainable (for example, why disease struck some but not others). For some common people, modernization, the expansion of trade, and new opportunities in cities softened these beliefs. However, for others, these changes were seen as turning an already dangerous world into one disrupted by more rapid economic fluctuations and the loss of traditional rights. Life was further complicated by religious discord, disruption, and war. Commoners struggled to understand and control their lives as they underwent significant change. Improvements in agriculture, population increases, and the growth of trade and cities created both opportunity and stress. Common people had few means to address their challenges and problems. Some of these means included revolt, attacking "witches," and blaming Jews. A subtle way in which commoners faced their fears, problems, and troubled times was through the stories they told and passed on, expressing warnings and hopes. Folklore and witchcraft trials are two examples of how illiterate peasants attempted to understand and handle their problems.

A belief at the time was that the devil himself directed evil forces, causing bad things to happen. Seeing these things occur, people feared evil would infiltrate their communities and control their lives. It comes as no surprise that witchcraft trials were most common in places where religious divisions and fears of spiritual and social deviance occurred. Trials were often held in places where people suffered most from wars and hardships. In some locations, especially in Germany, fears of evil and discord within the community were directed at Jews.

Early Stereotypes

The history of the Jews in Germany goes back to the year 321. Jews endured much persecution (as they did in Russia and elsewhere).

They suffered during the Crusades and were accused of well poisoning during the Black Death of 1346–1353 (leading to a massacre). The end of the 15th century was a period of religious hatred when all possible evils were attributed to Jews. From August to October 1819, pogroms that came to be known as the "Hep-Hep" riots took place throughout Germany. During this time, German Jews were stripped of their civil rights and began to emigrate.

Today, Christians and Jews live together in peace and general understanding, but that was not always the case. Jews were not officially cleared of the charge of deicide (crucifying and killing Jesus) until Vatican II's 1965 Nostra Aetate statement. The Church warned Catholics against thinking Jews were an accursed or rejected people. Numerous statements have also come from American and European Protestant entities condemning Christian antisemitism. However, these recent developments did not help the Jews of the 1930s and 1940s.

Long blamed and persecuted for the crucifixion of Jesus, the Jews' lot deteriorated in the medieval world. As the Crusades began, the Muslims were the "infidel" targets in the attempt to retake the Holy Land. However, Christian mobs also pillaged and slaughtered Jews. Supposed Jewish deicide fueled many Christians' belief that it was their duty to continuously punish Jews and that Jewish suffering was God's will. Many thought Jewish social degradation confirmed the superiority and legitimacy of the Christian faith. Persecuting Jews became a priority instead of mere cultural bias.

In Germany in the 1530s and 1540s, professor of theology and priest Martin Luther rejected the Catholic Church and denounced Jews as a damned people. He also hated Catholics, Anabaptists, and others.

From the early 1800s and on, Poles, Germans, and other Europeans practiced what we have come to know as antisemitism. Primarily politically and economically motivated, they targeted Jewish communities. The ancient Christian rhetoric of anti-Judaism was reinvigorated.

The theological anti-Judaism of the medieval Church formed one of the underpinnings of the atrocities the Jews would face in the

Holocaust. It gave credence to Christian xenophobia (the fear and hatred of strangers, foreigners, or anything strange or foreign) and anger at Jewish resistance to absorption into Christianity.

The Jews of Germany and elsewhere in Europe were accused of not only poisoning water wells but committing ritual murder. In the 1300s and 1400s, these baseless claims led to massacres. Many German Jews fled to the east, taking their Yiddish dialect with them. In May 1349, a law was passed by the leaders of Brandenburg, Germany, that read, in part, "it is said that the Jews have elsewhere dispatched many persons through poisoning." Many of these rumors started at the outbreak of the Black Death. Some thought the Black Death spread because of this sabotage or poisonings. Entire Jewish communities were blamed, burned, and massacred by enraged rioters. In 1348 and 1349, it is estimated 20,000 Jews were burned to death in Strasbourg, Germany. This event foreshadowed the Holocaust, with men, women, and children separated and killed, while some who converted to Christianity were saved. Most were tortured, then burned alive. The massacre was the result of the vicious and pervasive anti-Jewish sentiments that led many to believe Jews were responsible for the maladies, social problems, crises, and disasters that befell their society. Myths and rumors were used as evidence of the Jews' culpability because no evidence to support the accusations existed.

Another insidious rumor stated Jewish doctors killed Christian patients. The Church councils of Valladolid and Salamanca in Spain reinforced this rumor by explicitly warning Christians about Jewish doctors who would try and kill Christians by dispensing tainted medicines.

One story from European folklore was *Der Giftpilz* [The Poisonous Mushroom], in which a young girl ignores her friends' advice and visits a Jewish physician, only for him to transform into his true visage of the devil. Christian mythology includes the story of the "Wandering Jew," doomed to wander until Jesus's Second Coming for rebuffing and striking him during his trip to Calvary to be crucified. The legend reinforced the idea that Jews are wicked people cursed by God. This legend was a cause of antisemitic violence during the

Middle Ages, was adopted by German antisemites in the 19th century, and was used as Nazi propaganda.[2]

Usury or moneylending was a forbidden activity for Christians in the Middle Ages. Thus, it was controlled by the Jews (it was usually the only occupation the law allowed them to have). As a result, a great deal of medieval literature, including *The Merchant of Venice*, produced the conventional figure of the Jewish moneylender. The antisemitic and offensive term "Jew down" reflects this continuing belief that Jews are cheap, bargain, and haggle to obtain the best price for a good or service. I had never heard the term until I was an adult and didn't know what it meant at first. Interestingly, I don't believe the person who uttered the phrase knew either and was using it as an expression without understanding its darker roots.

Another stereotype was that Jews were greedy and untrustworthy moneylenders who took excessive interest in money loaned to Christians. During times of economic instability, many had to deal with Jewish moneylenders. These moneylenders often charged high interest rates. Usury was considered a crime by Christians, and high interest rates resulted in hatred and contempt. One example of this stereotype was in William Shakespeare's 1600 play *The Merchant of Venice*. In the play, a Jewish moneylender named Shylock demands a pound of flesh from the hero Antonio when he could not pay his loan back.

Beginning in the Middle Ages with William of Norwich's 1144 accusation and into the 20th century, Jews were accused of "blood libel," killing Christian children and consuming their blood. Some claimed that the Jews used the blood to make Passover matzah (unleavened bread). A famous example of blood libel was *The Prioress' Tale*, part of the 14th-century English poet Geoffrey Chaucer's *The Canterbury Tales*. In the tale, a seven-year-old boy is brutally murdered by Jews for walking down their street as he sings a Christian hymn. Somehow, the murdered boy's body continues to sing, drawing local Christians' attention, who hang the Jews for their crime. The blood libel was a leading justification for pogroms, other antisemitic violence, and hatred throughout the West. The Catholic Fourth Lateran Council, established by Pope Innocent III in 1215, forced Jews to wear distinctive clothing. This foreshadowed the Holocaust when Jews were forced to wear a yellow Star of David armband.[3]

"Host desecration" was another offense Jews were accused of in 13th-century Germany and elsewhere. It was said to be a disrespectful act against the host wafer, used by Christians during the Holy Communion or Lord's Supper (commemorating the last supper of Jesus with his disciples). For the next six centuries, suspected host desecration became one of the justifications for the persecution and expulsion of Jews. Jews found guilty of the crime were often executed.

When Hitler came to power, Germany was populated with more Jews than any other country in Western Europe. The short-lived Weimar Republic (1918–1933), which Jews strongly supported and helped by creating its constitution, could not protect Germany from its post-World War I severe economic hardships. Hitler capitalized on this fact, especially during Germany's inflation of 1923 and the 1929 Depression. The angry German public looked to the Jews for somehow causing or exacerbating these financial problems.

"Jew-Animals," and Other Monstrous Visages

A form of antisemitism is imagining Jews as animals or human-animal hybrids that pose a threat to their neighbors. The Nazis would later refer to Jews and other undesirables as *Untermenschen*, or subhumans. Jewish writers used these images as warnings to fellow Jews about this antisemitism.

In H. Leivick's early-20th-century Yiddish poem "The Wolf," a congregation is massacred, with the sole survivor being the rabbi, who turns into a werewolf. He then attacks other Jewish families who are trying to rebuild a temple on the same grounds. The imaginary rabbi is a warning sign to save the congregants from the same fate—to urge them to leave and not rebuild in the same place where they are unwelcome before they, too, are killed.

German Jewish novelist Franz Kafka used animal figures as warnings to Jewish readers about gentiles. In Kafka's 1917 "Report to an Academy," an ape turns into a human who learns to smoke, drink, and speak. The ape warns readers of the dangers of Jewish assimilation into gentile society by ridiculing the supposedly civilized Christian, but brutal, world. In German psychiatrist and author Oskar Panizza's late-19th-century published story "The Operated Jew," a Jewish man pays doctors and scientists to change his appearance, behavior, and speech to be accepted as a gentile in German society. He succeeds, but only for a while, as upon drinking too much alcohol on his wedding night, he transforms into his real essence of "the monstrous Jew." Panizza's antisemitic story, written from a supposedly medical perspective, warns of Jewish assimilation into gentile society. In the 1920s, the German Jewish philosopher Salomo Friedlander reversed the story in his "The Operated Goy." A Nazi supporter falls in love with a Jewish woman. The young man converts to Judaism and, in a series of similarly grotesque operations, alters his outward appearance, behavior, and manner of speech. Friedlander's satirical story shows how one can change, undermining nationalist and racist ideologies.[4]

Monstrosity is a term used to explain the unimaginable. Holocaust literature features many stories in which those experiencing horrible circumstances can be dehumanized, behaving in such a way that they themselves become monsters. In German Jewish writer and Holocaust survivor Edgar Hilsenrath's 1964 novel *Night*, the inhabitants of a fictional ghetto treat one another in increasingly inhumane ways to ensure their survival. They become dehumanized monsters in the process.

While this dehumanizing could have been left behind in the medieval world, as the Holocaust showed, the demonization of the Jews through antisemitic Nazi propaganda that depicted them as monstrous creatures prompted further horrific acts. The idea of "Jewish monstrosity" enabled the perpetrators to deny the humanity of their victims.

During the Middle Ages, from the fifth to the 15th centuries, the devil and demons were depicted with grotesque, animalistic physical features including horns and tails. Similarly, antisemitic caricatures of Jews included horns, tails, goats' heads, and pigs' ears, as some believed they worked for Satan. Other subhuman characteristics included flat feet, bowlegs, a slanted forehead, and puffy lips.

Folklore around the *Judensau* ["Jew's Pig"] depicted Jews suckling at the teat of pigs and eating fresh pig feces. These images frequently also included the devil consuming sow's milk and feces. These images first appeared in Germany in the 13th century and have appeared on public bridges, buildings, monuments, cathedrals, woodcuts, and newspapers. They further institutionalized antisemitism in everyday German life. Some 20 Judensau images remain on German churches and other buildings.[5]

German antisemitic folklore, legends, and belief in monsters contributing to the Holocaust

Interestingly, one of the first monster movies was the 1915 German movie *The Golem*. It was the first of a trilogy of Golem movies, with sequels in 1917 and 1920. The movie was based on Jewish and European folklore and points to the threat Jews were said to pose. The plot involves an antique dealer searching the ruins of a Jewish temple. He finds a golem, a clay statue that had been brought to life four centuries earlier by a rabbi using magic to protect the Jewish people from persecution. The dealer resurrects the golem as a servant, but the golem falls in love with the dealer's daughter. When the golem's love is not reciprocated, it goes on a rampage and murders innocent people. It is thought that *The Golem* was the precursor to the *Frankenstein* movies, based on Mary Shelley's 19th-century book.[6]

The 1922 silent German vampire film *Nosferatu* was based on Germans' fears of "the others." Unlike in Bram Stoker's *Dracula*, the physical appearance of *Nosferatu*'s vampire Count Orlok, with his hooked nose, long claw-like fingernails, and large bald head, was the German stereotypical caricature of Jews. He appears rat-like, an image to which Jews were often compared. Orlok wants to take German property, something invaders from Eastern Europe were said to want, and that struck fear in the German people. Further, Orlok spreads the plague through his subordinate rats, like folklore about Jews spreading disease. The movie reflects Germany's festering antisemitism. Interestingly, Jewish actor Alexander Granach, who emigrated to the United States before World War II in 1938, played the role of Knock, the blood-drinking, insane servant of Count Orlok (like the character Renfield in *Dracula*) who ate living creatures such as insects to obtain their life force. Again, shadows of antisemitic folklore.[7]

The real monster in *Frankenstein* is the fictional Dr. Victor Frankenstein (with a Germanic name given the real Frankenstein castle is in Germany), who attempted to play God by creating life from dead body parts. Dr. Frankenstein has been compared to the real Nazi monster Dr. Josef Mengele, who conducted barbaric and inhumane experiments on Jewish twins and other victims in concentration camps. The Nazis, and Mengele in particular, attempted to play God by deciding who should live and who should die. These efforts were part of the pseudoscience of eugenics, manipulating reproduction within the human population to increase the occurrence of desirable inheritable characteristics. Chilling fictional and horror stories and movies such as *Boys from Brazil* (Mengele emigrated to Brazil after the war and died there in 1979) portray Mengele as creating life in the form of "perfect Aryans." The 2017 book *Monstrumführer* by Edward M. Erdelac tells the fictional story of Mengele discovering Frankenstein's lab journal and being tasked by the Nazis with replicating the latter's reanimation procedure to create invincible Nazi warriors. Two Jewish brothers fight against Mengele's efforts by enlisting the creature created by Dr. Frankenstein. Again, these are examples of fictional and real-life horror stories reflecting each other.[8]

From the start of World War II, Hitler used Germanic folklore and beliefs in the occult to supplement the Nazi Party's efforts. High-level Nazis researched everything from the Holy Grail to witchcraft. Many Germans and Nazi leaders believed in monsters and other supernatural beings. Among those mythological fascinations were werewolves, which were seen as representing German strength and purity. Some described werewolves as bestial but well-meaning figures that are tied to the woods, blood, and soil. This refrain of "blood and soil" is often heard from modern-day neo-Nazis. The Nazis were so enamored with wolves they called their submarine fleet "the wolfpack." They named individual submarines "Wolf" and "Werewolf." They even named another "Grimm" in honor of the Brothers Grimm, who wrote many antisemitic folkloric stories in the 19th century. Vampires, on the other hand, were bad and represented the subhuman Jews and Slavs who flooded from the East, drained Germany of resources, and contaminated Aryan blood.[9][10]

The battle of werewolves versus vampires is ages old. The Greeks believed the corpses of werewolves, if not destroyed, would return to life as vampires prowling battlefields, drinking the blood of dying soldiers. The Roma believed werewolves served as protectors of caravans against vampires. Similarly, in Irish lore, there is a story of a priest stricken with lycanthropy (werewolves are termed lycanthropes from the Greek words *lucos*, meaning wolf, and *anthropos*, meaning man) who protects travelers from vampires while on the way to a monastery.

Dracula became the basis for an entire genre of literature and film. It is thought Stoker based the Dracula character on Vlad the Impaler (also called Vlad Tepes or Vlad Dracula), a Romanian leader who was born in 1428 and died in 1477. As his nickname suggests, he impaled his victims by piercing their bodies on top of wooden stakes placed in the ground. Modern-day stories and movies such as *Van Helsing* and *Twilight* continue the ages-old battle between vampires and werewolves.[11]

The demonization of one group by another—such as antisemitic Nazi propaganda that depicted Jews as monstrous creatures—prompted horrific acts of dehumanization. The assumption of Jewish monstrosity enabled the perpetrators to deny the humanity (*Mensch* —singular, or *Menschen*—plural, as it is in German) of their victims.

Importantly, in terms of the Holocaust, German stories before 1480 highlighted Vlad's cruelty, plundering, and blood-sucking nature in his campaign in 1462. While the Romanians thought of Vlad as a hero, Germans noted his cruelty and described him as a demented psychopath, sadist, and gruesome murderer. Again, the Nazis viewed Jews and invaders from the East (in this case Romanians) as vampires.

As the end of World War II approached and the Allies advanced on German territory, Hitler and his most senior advisers looked to the supernatural for inspiration. They created two separate movements, with nicknames based on wolves (e.g., "wolfpack"): one, an official group of paramilitary soldiers, and the other an ad hoc ensemble of partisan fighters. Both sowed terror and demoralized occupying soldiers.

Supernatural thinking was an inherent characteristic of the Nazis. The regime used astrology, the paranormal, paganism, Indo-Aryan mythology, witchcraft, miracle weapons, and the lost kingdom of Atlantis to reimagine German politics and society and recast German science and religion. The Nazis drew upon occult practices and related sciences to gain power, shape propaganda and policy, and pursue their dreams of a racial utopia and empire. Their belief in astrology was so strong, Hitler's deputy Rudolf Hess flew to Scotland in 1941 to negotiate peace with the United Kingdom based on his astrologer's advice. He was arrested and spent the rest of the war in prison. The Nazis even had biodynamic farms—a holistic approach to farming that incorporated spiritual, mystical, and magical beliefs —at the Dachau and Auschwitz concentration camps.

Another example of the Nazis' preoccupation with the supernatural was their fascination with Norse tales of frost giants or *Jötunn*. Some experts say Hitler's desire for his troops to be like Norse people—who appeared to be more immune to cold—led him to improperly equip his troops for winter conditions.

Hitler and his henchmen exploited a public fixation with the occult, paganism, and racial superiority. In Nazi Germany, the public fixations included werewolves, a preference for magic over science, and the influential Thule Society.

The Thule Society (named for a mythical, lost northern continent from which the Aryan race was supposedly descended) was a German occultist group organized in 1918, just after World War I. Membership required a "blood declaration of faith," in which the adherent "swears to the best of his knowledge and belief that no Jewish or colored blood flows in either his or his wife's veins and that among their ancestors are no members of the colored races." Rudolf Hess was a member. It sponsored the German Workers' Party, which was reconstituted by Hitler into the Nazi Party. It has been featured in several episodes of the American television series *Supernatural*, and in other stories and movies, as a conspiratorial Nazi organization intending to resurrect Hitler, fight against Jews, and in other ways accomplish Nazi goals.

Many leading Nazis believed in supernatural beings and forces and looked to those whose principles they believed in to support their claims and beliefs. Nostradamus, a prophetic French astrologer, was one such source. Nazi Propaganda Minister Josef Goebbels established a team of astrologers that created Nostradamus-based propaganda for use in foreign policy.

In times of crisis, supernatural and religion-based thinking often take hold under the guise of "scientific" solutions to life's problems. Such thinking, in turn, fosters bad societal outcomes. That is what happened to Germany's fragile democracy in the 1920s and 1930s after World War I. Cultural upheaval, abandonment of civic traditions, indulgence in fantasies, and loss of a sense of reality occurred. Instead of relying on science (which the Nazis believed failed them in World War I), they attached themselves to what historian Peter Staudenmaier calls "border thinking" and "supernatural imaginary." These approaches include astrology, folklore, and outlandish pseudoscientific theories. Another reason for the Nazis' rejection of traditional science was their belief that the evil, soulless Jews who held so many academic and scientific roles had corrupted it.[12]

Pursuing their supernatural aims, Nazi scientists hunted for "death rays." *Schutzstaffel* (SS) paramilitary death squads led by Hitler henchman Heinrich Himmler and responsible for mass killings—officers traveled to Tibet in the middle of the war to look for a lost Aryan tribe, and Himmler employed a personal astrologer. The Nazis explored the "importance of 'Nordic' blood purity," the monstrous Jew, mystical Eastern traditions, and the perceived deleterious effects of socialism, liberalism, and feminism. The Nazi swastika comes from an ancient religious good-luck symbol in Indian culture. The Nazis were open to supernatural theorizing, occult practices, and "miracle weapons" through which they believed they would win World War II. The Nazis' methods were not too different from the fictional Dr. Frankenstein, who, by attempting to imitate God by unnaturally creating life, was the real monster.[13]

While in the present day, we might think of the Nazis' supernatural aims as "crazy," if the Germans had won World War II, our society would no doubt be influenced by their efforts.

To gain a sense of why the Nazis viewed Jews as subhuman, it is important to first understand 19th-century German folklore and legends concerning Jews. Many of these stories were written or collected and published by the famous German authors known as the "Brothers Grimm" in their Grimm's Fairy Tales. In the mid-19th century, the brothers, Jacob and Wilhelm, wrote or collected some of the world's most beloved stories, including "Cinderella," "Hansel and Gretel," "Rapunzel," "Beauty and the Beast," "Little Red Riding Hood," "Rumpelstiltskin," "Sleeping Beauty," and "Snow White." Some of these stories were antisemitic, reflected and further incited German hatred of Jews, and were used later as propaganda by the Nazis. Two were "Little Red Riding Hood," which symbolized the German people suffering at the hands of the Jewish "wolf," and "Cinderella," in which her Aryan purity distinguished her from her mongrel stepsisters.[14]

Some believe that famed director and storyteller Walt Disney was antisemitic. This belief may be in part due to his prolific use of Brothers Grimm stories such as *Cinderella* and *Beauty and the Beast*. Further, Disney was associated with some known antisemites, including the CEO of the Motion Picture Alliance. Disney also welcomed Nazi director Leni Riefenstahl to his studio. However, of the Jews who worked for Disney, it would have been difficult to find any who thought he was an anti-Semite. In 2020, *The Jerusalem Post* found there to be no evidence of Disney being antisemitic. In fact, the

Nazis attacked Disney's work, including in a newspaper article of the 1930s that stated in part:

"Mickey Mouse is the most miserable idea ever revealed. ... the dirty and filth-covered vermin, the greatest bacteria carrier in the animal kingdom, cannot be the ideal type of animal. ... Away with Jewish brutalization of the people! Down with Mickey Mouse! Wear the Swastika Cross!"

Although the issue isn't clear cut, it appears doubtful Disney was antisemitic.[15]

A few of the Brothers Grimm stories that portray antisemitism most clearly are "The Jews' Stone," "The Jew Among Thorns," and "The Girl Who Was Killed by Jews."

"The Jews' Stone" is set in a village in the Austrian state of Tyrol in 1462. It tells of a boy who is sold by his father to Jews who martyr the boy to death on a stone in the woods and hang his mutilated body from a tree. The boy's father confesses to his wife what he did, and when he tries to show her the money he received in exchange for their child, it turns into leaves in his hands. The father dies and the mother brings her son's body to a church, where the stone on which the boy was killed—forever after known as the Jews' Stone—is also brought. The boy, a "holy child," is said to remain in the church to this day.

The story "The Jew Among Thorns" tells of a servant who is underpaid by his rich employer. The servant leaves and encounters a dwarf to whom he gives his earnings. The dwarf grants him three wishes (including a fiddle that makes people want to dance). When the servant later encounters a Jew listening to a songbird, the servant shoots the bird so the Jew can keep it. When the Jew enters a thorny hedge to retrieve it, the servant plays his fiddle, and the Jew is forced to dance in the thorns. The servant thinks the Jew, who in his mind has abused people, will be punished by being stuck by the thorns. The Jew has the servant arrested by claiming the servant stole money, and the servant is to be hung. The servant asks the judge for permission to play his fiddle. Spectators are forced to dance, and the servant only stops playing when the Jew admits the servant did not steal. The Jew was hung instead.

"The Girl Who Was Killed by Jews" takes place in Pforzheim, Germany in 1267. It tells of a greedy old woman who sold a young girl to a group of Jews who drained and collected her blood before discarding her body in the Enz River. A few days later, the child resurfaced alive and was pulled from the water but died after calling for vengeance. The Jews and the old woman confessed their crimes and were executed.

These and other stories were the results of and further fed the vicious and pervasive European anti-Jewish sentiments that led many to believe Jews were responsible for any malady, social problem, or disaster that befell society. In these Brothers Grimm stories, Jews were described as monsters who murdered children, drained their blood, and persecuted the innocent. Myths and unfounded rumors were used to support accusations, as no evidence existed.[16]

Jews' Search for Super Weapons to Protect Themselves

Throughout their history, including before the Holocaust, Jews understood the need to protect themselves. In ancient times, they were enslaved in Egypt, persecuted by various countries, and blamed for the Black Death and other calamities. In more modern times, the pogroms of the late 19th- and early-20th centuries demonstrated how Jews were persecuted by government authorities. These events, in part, resulted in modern Jewish nationalism (including Zionism) and the founding of Israel. The goal was to protect the Jewish community independently of state authorities.

At times in their history, Jews sought and employed "super weapons" intended to secure victory through the power of God. Some of the first super weapons, miracles, or plagues (depending on one's perspective) occurred in the lead-up to the Hebrews' escape from Egyptian bondage (celebrated as Exodus and during Passover). Moses employed God's will to turn the Nile River to blood and cause burning hail to fall from the sky as well as bring three days of darkness, the death of Egyptians' first-born sons (mirroring an earlier similar act by the Egyptians against the Hebrews), an infestation of frogs, gnats, and flies, the parting of the Red Sea, and the related drowning of the pursuing Egyptians.

A later super weapon was the Ark of the Covenant. According to Joshua 6:4, when attacking Jericho and wanting to strike terror in their enemies in 1406 B.C.E, the Israelites carried into battle the Ark of the Covenant, containing the Ten Commandments, and symbolizing God's presence. As described in Exodus 19:5–6, Yahweh (God) made a covenant with the Israelites:

"Now therefore, if ye will obey my voice ... keep my covenant, then ye shall be a peculiar treasure unto me above all people ... a kingdom of priests, and a holy nation ..."

Further, the Jews used the Ark to divide the Jordan River, allowing them to cross. They used the Ark and the trumpets of Joshua to bring down the walls of Jericho ("the oldest city in the world," dating to 9000 BCE and located northwest of the Dead Sea) and defeat the Canaanites (living in modern-day Israel, Palestine, Lebanon, Syria, and Jordan). The Bethsames (an ancient people from Palestine) were killed when they attempted to open the Ark. The Philistines, an ancient people from the Canaan region, suffered plagues after capturing the Ark, causing them to quickly return it to the Israelites.

In 1981, Steven Spielberg directed and George Lucas produced the movie *Raiders of the Lost Ark*. In it, the Nazis—forever trying to secure supernatural weapons to further their aims— attempt to steal the Ark. They are stopped and punished by God for it and, more widely, for the Holocaust. In *Raiders*, when the Nazis opened the Ark, ghosts (in true horror movie fashion) fly out and kill the evildoers by shrinking one's head, melting the face of another, exploding another's head, and sending a beam of energy through the remaining Germans. The area is then wiped clean of the Nazis by the hand of God. The heroes, Indiana Jones and Marion Ravenwood, are spared when they close their eyes to not look upon the avenging ghosts. This is like the Biblical Lot and his daughters (Genesis 19), who obeyed God by looking away from the destruction of the evil city of Sodom, while Lot's wife (who looked back) turned to salt.[17]

Other tales of employing supernatural forces include mentions of the golem, arguably one of the first "superheroes." In one classic tale,

Rabbi Judah Loew of Prague creates a golem to defend the Jewish community from antisemitic attacks. Eventually, the golem grows out of control, and the rabbi is forced to destroy it. Modern-day storytelling, including the 2009 movie *Inglourious Bastards* and the 2005–2015 American television series *Supernatural,* have featured a golem as protector of the Jewish community against Nazis and evildoers.

Unfortunately, the Jews did not have super weapons or other means to stop the horrors of the Holocaust.

THE KITMACHERS

"I fought a big black bird and won."
—Al Kitmacher

We will now move from discussing early Christian and German views of Jews to focusing on my father Al and his family.

My father lived with his father, Gershon; mother, Miriam; older sisters Frieda and Sarah, and his younger brother Yitzhak, first in Lublin, then in Warsaw. They were a close, loving, average, and poor early-20th-century Polish Jewish family. Each had desires, wishes, regrets, worries, virtues, flaws, fears, wants, and every other characteristic people have. They, like so many others, did not deserve to be persecuted or murdered. They didn't realize the depths of the monsters they would face.

"Our family was close and happy," my father said. "We lacked for everything—food, medicine, clothes, money, but we didn't lack for love of one another. We didn't realize how good we had it, how fragile it all was, and how easily it could be lost. I wish I could turn back the clock, appreciate everything more, love everyone a little more, and see more clearly the monsters who were gathering on the other side of the hills. I wish I could have warned my family and convinced my father, who was optimistic about and trusting of the Germans, that we needed to leave while we had the chance. It just never seemed that the horrors would be what they became. Despite all the pogroms and antisemitism, nothing like the Holocaust had ever happened. It just didn't seem real until it was."

Historically, Jews had first names followed by either "ben" or "bat," meaning "son of" or "daughter of," respectively. Ashkenazi Jews from Eastern Europe, like my father's family, didn't have last names until the 18th century. Many of those names were German, including "Kitmacher." This was because in 1787, Austro-Hungarian law, which was the first law mandating that Jews have last names, required Jews to adopt German surnames. Many Jews adopted last names related to their occupation, Jewish history, or roles within religion. Interestingly, whether Jews adopted German surnames or not, the Nazis did not spare Jews who attempted to convert to Christianity after January 18, 1871 (the founding of the German Empire). Only Jews whose grandparents had converted to Christianity before that date were spared.

As mentioned earlier, we believe the first Kitmacher ancestor in Poland was named Hershl. Being known by just a first name was common among European Jews of the time, usually followed by a description of their occupation. *Kit* in German means "putty," and *Macher* means "maker."[1]

Family knowledge and remembrance can be useful in making abstract history concrete. The experience of my father's European family reflects how tangled things could become in the untenable conditions created by the Holocaust. In the following pages, I tell the stories of my father's immediate European family members. As I never met them, I approximate their words and thoughts based on what I know of their lives and those around them. I intend to breathe life into them, giving a voice to those whose lives were stolen.

In recreating their backgrounds, I relied heavily on the study of birth order because it contributes to personalities. While birth order doesn't explain all differences in personalities the position in the sibling sequence has been found to help shape them. The size of the family and the relationship between the parents and the children are other factors and contributed to the "testimony" of these family members. The following comments from my father required the least expanding upon and include numerous stories and descriptions my father provided while telling his story to the 1994 San Francisco Bay Area Holocaust Oral History Project and our family through the years. His description of his upbringing, religious life, first encounter with antisemitism, and his family's early lack of concern over the spreading name Hitler are all elements my father discussed in his 1994 interview.[2]

Al (My Father)

My father's full name was Albert Leon (Abush Leib in Yiddish) Kitmacher. He was born in Lublin in 1920. From 1920 to 1933, my father and his family lived in an apartment at 3 Czwartek Street in the Jewish section.

From 1933 to 1940, my father (aged 13–20) and his family lived at 60 Chlodna Street in Warsaw until they were forced into the Warsaw Ghetto in 1940.

My father (late 1940s)

My father was 19 when the Nazis invaded Poland in 1939, Frieda was 24 (born 1915), Sarah was 22 (born 1917), and Yitzhak, for whom I am named, was 17 (born 1922). My father seemed to be unaware that he had an older brother, Moses, who died in Lublin at three months old in 1914, for he never mentioned him. My father was named after his paternal grandfather Abush Leib Kitmacher. My father had many other, more distant relatives in Poland, but none in Lublin or Warsaw:

'My early life was very difficult and it's very hard to talk about. I'll do my best. I was the second from the youngest in my family; I was the third born, but the oldest boy. This made me the 'man of the family' when my father was away for five years, and I took this responsibility seriously. We were a very close family. We loved each other very much. We didn't have much money or food, but what we had we shared willingly within the family. I still remember the wonderful smells and sounds of my mother cooking and baking. I was trained by my father to be a tailor from the time I was quite young. Men in our family were tailors. My two sisters worked as seamstresses.

I felt like I grew up with fewer restrictions than my older siblings.

My parents loosened the rules by the time I came along. As a middle child, I also felt like I received less attention than my older sisters and younger brother. I was always eager to please and be agreeable, showing off what I knew and what I believed I knew. Later in life, I would use the phrase 'I know exactly.'

I also felt a little lost and left out because I wasn't the oldest or youngest. I always made friends easily, trusting others, at least until the horrors of the Holocaust. I was a young man and, of course, was interested in finding a wife, having children, and raising a family. I was friendly with some of the girls who lived nearby and who I met, but there was little time for this as I spent most of my time trying to help the family survive. There were times that I felt like I was excluded and not understood compared to my siblings. I wasn't praised like my older sisters or coddled like my younger brother. But I tried to make my mark in the family by working hard. My father always warned us about doing 'half-assed' work, meaning work that wasn't complete and well done.

My first recollection of antisemitism occurred in 1932 when I was 12 or 13. I was coming home from Jewish public school in Lublin with a friend when a big fellow, a Polish man in his thirties, walked over to me and shook cigarette ashes into my eye for no reason at all. It burned and hurt very much. I didn't understand why he would do this to me—I didn't know him. This made me wary of other Poles, whose intentions I didn't know. We frequently heard the old saying 'Beware the ayin ha'ra.' We regularly spat ritually three times after a vulnerable person's name was mentioned and said, when making plans, 'Let it be without the evil eye—kinehora.' We were wary.

We grew up hearing horrible fables and stories about how Jews were to blame for everything from disease to unemployment. We knew of Polish folklore that painted a horrible picture of the Jewish people. But we assumed this was just folklore, imaginary worries of some but not most. I grew to think differently and believe these centuries-old tales sowed the seeds of antisemitism and the Holocaust. After the cigarette incident, it was difficult to trust strangers.

I didn't go too far in school, only through the sixth or seventh grade in a Jewish public school. Christians went to a separate public school. I never had thoughts of going further in school, let alone college—I needed to work and contribute to the family's well-being. Jews and Christians were segregated in Polish colleges. Jews were required to sit on designated 'ghetto' benches in the classrooms or just stand. Any Christians who dared sit with Jews were beaten by Polish nationalists. The Jewish community passed a resolution in 1936 protesting these ghetto benches.

I had Jewish classes from a rabbi on Saturdays to prepare for my bar mitzvah. In 1933, my father (who had just returned from Germany) threw a simple bar mitzvah in Warsaw for me. This was very different than the grand events that the few wealthy Jews threw for their children—but we had lots of fun! He invited some friends, they had a bottle of liquor, and my mother made a very special dessert—cheesecake! In Judaism, cheesecake is thought to represent the 'land of milk and honey' that Moses's liberated Hebrews searched for during the Exodus from slavery in Egypt.

My brother was there, but my mother and sisters, of course, had to watch my bar mitzvah from a different room, which was the tradition since the sexes were separated in synagogue, but they could see and hear everything. I saved some of the candies that were thrown at me, the bar mitzvah boy, and shared them with my siblings.

We were not yet concerned about Hitler; he didn't seem to have anything in mind then. The family didn't know of Hitler's book *Mein Kampf*, which had been published in 1925, and his rabid hatred of the Jews. Everything was OK in Poland until the Germans invaded in 1939.

Our primary concerns revolved around making a living. We had a reasonably normal family existence between 1933 and 1939, working hard, with no particular problems. We lived from day to day. Our family enjoyed good health and even had enough food (unlike when we were later moved into the Warsaw Ghetto and after), with matzo ball soup, sweet-and-sour rolled cabbage, and other favorites. I was born after World War I ended, so I grew up in the interwar period. Unlike my parents, my sisters, brother, and I had a whole new set of opportunities that being a citizen of a republic afforded us. There were also new challenges that we faced that our parents didn't have to deal with. The Great War with Germany, World War I, was over, and we weren't focused on Germany. Germany invading Poland was not yet on the horizon. We were living our lives, planning for our futures. Jews had a greater sense of community and belonging in the Polish Republic that didn't exist before World War I.

Occasionally, we encountered antisemites in Warsaw—it was not hard to find them. We faced new occurrences of persecution because of government policies and community flareups against Jews. Despite this, my father expected we would stay in Warsaw, working, for the foreseeable future. In retrospect, this was a mistake. We should have made every effort to get out while we could. Poland, and Warsaw especially, was the 'crossroads' of Europe; it seemed every army had invaded and marched through the area. I wish we could have foreseen what the Germans had planned.

Some of my friends described themselves as Bundists, embracing the idea of secular Jewish nationalism, including political, cultural, and social autonomy in Poland and the rest of Eastern Europe. They attended meetings in Lublin and Warsaw. They fought against the persecution of Jews, boycotts of Jewish goods, and the ousting of Jews from workplaces. They worked to set up Jewish trade unions, workers' kitchens, cooperative shops, and cultural institutions. They had youth, women's, sports, and other organizations. They campaigned against antisemitism, pogroms, and helped Jews emigrate. They even worked with the American Jewish Joint Distribution Committee, organizing artisans' and contractors' cooperatives. I would have liked to join their ranks, but had little time, needing to work and bring home food."

Grandfather Gershon

My father's father, Gershon "Gersh" Henoch Leib Kitmacher, was born in 1890 in Czemierniki, where the Jewish population in the 1920s numbered just over 01,000—two-thirds of the population. As the Holocaust progressed, most Czemierniki Jews were sent to Treblinka and few survived.

Gershon's parents and other relatives had lived in the shtetl of Czemierniki. It was a small, agricultural village outside of Lublin. His parents often told him how everyone worked hard, whether they were farmers, craftsmen, metalworkers, milkmen, or had other occupations. The town's rabbi was looked to for advice on everyday life, from raising children to getting married, finding happiness, and caring for the elderly. Even if people were not literate or formally religious, they still participated in the synagogue as a traditional way of helping each other. However, there was not enough work to keep everyone busy and not enough food to live on. Gershon was a very good tailor and taught his and his wife Miriam's sons and daughters to be tailors and seamstresses. Like the old Yiddish saying "mir zollen nit farnayen der saychel [one should not believe in superstitions, but still it is best to be heedful of them]." He always chewed on a piece of thread while sewing to keep his common sense with him.

Gershon had four brothers, one of whom was named Albert Leon [Abush Leib] Kitmacher—the same name he and Miriam would give their son Al upon his birth in 1920. Gershon's parents moved the family to Lublin, a much larger town, to find work and hopefully live a better life with more food, and improved living conditions.

In 1928, Gershon left Poland to work in Germany. It was hard to make a living in Poland and work was scarce. He felt that Germany's economy was somewhat better than Poland's in the late 1920s, having come back from its economic low following the end of World War I. For the good of the family, and thinking there would be more work there, in 1928 he went to work in Berlin. He opened a tailor shop and found customers—Jewish and non-Jewish. Berlin was a very big city, bigger and busier than Warsaw and Lublin combined. There were many more motor vehicles and things seemed more modern. There were also many more "fancy" people, wearing formal clothing, top hats, and other trappings of the rich. There was also much culture, beautiful music, good food, and excitement in the air.

Gershon's family was everything to him, he would have done practically anything to make their lot in life better. Being away for five years was very painful for him, as he was sure it was for his family. He missed his wonderful wife, Miriam, and the kids. He wrote often, and they were always in his thoughts.

Although looking back it may seem odd that Gershon chose to go to Germany to find work, he knew that Jews had lived there relatively peacefully for 1,000 years. He also personally knew several Jews who lived in Berlin, spoke the language fluently, and identified as German and Jewish. Jews felt comfortable in Germany. It was like any other place; there were problems and antisemitism, but nothing too bad. He was optimistic about the future. He had heard some of the folklore the Poles and Germans had about Jews but didn't know all the stereotypes and conspiracy theories that Germans were taught. If he had known, maybe he would have thought twice about living there.

Gershon thought his German last name helped him blend in—no one questioned whether he was Jewish. He regularly sent money home to support his family. He wished he could have been with them but felt good that he was helping put food on the table. He lived at 18 Charlottenburg Kantstrasse. Berlin was an ancient, big city, having been the German capital for as long as anyone could remember. At first, it was a nice, big city to live and work in.

Gershon knew of the *Gemeinde*, a Jewish organization and center of German Jewish life that embraced all Jews, including noncitizens. It helped the government organize communal and ritual affairs, build, and maintain synagogues, operate charitable institutions, and organize Sabbath and other religious services he attended.

While some German Jews were doctors, lawyers, and journalists, most were like Gershon, working with their hands, creating, and fixing things. He made friends with German Jews and Jews who, like him, were temporarily in Berlin to find work.

Other German Jewish organizations included the League of Jewish Women and the Reich Association of Jewish Front Soldiers. German Jews were more than proud that about 100,000 of their number served in the German military in World War I, and 12,000 died defending the homeland. Gershon knew one man who fought for the Germans and was injured; he received the highest decorations a German soldier could receive. This man was very proud of them but rarely put them on, though he occasionally brought them out of the cupboard and showed them to Gershon and others. The man also received a letter from the German government thanking him for his military service. The increasing dark clouds over Germany's Jews angered and saddened the man greatly. Gershon didn't know at the time that some Germans blamed the Jews for their having lost World War I. When he heard this, it seemed crazy to him, and he thought it must have been only very few hardheads who would think this.

The year 1933 was a turning point. The Nazis came to power in Germany and named Hitler as chancellor. Nazis boycotted Jewish shops and businesses, denied non-Aryans [non-Germans] admission to the legal bar, denied the repayment of non-Aryan medical expenses, and restricted Jewish enrollment in German schools. Before all of this, there had been some discrimination and antisemitism, but Germany seemed to be generally tolerant and accepting. Now, brown-shirted toughs with swastikas intimidated, screamed, and spat at Jews and other non-Germans. They carried signs saying horrible things about them and drew Stars of David with lines through them on storefront windows. One could feel the hate and rage. Before, Gershon felt safe walking on the streets in Berlin. People were people, whether German or Jewish. But now, one could feel the tension and the hate. He saw thugs yelling insults at people they thought were Jewish. Germany was not a safe place for Jews.

Before, Jews enjoyed rights like German citizens. Now they were kept out of many activities. Laws were enacted to segregate and impoverish Jews, and the German government, which had been accepting of Jews, now demonized them. Germany teetered on the brink of civil war, with daily bloody street battles between Nazis and communists. This is when Gershon was given the order to get out of Germany. He was forced to leave his tailor shop and return to Lublin, 463 miles away. It was his first time back home in over five years. He looked forward to getting out of this quickly worsening situation and back to Poland where he hoped there would be greater stability and peace.

Upon Gershon's return from Berlin, he moved the family to

Warsaw. He hoped there would be more work and greater opportunities there like there had been in Berlin.

Berlin has been a center of science, technology, arts, the humanities, city planning, film, higher education, and industry. It was also the Nazi capital, with a population of about four million. Before World War II, Albert Einstein rose to public prominence there, being awarded the Nobel Prize for Physics in 1921. After Hitler came to power in 1933, Berlin's Jewish community was reduced through emigration from 160,000—one-third of all Jews in the country—to about 80,000. After Kristallnacht—the violent anti-Jewish demonstrations that destroyed 1,000 synagogues and over 7,000 Jewish businesses, hospitals, schools, cemeteries, and homes on November 9, 1938, killing thousands of the city's Jews, 96 were imprisoned in the nearby Sachsenhausen concentration camp. Starting in 1943, many were shipped to Auschwitz and other death camps. The April and May 1945 Battle of Berlin resulted in the surrender of the German army and Hitler's suicide.

The city was reduced to rubble and about 22,000 German civilians were killed. Berlin is the most heavily bombed city in history.

My Father's mother Miriam (date unknown)

Grandmother Miriam

My father's maternal grandmother, Ruchla ("Rachel") Neiman (maiden name) Rosenblatt was born in Poland in the 1800s and lived with my father's family. She was living in the Lublin Ghetto in 1943 when she and two of her grandchildren were shot and killed in the courtyard of her house. She had three brothers, Chaim, Isaak, and Lipa (my father's great uncles), all of whom moved to Krasnik, Poland (the date is unclear). Her three brothers and their children died either in the ghettos or camps. Ruchla's husband's (my father's maternal grandfather) name was Gersz Leizor. He was born in 1860 in Poland and was serving as a Polish reserve soldier in 1889 when he married Ruchla.

My father's mother (Rachel's daughter), Miriam Brandla Neiman Kitmacher, was born in Lublin in 1890.

Gershon and Miriam met in Lublin, introduced by a matchmaker employed by their parents. They married when they were both very young, barely 20. They were fortunate. They got along well and built their love by building a life together. Miriam knew many young women in arranged marriages who didn't fare as well. Gershon and she had four children—two boys and two girls.

When Gershon went to work in Germany in 1928, Miriam stayed behind to take care of the family. She agreed with his decision to go as their family was very poor and there was never enough food. If Gershon could make more money in Germany, it seemed like the right thing to do. She missed him terribly, but it helped the family survive. She never told him, but before he left, she attached a pin on his clothing to repel any evil spirits.

Despite the lack of food and necessities, they were a happy family. At the time, Miriam didn't know that Germany could be dangerous for Jews. The family had experienced pogroms and antisemitism in Poland, and she was sure it existed elsewhere, but there was nothing about Germany to fear—or at least she thought there wasn't.

They had a close family. They often didn't have enough money, but they found a way to survive. They were not very religiously observant, going to synagogue on the high holidays but not every Sabbath. Despite this, they were Jewish in every way possible, from the type of food they ate, to what they believed, to how they raised their children. They were proud of their heritage and traditions. Like others, they enjoyed Klezmer music, dance tunes of Eastern Europe, and other distractions from everyday life.

They mainly spoke Yiddish at home and Polish outside the home. They didn't speak Hebrew but used a bit of German because of Gershon's familiarity with the language. Miriam loved the sound of Yiddish; it was comforting to have their own language. Some of the Yiddish words they used, included *bissel* [a little bit], *chutzpah* [nerve], *feh* [disgust], *goy* [Gentile], *kibbitz* [talking and joking], *kvetch* [complain], *l'chaim* [to life], *mazel tov* [good luck], *mensch* [decent person], *meshuggeneh* [crazy], *mishigas* [craziness], *nosh* [eat or nibble], *nu* [so, said in a questioning way], *oy vay* [woe], *plotz* [aggravation], *schlep* [move slowly], *schmooze* [chat], *shmaltzy* [sentimental or fancy], *spiel* [a long story], *shmatte* [rag], and *tatela shind* [golden child].

Yiddish is the language of the Ashkenazim central- and eastern-European Jews. The origin of the language has been dated to the ninth century CE. Written in Hebrew, Yiddish became one of the world's most widespread languages, appearing in most countries with a Jewish population by the 19th century. Millions of Yiddish speakers were victims of the Nazis. The number of speakers was further reduced by the suppression of the language in the Soviet Union. The language nevertheless continues to flourish among the ultra-Orthodox in numerous countries, and among secular students of Yiddish at leading universities.

Jewish life was vibrant and exciting. Miriam remembered the day a new movie theater called The Palladium opened in Warsaw. There were advertisements for it and even a spotlight that lit up the sky in front of the theater, announcing its presence. Everything seemed so modern. Despite their struggles, they had great hope for their future and their children.

The family lived and worked in a mostly Christian neighborhood, although there were some other Jews. Their tailor and seamstress shops were in the house. Miriam was friendly with some of the Christian women who lived in their apartment buildings. They'd offer each other sugar, flour, and other baking and cooking goods.

It seemed like there was the nonstop and deafening sound of hammering and sawing after Yom Kippur, preparing for Sukkot. Soon, there were palm branch roofs erected as far as the eyes could see. Purim was an occasion for the children to dress up and perform before their admiring parents. Miriam and Gershon made their children's costumes, and the children would rehearse their parts until they were perfect. On Passover, the family would buy special matzo bread with holes. Sometimes they would celebrate Passover with extended family. In the spring, the smell of fresh paint used to spruce up neighboring buildings, blended with the fresh scent of the new season. Spring, warm and gentle, brought the beautiful holiday of freedom: Passover.

Although Miriam didn't believe in all the old ways, she did believe in some of the folklore and sprinkled a little salt in the corners of their rooms to ward off any evil that may have wanted to get in.

She took great pride in being a good mother to their four children. After baby Moses died at three months in 1914—thank God

Lilith didn't take him from them at birth so they could enjoy a little time with him—Gershon and she were secretly hoping their firstborn would be a boy. But they couldn't have been happier with their two girls and two boys. She tried not to leave any of the kids out, paying attention to each although, as was the custom, boys were paid more attention than the girls—that was just the way it was. They always ate their meals together and she asked how each child was doing. She congratulated them on their accomplishments and encouraged their dreams.

Miriam prayed that their children would grow up happy, healthy, and fulfilled. After any sneeze, she'd repeat the phrase "long life," "good health," or "God bless you." They didn't have much money, and their kids had to leave school to help the family, but she still wanted the best for them. She thought the future was bright for those who worked hard. She would have done anything for their kids.

Aunt Frieda

Frieda's parents, Gershon and Miriam, were always busy working and trying to put food on the family's table. As the eldest, she was given extra responsibilities. She acted as the disciplinarian, enforcing the rules of the home. She monitored her siblings' actions at home and in the courtyard, keeping them safe. She also ensured each associated with the "right people:" no ruffians, bad kids, or those who might share unwholesome habits, foul language, or diseases. Along with overseeing her siblings' playtime, Frieda ensured each studied and did their work. She tested them on schoolwork and looked at their tailoring and seamstress work. As they got older, Frieda's siblings didn't appreciate her help as much.

While other children played, Frieda read books and cleaned, washed, and cooked alongside her mother. She always felt a lot of pressure to do the best that she could. She was always a perfectionist and an overachiever, striving to please their parents. She was diligent, wanting to excel at everything she did. She was the reliable and conscientious one, but she also tended to be cautious. Frieda stuck to the straight and narrow and didn't like change or stepping out of her comfort zone. Her siblings said she was bossy and controlling, but she had to take charge, whether it was on chores or other family responsibilities.

Sarah and Frieda, as the daughters, couldn't get away with the things that Al and Yitzhak, the "beloved sons," could. It wasn't fair, but it was the way the world was. While Sarah had time to think about relationships, Frieda didn't have that luxury. She had an important role in the family and had to act like a third parent.

Before World War II, the family lived in enormous, multistory apartment buildings housing more than 100 families in both Lublin and Warsaw. The front apartments where the windows looked out onto the street were occupied by doctors, lawyers, teachers, and other professionals. Tradesmen, including tailors and seamstresses (like their family), shoemakers, milliners, and others, who worked from home, resided in the rear apartments.

The buildings also housed bakeries, mattress factories, chicken-wire fence factories, and blacksmiths. One building had a school for ballroom dancing, a trumpet school, and a merchant's organization. The other building housed a private school for girls, a sports club where Frieda had exercised when she was young, and a *cheder* (a small religious school), where a rabbi taught young boys to read the Torah. There seemed to be whole cities within the confines of these densely populated urban dwellings. Frieda never forgot the sounds, smells, and characters. All the sounds and smells blended together, the baked goods, the music, the hammering. Most of the tenants were Jewish and everyone knew everyone else.

They were not a well-to-do family. Their father Gershon's income barely covered living expenses, which is why they needed to take in seamstress and tailoring work. The children each attended Jewish public school for as long as they were in school. Other Jews had to attend more expensive private school because admission quotas restricted the number of Jewish students who could attend public schools. The Christian children went to their own schools. The family didn't let this discrimination dispirit them, and Frieda didn't know if they really thought of it as discrimination. It was just the way things were. The children were energetic and earnest.

Many of the young people Frieda knew had joined and belonged to Zionist organizations and sports clubs. When she was 11, she joined a Zionist group called *HaNoar ha-Tsioni*, Hebrew for Zionist Youth. They would meet, learn, and engage in Hebrew songs and dances like the *hora*. Their young instructors took them camping and introduced them to Jewish history, literature, and Zionism. From their instructors, they learned that the Jewish people must have their own country—that they must return to Palestine, their Biblical homeland—because the dangers of antisemitism in Europe were too great. She decided that once she was able to help the family get to a good place living-wise, she would look into moving to Palestine to help build a new Jewish homeland. This desire to build a new homeland ran contrary to their attachment to their native soil. Jews had lived in Poland for hundreds of years. This made Frieda feel conflicted.

While their parents clung to the traditional ways, the children—as younger Jews, fully embraced the country's culture while simultaneously observing some Jewish traditions with the family. Everything around them seemed to be evolving and modernizing, and despite all the hardships, they had hope for a brighter future.

Aunt Sarah

Sarah was a middle child along with Al, although he was three years younger than she was. She thought, as the middle girl, she was under less pressure than Frieda to help run the household. But she felt like she received less attention than her older sister and her younger brothers, which made her want to please everyone. Sarah sometimes felt left out. She wasn't the oldest or the youngest, so who was she? Frieda was often praised by their parents, and Yitzhak was coddled. Sarah thought if one were to ask her family and friends, they'd describe her as agreeable, a little rebellious, a good friend, a peacemaker and negotiator, and someone who "goes along to get along." Changes didn't bother her much, as she would "go with the flow."

Whereas Frieda's and Yitzhak's attentions were mainly focused on the family, Sarah, like Al, had some close friends. There was even a neighbor boy who she liked. They gave each other affectionate glances and said hello to each other and even touched each other's hand in passing, but that was as far as it went. They understood that a more serious relationship was something their parents would need to arrange. Their parents were too busy working and finding food for the family to eat to focus on boyfriends or girlfriends. But someday Sarah knew her parents would find her the right boy and she would settle down and create a home for themselves. She planned on having children of her own! While growing up, at the end of summer, the children returned to school bursting with delight and eagerness. Sarah was an excellent pupil and loved school. She attended a Jewish public school and afternoon Hebrew school. Although the family was at times hungry and lacking material goods, there also seemed to be much joy and freedom.

Winter was a particularly happy time for Sarah. She would sit by the window and watch the snow fall. It gave her a feeling of warmth and safety. She especially loved the smell of wood-burning fireplaces as people tried to keep their homes warm despite the freezing temperatures. Kids got into snowball fights up and down the street and sometimes their parents would play. Lublin and Warsaw were fun places to grow up in and call home.

Sarah always seemed to be smiling and happy, and people liked her. People who knew her would stop and ask how she was and pat her on the head or pinch her cheek. She had a few Polish non-Jewish friends. They played hide and seek and other games together in the garden behind their apartment building. When Passover came, other children didn't understand why the Jewish children couldn't play. Sarah remembered one girl saying that Jews drank Polish children's blood—so stupid! She could never understand how people could be so mean to each other. She even knew a Jewish girl who some Polish people threw stones at for no reason. It didn't make any sense. Couldn't they all be nice to each other?

Sarah loved to recite poems and sing. When they visited friends or relatives, Gershon and Miriam would ask Sarah to sing or tell a story. Sometimes she didn't feel like it and just wanted to play with the other children outside. But she was a natural entertainer, bringing laughter to others. Maybe someday she would be an entertainer for real!

Sarah always kept busy, visiting with relatives, playing, going to school, and ice and roller skating on Saturdays. Her favorite photo was of her mother, father, sister, brothers, and she enjoying being a family. It was 1933, she was 16 years old, and their father had just returned from Germany after being gone for five years. The family looked so carefree. It was midsummer, the trees were in bloom, and they were all wearing their best clothing. They were moving from Lublin to Warsaw, and one wouldn't think anybody had a care in the world.

Uncle Yitzhak

Yitzhak's childhood was happy, and he felt secure in the love and affection he received from his parents, brother, and sisters.

After school, other children and Yitzhak played ball, hide and seek, and hopscotch in the courtyards. He loved the excitement of picking players and sides, running, and jumping. He remembered Gypsy men and women visiting their neighborhood and playing folk music. Other times, a blind man and his son sang and played the accordion. The children would circle around to watch a performance and scramble to pick up and drop into the musicians' hats the coins that women tossed from their apartment windows. It all seemed so otherworldly. Some seemed to resent the Gypsies, saying they brought bad luck and illness. Yitzhak thought that the only thing they brought was a sense of fun! It seemed like there was always something fun going on in the neighborhood. He didn't think his older sisters and brother felt the same way, especially Frieda. They adamantly kept their distance from others and tried to restrain his friendships in the apartment building.

The family never had birthday parties and Yitzhak didn't remember going to others' parties, so maybe it just wasn't the custom. He did go to Al's bar mitzvah, and it was a lot of fun dancing, enjoying music, and eating good food. He wished his sisters and mother could have participated, but they had to watch from a distance as was the tradition.

One of the most popular games was *volkerball*, a type of handball game with two teams and complicated rules. The older children played this, and it was a great day when they allowed the younger children to play too. As the baby of the family, Yitzhak was fun-loving, outgoing, and often the center of attention. He was always agreeable and went with the flow. He felt like he could always charm his way through difficult situations. On the other hand, he felt like he was not taken as seriously as his older siblings. Things he accomplished weren't seen as being as big as their accomplishments. He thought others would describe him as free-spirited, with fewer rules to follow compared to his sisters and brother. Honestly, and maybe it's because of the consistent love he received from his parents, he believed he was destined to do great things.

Yitzhak's siblings, although they loved him, also thought he was too coddled by their parents. Less was expected of him than the others. The other children complained about their workload, sewing clothing, and working around the house. They did this while he got to go out and play. It's not that he was lazy. It's just that there were so many other things to do besides work. He sometimes wondered if the Biblical Joseph, with his multi-colored coat and all those brothers, felt like him, envied by his siblings. He was the tatela shind.

Yitzhak was especially close to his father. Gershon always seemed larger than life and able to accomplish great things. Yitzhak thought Gershon was very brave when he went to Germany for five years to make money to send home for the family's comfort. Yitzhak missed him terribly and often wondered what Gershon was doing in far-off Berlin. That seemed like a whole other world. Yitzhak was so happy when his father came home! Gershon was the smartest person Yitzhak knew—not through book learning but real-life lessons. Gershon and Miriam were Yitzhak's heroes!

THE HARRIS FAMILY

"If I had said I was a tailor, I would have been killed."
—Al Kitmacher

My Mother the Angel

My mother, Pearl Harris, was born in October 1922 in Schenectady, New York. She lived with her father, Louis; mother, Rose; and older sister, Celia. They moved in 1929, and my mother (and subsequently her married family) lived in Pittsfield, Massachusetts, to 1987. My mother and her family reflected the history and lives of many Jewish Americans. European Jews, like my mother's ancestors, often escaped the horrors of persecution and programs in Poland and Russia to immigrate to America, the land of "milk and honey."

"We were Jewish and Americans; we were proud of both," Pearl said. "We heard that Jews elsewhere suffered abuses and discrimination and wanted to help, but it all seemed so far away. My father was born in Poland in the late 1800s. He came to the U.S. with his father, brothers, and sisters; his mother had died in Poland. They left as antisemitism was rising and the First World War was raging. He used to tell us about antisemitism, pogroms, and deprivations that he, his family, and other Jews faced. I felt very fortunate being born and growing up in the US, but I often wondered how my fellow Jews were doing in Poland and elsewhere in Europe. If I knew how to help them, I would. I would soon have the chance."

My mother never had a cross word or negative wish for anyone. She was a human angel who grew up in a loving, average, and poor early-20th-century American Jewish family.

My mother as a baby, circa 1923

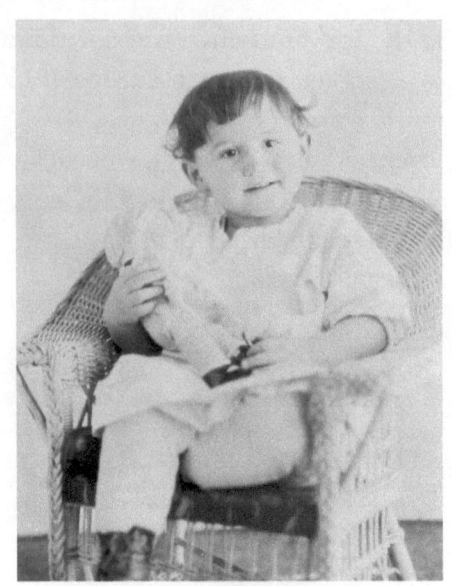

My mother at 2 years old, 1924

My mother on a pony, circa 1928

The Harris family (early 20th century)

"I was the younger of the two children in our family. I always looked up to my big sister Celia, or 'CeCe,' as I called her. I couldn't have asked for a better sister. I remember my childhood as a happy time in my life, surrounded by my loving family and a supportive community. I remember my mother telling me how lucky both of us were to be healthy and alive as I had fallen horribly ill as an infant. I was poisoned as a baby by her breast milk, which had thickened and spoiled in her breast. I've been told since then that milk can't spoil in the breast, but this was what the doctors said at the time. The doctors told her she needed to have a radical mastectomy, which was the common approach. She was in pain for the rest of her life.

Our family moved from Schenectady to Pittsfield, in the Berkshire Hills of western Massachusetts, when my dad was offered a new job. We moved to the upstairs apartment of a two-family house on Crane Avenue in Pittsfield. My best friend up until high school was Lillian Samel. Next to her four-foot, ten-inch frame, I seemed tall at five feet, four inches. I was skinny, although I always ate well.

I remember the early 1920s as an exciting time with new, modern conveniences like refrigerators. Our radio connected us with the rest of the country and world! New motorized vehicles had long since replaced horses, and the air was thick with smoke from their exhausts. My mom was a great cook but never let me help her in the kitchen. I'm not sure why. Years later, when I married, I didn't even know how to boil water!

Then, in 1929, the Great Depression hit. We were very poor, and everyone was scared. Businessmen and other successful people were now selling apples and pencils on street corners. It was a very sad time."[1]

The Great Depression was the worst economic downturn in the history of the industrialized world, lasting from 1929 to 1939. It began in the United States with the stock market crash, and by 1933, at its lowest point, some 15 million Americans were unemployed and nearly half the country's banks had failed. The massive spending during World War II ended the Depression, with more than 12 million Americans serving in the military, and a similar number in defense-related jobs.

In response to the Depression's massive bank failures, President Franklin Delano Roosevelt (FDR) in 1933 established the Federal Deposit Insurance Corporation (FDIC) to protect U.S. bank depositors' accounts. I rose to the senior executive level as FDIC's chief human capital officer before retiring in 2019. I was with the agency for 16 of my 36 years in government service.

"I took pride in learning how to save a penny! I developed frugal and careful habits, like patching clothes, scraping the inside of eggshells to get every last drop of egg, clipping coupons, and saving Gold Bond trading stamps. When walking outside, I always kept a look out for coins people may have dropped. I faithfully continued these habits my whole life.

Our family was Reform, observing the major Jewish holidays but otherwise was not traditionally religious and didn't go to services regularly. We celebrated Rosh Hashanah [New Year], Yom Kippur [Day of Atonement], Passover [to remember the Hebrews' liberation from ancient Egypt], and Hanukkah [the Festival of Lights commemorating the recovery of Jerusalem and rededication of the Second Temple at the beginning of the Maccabean revolt].

I was involved in activities at the local Hebrew school and Jewish community center. Like other Americans at the time, I heard stories about European Jews being mistreated. I was concerned for them, but there were problems much closer to home like the Depression. We didn't understand the seriousness of the Nazi threat yet. We knew of antisemitism, but I didn't personally experience it. My father told us how antisemitism was much more prevalent in Europe than in America. It was hard to believe that people could be so cruel to each other just because of what they believed.

I loved the Berkshires—it was home. There were four seasons, with beautiful fall foliage, snowy winters, lovely springs, and warm summers. There were forests, mountains, and lakes. Even the wealthy from New York City built mansions and estates in the Berkshires! It was a warm, welcoming place.

I fondly remember sitting near our little fireplace in the living room, all four of us talking about our days and the future. Although we lacked much, mostly the things I remember are the warmth, the smells of the food my mother was baking and cooking, and the love we had for each other.

When I was a young child, my mom, dad, sister, and I often went blueberry picking in the hills near Pittsfield. There were blueberries, blackberries, apples, and all kinds of fruit growing in the Berkshires. We didn't own a car, but we didn't need one because we went with friends. I vividly remember one time we rode in the open back of their pickup truck and sat on a board that they had placed across the back, directly behind the cab. The weather was pleasant going there, but coming back, the sky darkened, and it started to pour! The rain hit the cab slanted over us, and not a drop touched us—a miracle! Times seemed much simpler then, and it didn't take much to keep entertained.

Growing up, I used to take the young daughter of my parents' friends to the movies on Saturdays. The friends gave me ten cents for a ticket, and there was no charge for the child. It was a losing proposition for me, as the ticket price in the early 1930s was 25 cents, and I always bought candy and drinks for the two of us. I remember one time the child got very tired, became too noisy, and we left without watching much of the show. I never did finish seeing that movie, whatever it was!

Some wonderful movies came out during my teenage years, like *Snow White and the Seven Dwarfs, The Wizard of Oz, Tom Sawyer, Gulliver's Travels, Heidi, Alice in Wonderland,* and *Babes in Toyland.* At the time, I had no idea that a number of these movies were based on German and European folklore and tales as written by the famous Brothers Grimm. If I had known their stories in their original forms, with their horrible antisemitism and hateful lies, I don't think I would have enjoyed them nearly as much.

I remember going to see 1931's *Frankenstein* and 1933's *King Kong* at the movies. They were both scary and impressive in their own ways. How did they create Frankenstein's monster and the lifelike Kong and dinosaurs? But what struck me was that the real monsters were the humans who manipulated Frankenstein's creature and Kong for their own purposes. Dr. Frankenstein was trying to play God by creating life, and it was this new creature that paid the price due to the humans' ignorance and lack of tolerance. The 'monster' was a simple, lonely being who just wanted to be liked. Likewise, Kong was used by humans as a sideshow act to make money. I felt bad for both the creature and Kong. The messages of these movies were clear to me: don't try and play God and make sure you know your place in the scheme of things.

I loved to read as many books and 'funnies' [comics] in the newspaper as I could get my hands on. I remember reading *Winnie the Pooh, Bambi, Doctor Doolittle, The Wizard of Oz, Raggedy Ann and Andy,* and others. *The Wizard of Oz* especially had an impact on me, with its message to stay close to home and family. It also warned not to trust far-off people and lands, though at the time I had no reason to take this part of the message to heart. I had dolls and other toys, and as a family, we played Scrabble, Monopoly, and other board games. My sister Celia was my best friend!

There were two major lakes in Pittsfield: Pontoosuc and Onota. They were both big and beautiful. One vivid memory I have is from when I was 12 years old, in 1934. Though I had swam in lakes before, I had never been in a swimming pool, so I started diving and swimming at the YMCA pool. YMCA stands for Young Men's Christian Association, and although it was a Christian organization, it allowed individuals of all faiths, including Jews, to attend and work on their 'body, mind, and spirit.'

I remember when the instructor told me to start by jumping off the diving board. I was taken aback. As I approached the board's ladder, I waited a few moments to watch others jump off and into the water. While it looked kind of fun, I was still a young girl, and a jump that high was scary. When no one else was in front of me and a line had formed behind me, I decided I had no choice but to jump. I hoisted myself up the metal ladder and felt the blood rushing to my head, leaving my body cold and shaky. I was terrified. Standing on the board for the first time, I looked down into the water, which seemed to be 20 feet below me. Gingerly, I walked out to the edge of the board. Standing still, feet locked together, I contemplated whether I really would jump. The water was a formidable enemy, and I didn't feel strong enough to beat it. Reaching deep inside myself, I locked away my fear and nervousness and pulled out the small threads of strength and courage I had. I took one last step, which left me at the very edge of the board.

Per the instructor's directions, I bounced once, breathed deeply twice, and leaped from the end of the board. Though the deep end was most likely around ten feet deep, I swear I sank at least 20 feet before my feet touched the bottom. Frantically, I pushed off the floor of the pool. The surface couldn't come fast enough, and I was frightened. It took a long time to come back up, which made me feel like I wouldn't reach the top. When I finally reached the water's surface, I gasped for breath. Flailing around in the water, I finally found myself at the edge of the pool. Thankful to be alive, I pulled myself out of the pool, as the instructor was too distracted to assist me.

I hated the water for the rest of my life and avoided lakes and swimming pools, so I never could have predicted that I would have a similar experience some ten years later when I joined the U.S. Navy.

My family was surprised when I joined the Navy as I was always the quiet little one. I think my parents and sister were proud of me. These were extraordinary times and I needed to push myself well beyond my comfort level. We all had to pitch in, do our best, and make this a better world."

My Grandfather Louis

In the following pages, I tell the stories of my mother's father Louis, her mother Rose, and her sister Celia. As I never met my maternal grandparents, I approximate their words and thoughts based on what I know of their lives and those around them. I knew my aunt Celia well and we had a close, loving relationship.

Louis was born in Poland in 1898. His schooling in Poland was through the third grade. He came to the U.S. in 1916, at age 18, with his father, Julius, and his five brothers and two sisters. The family left Poland because anti-Jewish feelings and rhetoric were rising during World War I and they feared what would happen to them if we stayed. Numerous pogroms against Jews were initiated in Eastern Europe following the end of the First World War in 1918. It was a scary time in Europe, and it seemed much worse than it was in the earlier 1900s. So much intolerance and hatred towards Jews and others who were "different"!

Louis observed that, in Poland, the monsters born from folklore as well as men wishing the family harm seemed to be around every corner. They needed to get away from that land of horrors. They heard stories of how open and tolerant America was: a land of milk and honey! The family set its sights on immigrating to the great land of freedom, the United States.

Louis' mother had died in Poland in the early 1900s. She was a wonderful and loving woman. He remembered the wonderful smells as she cooked traditional Jewish and Polish foods. The family missed her dearly and wished that she had lived to move with them to America. Later, at one time, nine grandchildren were named Pearl in her memory.

Upon entering America, the Ellis Island officials shortened and

Americanized the family's last name from Hershkovitz to Harris. Harris is an English, Irish, Scottish, and Welsh last name; none of the Harris' ancestors had lived in those countries. The officials explained that Louis' surname was difficult to spell and say, and they wanted to make it easier for him to fit in. Later, Louis heard an old American Jewish joke which made him think of the name change:

"A Jewish immigrant landed at Ellis Island in New York. The procedures were confusing, and he was overwhelmed by the commotion. When one of the officials asked him 'What is your name?' he replied, '*Shayn fergessen*' which in Yiddish means 'I've already forgotten.' The official then recorded his name as Sean Ferguson!"[2]

Ellis Island is an island in the New York City harbor that served as the busiest immigrant inspection station in the United States. From 1892 to 1924, approximately twelve million immigrants, including Jews, arrived at the Port of New York and were processed there under U.S. law. Today, it is part of the Statue of Liberty National Monument and houses the Ellis Island National Museum of Immigration.

Louis settled in Schenectady with his family. Soon after arriving, he met Rose, and they married in early 1918. They had Celia in November 1918 and Pearl—named after Louis' late mother—in October 1922. For a while, the family lived in the same town as Louis' father and siblings.

Louis made feather mattresses by hand. It was difficult work, and he remembered always coughing and wheezing from breathing in the feathers and dust. He didn't know that breathing in dust for so many years could damage his lungs as if he had been a smoker, which he wasn't. His bosses in Schenectady opened a feather-mattress factory in Pittsfield and asked him to work for them there. They offered him a small pay increase, so he moved the family to Pittsfield in 1929 to 168 Dewey Avenue.

Louis and Rose (early 20th century)

Louis commented and no one seemed to foresee the stock market crash in 1929. He was not a gambling man, and he didn't have much money saved, but his bosses persuaded him to put all his savings into Wall Street. He remembered President Hoover saying on the radio, a few months before the stock market crash, that America was close to triumphing over poverty. The famous Jewish economist Irving Fisher stated his belief, just three days before the crash, that stock prices had reached a permanently high level.

Thinking back, Louis thought investing in the stock market demonstrated an optimism and belief in permanent prosperity. Maybe people should have known better—if it seems too good, it probably is. He went from having very little to having nothing.

Louis lost everything on Black Thursday, October 24, 1929. He was in despair; he had lost the family's entire savings. Almost immediately, bread lines formed, shantytowns sprang up, and many people were unemployed. He went to the local bank to withdraw the little money he had left. The bank president came out of the building with a loudspeaker and told everyone to come back in a week, when he'd give them " ... a penny on the dollar [meaning much less than what the money was worth before the stock market crash]." Louis couldn't believe it. Fear and panic were thick in the air. As bad as it was for the family, it was even worse for those who had lost more due to the crash. There were stories of formerly wealthy men jumping from windows and rooftops out of despair. Louis would have never contemplated such a thing, as his faith in God was too strong.

Somehow, the family got by. They owned their little house and didn't have a car to worry about. They ate rice, oatmeal, sauerkraut, and beans several times a week. They waited in line for flour instead of buying bread. They ate meatballs made from breadcrumbs. They played card games and had singalongs. They patched old shoes with cardboard and put them back on, and they wore clothes long beyond their usefulness, sewing holes and tears to keep wearing them.

As Louis told Rose, Celia, and Pearl, and as a common phrase of the day said, "There are only three things you can do in life: eat it up, drink it up, or wear it out." He knew they would make it; they loved each other, lived in a nice town, and had helpful neighbors. Louis came to America from Poland to build a better life, and he would see that through. No matter how difficult things became in the US, things were still much better than in Poland; no one was trying to kill the family for the economic turmoil they were all experiencing.

My Grandmother Rose

Rose was born in Glens Falls in 1895. She married Louis on February 17, 1918, in Schenectady, where they settled. That's where they raised their wonderful daughters, Celia, and Pearl.

Rose's father Sam had come to the U.S. from Russia. Jews were often treated badly in Russia in the late-19th and early-20th centuries. Russian Jews were forced to attend special "assimilation" schools, suffered pogroms and violent attacks, and were blamed for the czar's assassination in the late 1880s. Like other Jews, Rose's father's family had been restricted in where they could live. Russia was a good place to get away from as Jews had no real life there. Fortunately, many were able to get out to more open and tolerant countries like America.

Rose's father was part of the mass Jewish migration from Russia to the U.S. At that time, it was easier to immigrate to America than it later became.

Rose's father's nickname was "Big Sam" because he was six feet, eight inches tall and had to duck down when coming through doorways. He was truly a giant. He became a Republican and took great pride in being part of the party of Abraham Lincoln. As a Republican, Sam believed in business and the need for people to pull themselves up by their bootstraps to achieve the American dream. He always worked hard and taught the family the importance of doing so.

Rose's mom's name was Cecilia. She and Rose's father married after they arrived in the U.S. in the late 19th century. She was three years older than Rose's dad. She died when Rose and her siblings were young—Rose wasn't sure of the cause—and her dad remarried a few years later. Rose didn't have a lot of memories of her mom because she was so young when she died. Rose still missed her.

While Rose's father came from Russia, all of her siblings, like her, were born in Glens Falls. In the late 1800s and early 1900s, Glens Falls had a sizable Jewish population. The local temple was built in the 1890s and the Jewish community center in the 1920s.

Growing up, Rose recalled her family was poor and each had to pitch in to help support the family. She had to quit school at age 12 to work as a seamstress, sewing buttons on clothes by hand in a factory. It was 1907, and it was common for children to work outside the house. Rose never thought twice about it, as it was what was expected of children to do—help the family. Of course, she would have rather been playing with friends and reading books, but that just wasn't doable.

Rose had two sisters and three brothers, but she never really knew her younger brother; he was injured as a baby when a window fell on his head. His mind was never right after that, and he lived in an institution for the rest of his life, as was common practice in the early 1900s.

Rose's Family (early 20th century)

When Rose was 22, her brother Julius began serving in World War I with the Army. The family was very proud both of his service and that American Jews were serving the cause of good. Unfortunately, Julius was horribly injured by German mustard gas in 1917. The Germans seemed like monsters—why would they make and use such horrible weapons? Julius's stomach never healed properly, even after surgery, and he suffered from pain for the rest of his life.[3]

In April 1915, German forces shocked the Allies on the Western Front by firing more than 150 tons of lethal chlorine gas, devastating the Allied lines. France, Britain, and later the United States developed their own chemical weapons and gas masks. Although chemical warfare caused less than 1 percent of the total deaths in World War I, the fear factor was significant. Chemical warfare with gases was prohibited after World War I by the Geneva Protocol of 1925. While it is still occasionally used, it has not been used to the extent it was in World War I.

Rose's father Sam lived into the early 1940s. Her husband Louis and their daughters got to know him a little bit before he died. As the family didn't own a car, it was difficult to get to Glens Falls from

Pittsfield, but Rose remembered Pearl visiting with Sam in Glens Falls in the 1940s. Pearl was in the Navy at the time, and Rose's father was very impressed with her. Pearl thought he was very talkative and pleasant to be around.

Rose used to love to cook and bake, as she grew up believing that filling empty stomachs with good food was one of the best ways to show love. She cooked traditional American foods like meatloaf, fried chicken, and macaroni and cheese, but she also cooked traditional Russian and Jewish foods like matzo ball soup, rolled cabbage, dumplings, and borscht.

My Aunt Celia

Celia was the oldest child in her family. Pearl and she were always very close; Pearl called her CeCe, and Celia called her Pearlie. Celia was the outgoing one, and Pearl was shy and quiet. Celia enjoyed being the older sister, as she was four years older.

Celia was very artistic and created many beautiful vases, lamps, and works of art. She was always interested in fashion, while Pearl was more modest. She described herself as full of life. Later in life, Celia worked at a large department store in Pittsfield called Zayre, selling hats and other fashion items. She enjoyed meeting and interacting with new people. She remembered that Zayre was one of only a few stores which stayed open 24 hours a day during the weeks leading up to Christmas each year. It was a lot of fun!

Celia remembered her parents as always working, trying to put food on the table. Her dad hand-stuffed feather mattresses, while her mom took in seamstress work, always keeping busy. As the older child, Celia was given extra responsibilities. Many times, she had to act like the parent, keeping the day-to-day household going. She was always there for Pearl, introducing her to other folks and keeping her safe. Celia commented that Pearl was her best friend.

Celia was always an overachiever, trying hard to please their parents. The downside was that she had little time for a childhood. She felt like she always had to be the grownup. She was diligent, always wanting to excel at everything she did. She was reliable and conscientious.

Celia mentioned that Pearl would probably say that she was bossy, but she had to take charge when it came to chores and family responsibilities. She helped their mom with the cooking, baking, and cleaning. It was stressful at times having to be so responsible. While it's fair to say she took on more responsibilities than Pearl a lot of the time, she never resented Pearl for it.

They were a poor family, especially during the Depression. Louis' income from making mattresses barely covered their day-to-day expenses, and he lost his savings in the stock market crash. Rose pitched in with sewing other people's clothes, and Celia and Pearl worked at five-and-dime retail stores.

Celia and Pearl both attended Pittsfield High School, though Celia was a few years ahead of her, paving the way! They went to Hebrew school a few afternoons a week, but it wasn't a common practice at that time for girls to have bat mitzvahs. Celia and Pearl were proud of their family's Russian and Polish roots but were grateful to have been born in America. From all the stories, it was clear America was far more tolerant and open than Europe; they didn't have to worry about pogroms and persecution. There was antisemitism, but Celia and Pearl felt protected by their loving parents. Because of their Polish and Russian ancestry, they were sensitive to news about the persecution of Jews in Europe.

Later, Celia met a wonderful man named David Cohen. He was kind, gentle, and responsible. They married in September 1941 (three months before the Japanese attack on Pearl Harbor), and he served in the Navy during World War II, doing his part to protect America and end the horrors in Europe. Dave was very patriotic, serving years later as the announcer for Pittsfield's annual Fourth of July parades, a local celebrity! Pearl asked Dave about the Navy and he explained that he was having a great experience and that the Navy WAVES he served with all seemed very nice. Celia was surprised when Pearl joined the Navy, as she always thought Pearl was too shy and quiet to join the military and move away from home, but she showed the family! They were all very proud of her.

PART II
EVIL AT THE GATE

NAZIS INVADE AND THE HOLOCAUST BEGINS

"On the day he was supposed to kill me, he was taken away."
—Al Kitmacher

Meet the Monster

As the Nazis invaded, horrible darkness descended upon Poland and other conquered lands and people. The main monsters of the Holocaust were Hitler, his henchmen, and his followers.

The Nazis invaded Poland on September 1, 1939, in their "blitzkrieg" or lightning attack. Poland's allies Great Britain and France declared war on Germany two days later. The Holocaust and systematic murder of Jews and other "undesirables" began. My father and his family were forced to give up their home and belongings and relocate to the Warsaw Ghetto and, later, to concentration camps.

The Nazis were a rogue's gallery of evil. Their unholy propensity was reflected in the uniforms they wore, including that of the SS, which featured a *Totenkopf*, German for skull and crossbones or "death head" (this symbol has since been adopted by neo-Nazis and other white supremacist groups). In the 1930s, the SS wore black uniforms with shiny black helmets that were intended to intimidate.

Hitler and many of his henchmen were raised on, had a great

interest in, and used antisemitic folklore and the occult, as well as neo-pagan, mystical, and supernatural teachings. They attempted to create their own brand of folklore through their stories of Germanic superiority and the inferiority of Jews and other people. The Nazis' hatred of the Jews and other vampiric "subhumans," together with the Nazis' supernatural leanings, posed the gravest threat to humanity the world had ever seen. They were passionately devoted to their grotesque world views and hatred.

Hitler was born in Austria in 1889. In 1907, he applied for admission to study at the Academy of Fine Arts in Austria but was rejected twice. Hitler was destitute and lived in homeless shelters. He earned money as a casual laborer and by painting watercolors, and he had a growing passion for architecture and music. It was in Vienna, between 1908 and 1913, that Hitler was introduced to racism and antisemitism.

There are many theories why Hitler hated the Jews. One is that a Jewish man named Leopold Frankenberg was Hitler's grandfather and Hitler was ashamed of it. Though Hitler's personal lawyer, Hans Frank, made this claim during the 1945–1946 Nuremberg trials, its validity is unclear. Another theory is that Hitler held animosity against the Jewish physician, Eduard Bloch, who cared for Hitler's beloved mother, Klara, before her death from breast cancer in 1907. This theory is more lacking in validity—Hitler thanked Bloch and spared him from the worst measures of the Holocaust. The theory with the greatest validity is that Hitler saw the Jews—who were prominently represented among Bolsheviks (the Russian revolutionary forces who rebelled against the czar and would later become the Communist Party), socialists, social democrats, and leaders in international finance and industry—as the cause of Germany's decline and loss of World War I, believing they "stabbed Germany in the back." He also blamed the Jews for the unfair terms imposed on Germany when it lost World War I, which was followed by economic collapse.[1]

During World War I, Hitler served in the Bavarian Reserve Infantry Regiment 16 as a dispatch runner on the Western Front in France. He was wounded at the Battle of the Somme and decorated for bravery with the Iron Cross. Ironically, he was recommended for the honor by his Jewish superior, Lieutenant Hugo Gutmann.

Hitler became involved in the Nazi movement, and through his ambition, opportunism, charisma, effective use of propaganda, and leadership climbed the ladder to become chancellor in 1933. In 1934, Hitler became known as Führer, German for leader. He described his hatred of Jews in his 1923 manifesto *Mein Kampf*, meaning "My Struggle." Hitler was obsessed with the practice of magic and avidly read *Magic: History, Theory, Practice* by German parapsychologist Ernst Schertel in 1923. Two lines in that book that appear to have captured Hitler's attention—he reportedly underlined them in his personal copy—are as follows:

"All men of genius possessed the ability to harness 'para-cosmical [demonic] forces' which can be combined with a lot of misery and misfortune but always leads to a consequence with the deepest meaning."

And ...

"Every demonic-magical world is centered towards the great individuals, from whom basic creative conceptions spring ... Individuals infected by the magician would henceforth form a 'community' or his 'people' [Volk] and create a complex life of a certain imaginative framework which called a culture."[2]

Hitler was truly a monster, with the bloodlust of a vampire, a god complex like Dr. Frankenstein, and a ghoul-like desire to murder and experiment on the living. Yet he had a cleanliness obsession and preferred others to do his dirty work. Through his charisma or "magic," and his use of longstanding antisemitic folklore and conspiracy theories, Hitler was able to rally and manipulate the impoverished German people. He encouraged them to believe in a bogeyman, a scapegoat—they needed to overcome the "deprivations" of World War I and he alone could show them how. He succeeded in building Germany into a great power that soon threatened the world.

Hitler practiced his heroic poses and rhetoric in front of cameras and mirrors, helping him perfect his cinematic style. Interestingly, mirrors play a prominent role in horror movies and stories. In ancient times, mirrors were thought by some to be "demon doors," or gateways through which evil could enter. Some stories use mirrors as portals through which ghosts and demons can be seen and communicated with. A prominent example is the urban legend of Bloody Mary, which says that if you say "Bloody Mary" three times in front of a mirror, she will appear and put your soul at risk. In other stories, mirrors are shown to possess the ability to display alternate realities, such as the "melting face" in the 1982 American horror movie *Poltergeist*. The Nazis made use of movies and other means of communicating to justify the Holocaust. An example is 1940's *The Eternal Jew*, which claimed Jews were genetically destined to be wandering cultural parasites.[3]

One description of Hitler posited that he was the "anti-Christ," a person prophesied by the Bible to oppose Jesus and substitute himself in his place before his second coming. This idea seems to be borne out of Daniel 8:23–25, which in part states:

"A king shall arise, having fierce features, who understands sinister schemes. His power shall be mighty ... he shall destroy fearfully and shall prosper and thrive; he shall destroy the mighty and also the holy people [the Jews] ... Through his cunning he shall cause deceit to prosper under his rule ... He shall destroy many ..."

Similarly, 16th-century French astrologer, physician, and reputed seer of future events Michel de Nostredame, or Nostradamus, wrote the following two passages, which some believe predicted the rise of Hitler:

"From the depths of the West of Europe, A young child will be born of poor people, He who by his tongue will seduce a great troop; His fame will increase towards the realm of the East."

And ...

"Beasts ferocious with hunger will cross the rivers, The greater part of the battlefield will be against Hister. Into a cage of iron will the great one be drawn, When the child of Germany observes nothing."[4]

The use of the word "Hister" in the final quote is believed to be either a prediction of Hitler or a reference to the Danube River, which in Latin is called Hister. Early Hitler supporter Erich Ludendorff, a German general, warned President Paul von

Hindenburg in 1933 of Hitler and Hindenburg's seemingly allowing him to rise to the level of Chancellor of Germany, before becoming Führer in 1934, stating:

"I solemnly prophesy that this accursed man will cast our Reich into the abyss and bring our nation to inconceivable misery. Future generations will damn you [Hindenburg] in your grave for what you have done."

Ludendorff unsuccessfully ran for president of Germany, retired, and died in 1937 before the war started. He was proven right, as Hitler did lead Germany to ruin in World War II.

One of the primary antagonists in the 2017 American superhero movie *Wonder Woman* was based on Ludendorff, who was portrayed as a monstrous World War I German general who used supernatural means to ensure German conquest.[5]

Hitler viewed the world as a Darwinian ("survival of the fittest") struggle for existence between races, with the Germanic Aryan race as the highest race—the only one capable of creating advanced culture. The archenemy of the Aryans, Hitler believed, was the Jewish people. Hitler described Jews as disease-causing bacteria, the masterminds behind the Bolsheviks, and the economic driving force behind Churchill and Roosevelt, whom Hitler believed to be Germany's primary enemies. Hitler saw the world's twin evils as Bolshevism and the Jews.[6]

Hitler identified with the theories of Darwin, a British naturalist, geologist, and biologist best known for his contributions to the science of evolution. Darwin indicated that all species have descended over time from common ancestors. He theorized that evolution resulted from natural selection in which the struggle for existence is won by the strong and not the weak.

We must not forget that, at its core, the Nazis' persecution of the Jews was based on the belief that Jews (and other undesirables) were an inferior "race." Hitler saw it in Darwinian terms: the superior Aryans must survive, win out, and vanquish the inferior Jews. Hitler and other Nazis considered the Jewish race to be disease-carrying vermin. Hitler saw it as a war for biological progress, with the Aryans needing to exterminate the Jews and other inferior races to improve the human species.

Hitler embraced the pseudoscience of eugenics and the racial extermination of what he viewed as inferior races. Such policies equated with survival of the best and fittest to improve the human race. Hitler insisted Jews could not be true Germans and spread the lie that Jews were dangerous enemies to Germany. Jews made up less than 1 percent of Germany's population when the Nazis took power. Despite their small numbers, Jews were portrayed as the force that caused Germany to suffer economically and otherwise.

In the science fiction and horror story by author Ira Levin and subsequent movie *Boys from Brazil*, a fictional Dr. Mengele genetically clones Hitler ninety-five times in hopes of creating boys who will become new leaders to continue the work of Nazi Germany. He gives the boys childhoods like that of Hitler. He is opposed by a Nazi hunter, loosely based on Simon Wiesenthal, who is mostly successful in his efforts. Other science fiction and horror stories and movies have followed a similar script, with new Nazis being created through scientific means.[7]

The Nazis themselves created propaganda promoting eugenics. The Nazi Office of Racial Policy (*Rassenpolitische Amt*) created a movie entitled *Erbkrank* (Hereditarily Diseased) about German mental hospitals and patients, including Jews, in which the patients live in "luxury." It argues that the genetics of idiocy create an unfair burden, financially and morally, for the German people.

Eugenics has been discredited as a science, with the Holocaust strengthening objections to it and sterilization.[8][9]

Hitler denied the existence of God, and through his actions, made clear his lack of belief in transcendent moral standards, humanity, empathy, and human rights. He had acolytes but very few friendships or close relationships.

It wasn't just Hitler and other senior Nazis who carried out the Holocaust. They were assisted to varying degrees by ordinary citizens who accepted and even promoted a depraved ideology.

Hitler ruled Germany until 1945. He directed the invasion of numerous countries and the murder of millions. No European country was able to withstand his onslaught except for Great Britain, which he attacked by air starting in 1940, and the Soviet Union, which Hitler tried to invade in 1941. There has been much conjecture about what would have happened had Hitler not tried to attack them, forcing them to react as they did. It appears his overall efforts could have been successful if not for his failure on these two fronts.

Hitler shot himself to death on April 30, 1945, in his *Führerbunker* in Berlin. Many unfounded theories suggest Hitler did not kill himself but instead escaped Germany and settled in South America. Several horror stories and movies have been made that hypothesize Hitler's escape and describe subsequent attempts to replicate and continue his evil through progeny or by other means.

Poland Invaded

Antisemitism swept across Poland in the late 1930s, both through an active antisemitic press and by way of orchestrated physical attacks on Jews. In some places, Jewish traders and peddlers feared traveling to area markets as bands of ruffians were known to attack on isolated roads.

Though Hitler is sometimes referred to as a madman, it is unclear how much of his evil can be attributed to mental illness. Experts say that while Hitler exhibited many psychiatric symptoms, including extreme paranoia, he most likely was not truly mentally ill. Hitler murdered with great pride and enthusiasm and with full knowledge of what he was doing.[10]

In the late 1930s, rumors spread that Germany was planning to invade Poland, and some urged Jews to move away from the Polish-German border. But most did not believe Hitler would dare attack Poland because of its treaties with Great Britain and France.

Some Jews did heed the warnings and fled, along with non-Jewish Poles. Families traveled by horse, cart, and on foot to escape. In the chaos of travel, many families were separated. Hearing German troops were close, others ran on foot away from the border. They soon saw a red sky in the distance and heard gunfire and bombing; the Germans were invading. There was shock and fear as the monsters in this horror story entered Poland. Soon, people's worst fears would be realized.

Though Poland and the Soviet Union had signed a nonaggression pact in 1932, Hitler and the Soviet Union's leader Josef Stalin signed a "secret agreement" in 1939, and both invaded Poland that year. The Nazis invaded Poland from the west on September 1, and the Soviets invaded from the east on September 17.

On September 8, 1939, German airplanes flew over Warsaw, dropping cinder bombs on the rooftops.

My Father's Words

"I remember the Nazis invading, dropping bombs on houses, and killing people in the streets. I had never experienced such horrors, but I soon realized that it was just the beginning. We lost all hope that Britain and France would keep Germany from attacking. I remember thinking, so these are what monsters really look like. The Poles fought back from horseback like it was still the 1800s; thousands of dead horses filled the streets after the battle was over. We didn't stand a chance.

It was horrible, many people lost their lives, and many buildings were destroyed. We were shocked when we saw German troops march in, and the Poles seemed to see the Nazis as conquering heroes instead of invading monsters. This didn't make sense to me. No doubt there were good people in Poland who wanted to resist the Germans and help Jews and other victims hide and get away, but often, the Poles seemed to want to collaborate with the Nazis; our Polish neighbors pointed us out as Jews. Whatever feeling of neighborliness that may have once existed was now gone for good.

I remember hearing when Poland's allies, Great Britain and France, declared war on Germany a few days after the Nazis invaded. World War II had started and within weeks, the Polish army was defeated. A few weeks after that, the Soviet Union invaded Poland. Poland surrendered to Germany in late September 1939 after losing tens of thousands of soldiers and countless civilians. Later, the Nazis betrayed and invaded the Soviet Union.

The Nazis established laws nullifying Jews' rights. If someone hit you, you had no right to complain. If someone came into your home and took anything he wanted, you couldn't go to the police and complain that you were robbed, because you had no rights. Jews, starting at age 12, were forced to wear yellow Stars of David and go to work. Many cleaned the rubble left by the Germans' bombing. We had to walk on the pavement and not in grassy areas. We were treated like aliens instead of people.

The Soviets came into Bialystok, a town in northeastern Poland. I had a friend driving a truck between Warsaw and Bialystok, smuggling things. My friend asked me to get my mother, father, and family and come with him. I was 18 or 19 years old and wanted to go; why would we wait with the monsters descending on us? But my father argued against it. He, like many older Jews, believed too much in the Germans. He said they were not bad people, and there was no reason for us to run. He said if there were bad ones, the German leaders would get rid of them. I didn't know any Germans and didn't believe, with what I'd seen and heard, that they would rein in their troops. Even though I wanted to leave, I couldn't leave my family behind. There is a saying in the Talmud: 'Who is wise? He who foresees what is about to happen.' It was difficult to know what to do. There is also an old proverb: 'He who puts up with insult, invites injury.' Our family had no idea how horrible the injury would be.

You could say I was a pessimist, expecting the worst, while my father was an optimist about what came next. There's a saying when tragedy is about to happen: 'pessimists flee, optimists die.' Against my better judgment, we remained in Poland, waiting for whatever would come next. I wish I had argued more strongly against my father. But our tradition called for the children to follow their father's wishes, as he knew best. It wouldn't be long before we discovered the mistake that we made in staying.

When the Germans came into Warsaw, they grabbed young, strong men to do their work. I was grabbed by a German soldier and a Polish man. My mind raced with what it was they wanted me to do

—they looked at me like I was just a body they were going to use to carry out their work. I was put to work unloading cases of beer from a truck. The cases were very heavy, and I was carrying them to the fifth and sixth floors. After many hours, my arms, back, and legs were giving out; I couldn't take it anymore and escaped. When I got home, I was exhausted and sick for two weeks and didn't remember anything that happened while I was sick. I slowly came back to himself."

My Grandfather Gershon

Gershon noted that Jews of his generation had a deep-rooted belief that the German people were highly cultured, liberal humanitarians —a nation of poets, philosophers, and composers! He recalled encounters with pre-1918 Germany that inspired trust and respect. He knew of Jews who served in Germany's military in World War I. Gershon said, in some ways, he had greater respect for the Germans than the Poles. The Germans always seemed to be ahead of other people, accomplishing great things.

Gershon observed that he and others felt if the rumored German atrocities were committed, they were done by a few unruly frontline soldiers. He was sure the Germans were good people, and once their economy improved and they gained the living space they desired, things would return to normal.

Holocaust Begins

The word "Holocaust" is Greek for *holo*, meaning "whole," and *kaustos*, meaning "burnt." The word was originally used about animal sacrifice. In terms of World War II, *holo kaustos* refers to the genocide perpetrated by the Nazis. Jews call the Nazi extermination of the Jewish people *Shoah*, meaning catastrophe. The Nazis called it the "Final Solution." The Roma, also victims of the Nazis, called it *Porrajmos*, meaning the "devouring."

The Nazis systematically murdered six million European Jews and about five million non-Jews during World War II, totaling 11 million people. The non-Jews murdered included Roma, Catholics, Jehovah's Witnesses, gay men, and those perceived to be undesirables, a group that included mentally, developmentally, and physically disabled people. Their murder was both a horrendous crime and an enormous tragedy. It was only through a series of miracles that my father survived.[11]

From 1940–1945, between the ages of 20 and 25, my father was imprisoned in seven slave labor and concentration camps. At the time, he didn't know there would eventually be more than 1,000 camps in Europe. The camps were established, in part, to achieve efficient, systematic, and impersonal mass murder.

There was an SS saying: "There's only one way out of the concentration camp—up the chimney." Jews were told they were being evacuated, resettled, or taken to work locations, hence the sign over the entrance to Auschwitz concentration camp that read *Arbeit Macht Frei*, German for "Work Will Make You Free."

Auschwitz sign, 2020. Courtesy of DzidekLasek, Pixabay

Some prisoners were given train tickets and receipts for their luggage to provide the illusion of normalcy. Of course, any belongings were confiscated by the Nazis. Signs at other camps read "baths and disinfecting rooms," and "cleanliness brings freedom!" Upper-class women were allowed to put on makeup before reaching their destination. Soon after, they were told to strip naked and marched into "shower rooms" (gas chambers), where they were killed. As they marched in, an SS man in a white coat—seemingly a medical professional—would utter soothing words. Their real role was to spot victims with gold teeth that could be collected following their death.

A "Special Detachment Team," which included other Jews, helped to keep prisoners calm. At Auschwitz, the Nazis had a Jewish orchestra play lively music while victims marched to their deaths. Some gas chambers had flower boxes outside to appear "pleasant." The Jews who were dressed were asked to take off their clothes and place them with any other belongings in a pile. They were given a receipt and told the clothes were to be washed and be disinfected. Women and children were separated from men.

Death by gas took 20 minutes. Gas entered the lower layers of air first, slowly rising to the ceiling, causing victims to trample one another as they tried to breathe. Often, stronger victims were found on the top of the pile of bodies. The Germans perfected the use of chemicals to kill during World War I. The first form of gas used in the chambers was carbon monoxide. Later, the insecticide Zyklon B was used. Dead victims were found with blood coming out of their ears and foam from their mouths. At Treblinka, where most Jews from Czemierniki, my father's ancestors' home, were sent, the victims were marched on a road called "the road to heaven" to a building with a Star of David on it. This approach was intended to—and did—reduce chaos, hysteria, and resistance.

Other Jewish prisoners were forced to take away the bodies. They were called *Sonderkommandos* and were not allowed to call the bodies "victims" or "corpses." Rather, they were to be referred to as "pieces of wood," "rags," or "excrement." Prisoners who cried while doing this work were severely beaten, and Sonderkommandos were generally killed within ninety days of their disposing of bodies. This pattern continued for the course of the war. Some Sonderkommandos wrote down their experiences and buried them in jars before their deaths.

When getting victims to the camps was not convenient, the Nazis would employ *Einsatzgruppen*, or "task forces," with mobile killing vans. These were trucks with their exhaust pipes redirected into the cargo hold. Jews were herded into these mobile killing machines, ninety at a time. Over 1.2 million Jews were killed this way.

After word of the "Final Solution" leaked to the Red Cross, the Nazis allowed the Red Cross to inspect a "mock concentration camp" with fake stores, washrooms, a hospital, classrooms, and gardens.

They even minted special money to make it look like the Jews were being paid. All was made to look innocent and pleasant. There were real prisoners present, but another half had been killed before the visit to reduce overcrowding. The children staged an opera called *Brundibar* about children who defeat an evil creature to save their mother. Of the 15,000 children held captive at this mock camp, only 100 survived.[12]

Antisemitism had a significant presence in Poland before World War II. While many were comfortable with Jews, some Polish politicians were disturbed by what they considered to be too much Jewish influence. These politicians pushed for Jews to leave Poland. When the Nazis invaded and began their killing, they employed Polish police and other officials. Some Poles identified, denounced, and exposed Jews in hiding. Others, including two Polish doctors who heroically saved the lives of 8,000 Jews by faking a typhoid outbreak, tried to help them.

About half the Jews who died in the Holocaust were killed before the Nazi gas chambers were operational. Many were tortured and killed by nonmilitary, "ordinary" non-Jews who drowned and beat them to death and used guns, axes, crowbars, bricks, and fire as weapons. As gruesomely described by Polish historian and Holocaust survivor Szymon Datner:

"Women were raped, their breasts cut off, little children were smashed on the walls, the fingers of the dead were cut off along with their gold rings, gold teeth were torn out of mouths; when in a house children were found with their parents, they would torture the children first, and then the parents."[13] [14]

Other monsters persecuted Jews in addition to the Nazis. Long-simmering antisemitism, which had been mostly hidden from obvious view, came out of the shadows as the Holocaust approached.

The Warsaw Ghetto

Though Jewish ghettos existed in the Middle Ages, they were closed by the beginning of the 19th century, in part by Napoleon. The Nazis reinitiated ghettos and used them to restrict undesirables. Four of the largest ghettos were in Poland: Warsaw with 400,000-500,000 people, Lodz with 205,000, Bialystok with 35,000-50,000, and Lublin with 34,000.

The Warsaw Ghetto was the old Jewish quarter of the capital, which the Nazis surrounded with a 10-foot-high, 11-mile-long brick wall. The ghetto was divided into two sections, with one side holding Aryans and the other Jews. Over 100,000 non-Jewish Poles were resettled to the Aryan side and were replaced with Jews. Just before the Nazi occupation of Poland in 1939, about 3.3 million Jews lived there. By the end of the war, only 380,000 Polish Jews were still alive. It is estimated that 13,000 Jews were killed by the Nazis in the Warsaw Ghetto. Almost 50,000 survived, only to be sent to death camps.[15]

My Father's Words

"At the beginning of their occupation, the Germans didn't do anything horrible to our family; there was little outright brutality. We heard stories of how monstrous the Nazis were, but we hadn't yet personally experienced it. We had many neighbors in the buildings where we lived, not friends, but cordial, they said hello and we said hello. I spoke with other Jews my age. It was too late to leave Warsaw; we knew people who left but they couldn't cross the borders and came back.

We didn't have much time. All of Warsaw's Jews had to relocate to the ghetto by November 15, 1940, six weeks after the order was given.

Life changed immediately for us. The orders came from the Judenrat: you must give up your radio, you must give up your electric iron, you must give up this, that, and the other. We were scared and confused. Why was this happening? And so, we had to give up the few comforts we had. Life stopped. The normal life stopped immediately.

Our apartment was taken away and we were forced into a little room in the ghetto. Everyone was crying. Although we hadn't lived in luxury, we had had a private apartment, we had work, and suddenly, we had to move. Everyone carried something, but we had to leave most things behind. We didn't have any valuables, no candelabras.

We mostly carried the materials we needed to do our tailoring and seamstress work. We also carried the clothes and food we had. We didn't know what to expect but knew it wouldn't be good.

We had a toilet in the little room we were forced into but had to share it with three other families. There was no shower—we had a *shitzel*, a big pot where we would warm up water and wash ourselves. There was no space, no privacy. I remember huddling with my family in one small corner of the room, trying to maintain some sense of normalcy in this very abnormal existence. No one was thinking about cleanliness. There were no books, no reading, no one thought of any holidays. It was 'let's get through the day.' In the ghetto, on average eight to ten people lived, if you could call it living, in each room."

The *Judenrat* or Jewish Council was an entity imposed by the Nazis on Jewish communities across Europe, mainly in Nazi ghettos. As early as 1933, the Nazis began to discuss establishing Jewish-led agencies to carry out anti-Jewish policies. As the German army invaded Poland, they required local Jewish populations to form Judenrat as go-betweens. The Judenrat organized the orderly deportation of Jews to the concentration camps, controlling Jews' numbers and occupations, distributing food and medicine, and relaying orders. The Nazis threatened and carried out violence against Judenrat members if they did not comply. The Judenrat also provided local police, fire, postal, sanitation, transportation, and other services. The Judenrat police were known as the Jewish Ghetto Police. Although their service was mandated, fellow Jews resented the actions of the Judenrat.

"At nighttime, I could hear the German motorcycles come in and then shotgun and machine-gun blasts. Some people were trying to escape. The Nazis killed them right on the spot. There were blood-curdling screams, crashing noises, and the smell of smoke from guns. The Nazis could not be human—they must be monsters. Human life —women, children—meant nothing to them. My mother would say, 'May the *mazikin* get the Nazis,' mazikin being the invisible demons of the Polish countryside. I didn't believe we'd be that lucky. But a golem or two to protect us wouldn't have been a bad thing!

There was no bread, no food, no nothing. It was just terrible.

Conditions were very harsh. People grabbed packages from other people, thinking maybe there was food. I remember seeing a girl about 14 years old grab a package from a woman and bite into it, thinking she would eat whatever was in it. But it was a light bulb. She was horribly injured."

To try to establish some sense of normalcy, those in the ghetto organized orchestras, chamber groups, choirs, concerts, theater, and other cultural escapes. Some songs expressed wishes for home, community, and family. Marysia Ayznshtat, the "Nightingale of the Ghetto," was one of the most popular singers. She was murdered by the Nazis at age 21 when she tried to save her parents as they were taken away.[16]

"In the spring of 1941, the Germans set up factories within and just outside the ghetto, using forced, slave Jewish labor," my father said. "These factories supported the German war effort, and Jews working for them were spared the first deportations to the death camps. How ironic that we were forced to support the Nazis' antisemitic, Jew-hating war efforts.

I was forced to work for the Germans outside the ghetto, at the Luftwaffe's Okecie Airfield, for about a year until our family escaped from the Warsaw Ghetto. I walked there every day. The Germans didn't talk directly to us, the airfield workers; they communicated through the Judenrat. I worked every day to have a piece of bread. The rest of the family had no work to do and stayed in the little room, praying for food. Other than the little pot with water, I had no way to wash away the sweat and dirt from the day's work. I would meet with a group of young men from the Judenrat in the morning to go to work at the German airbase. I worked for ten hours, then came back at night. It was hard labor—cleaning, carrying things, whatever they'd tell me to do. There was no outright abusive treatment at that time—it was not horrible yet. But there was no kindness either."[17]

It was the Nazis who reintroduced slavery into Europe. During World War II, and in part because Germany lacked manpower as so many German men were serving in the military, over seven million people served as slaves. They worked for Volkswagen, BMW, Mercedes, and other well-known companies. Slaves were seen not as human but expendable commodities. The hair of dead slaves was used to stuff mattresses and was made into felt and thread. It was also used to make submarine crew socks, as well as ropes and cords for German military ships. The ashes of slaves were used as fertilizer and to salt roads. Though it is a point of contention and rejected by some scholars, some claim the Nazis used the skin of Jews to make lamp shades. In 1974, the man helping me prepare for my bar mitzvah, Dr. Goldbloom, showed me a lamp on his desk and described the shade as being made from the skin of Jewish concentration camp victims. He said he kept it on his desk to remind himself and others of the atrocities the Nazis committed.

"I was searched every time I came back into the ghetto. No one could bring back food. Some attempted to bring things in, but they were searched by the Jewish kapos and Germans, and the things they carried were thrown aside. Life in the ghetto was terrible. The kapos were also prisoners of the Nazis, appointed as guards to oversee fellow prisoners. They were given better treatment.

I remember people lying on the street, dying on the street. If someone died, their family would put them on the street and still collect their ounces or ration of bread. Our family ate once a day, in the morning. We ate together and starved together; it was horrible watching your family starve. Everyone in the house survived, no one was sick. My parents weren't young or old—they were in their fifties. No one had friends in the ghetto.

Life in the ghetto was unbearable despite the occasional pleasant distraction like touring theater groups and concerts. Overcrowding was common. Plumbing failed and human waste was deposited into the streets along with the garbage. The smell of human waste was almost as unbearable as the conditions themselves. I've never seen or smelled such filthy, stench-filled conditions. Diseases spread in these cramped, unsanitary conditions. Those who still owned anything of value traded it for food. Those who didn't stole to eat. The extremely few people with money could purchase food on the black market, but that was not a reality for the overwhelming majority of those in the ghetto. Starving people walked slowly through the streets like barely living skeletons. Those carrying packages that might contain food were in danger of being attacked by the starving. No imaginary horror story or movie could be as unsettling."

The Nazis starved ghetto prisoners by limiting their daily intake of bread, potatoes, and fat to an estimated 800 calories a day. Most adults need a minimum of 2,000 calories to sustain metabolism, muscle activity, and brain function.

"During the long Polish winter, there was little heating fuel available, and people lacked adequate clothes. Thousands died from illness, starvation, and exposure to the cold. We knew many people who died in these ways. It was horrible. Some committed suicide, a sin in Judaism, to escape their miserable lives. As parents died, children became orphans who frequently were forced to live on the street. They begged for bits of bread from those who had none to give. Many of these children froze to death. Some children were able to help their families by crawling through small openings in the ghetto wall, smuggling food. Those who were caught were killed.

Education is an important part of Jewish culture. Despite the Nazis forbidding classes, adults organized and secretly conducted classes. Some students continued to play with any toys they had; those who didn't have toys made them out of cloth, wood, or anything else they could find.

We often described children as 'old people with children's faces' due to the toll of the monstrousness of the Nazis was taking. Most children lacked joy, happiness, or childlike innocence. Life was filled with pain and boredom. These children shared in the families' chores and work. In rural areas, they tended animals and helped with the crops. In urban areas, they worked in factories and sold food and other items in the marketplace. We all pitched in by doing tailoring or seamstress work.

Children and adults kept diaries describing their lives. We also created art, music, and other forms of self-expression. This helped us retain a sense of self in these hell-like conditions. I knew I had to find a way to get our family out of the ghetto before it was too late. I prayed to God for another miracle.

Through a combination of bribes to train conductors, tricks played on a Polish man demanding money to not turn us in, and other means, we were able to escape in the spring of 1942, just a year before the Warsaw Ghetto Uprising."

Uprising

In 1942, Hitler liquidated the ghettos and more than two million Jews were deported to death camps, including Treblinka. The Jewish Council of Warsaw published a notice on July 22 to ghetto inhabitants stating, regardless of age or gender, they would be deported to camps in the east.

In April 1943, 750 Warsaw Ghetto Jews formed a fighting group, led by Mordecai Anielewicz, to fight back against the Nazis. This group was known as Zydowska Organizacja Bojowa, or ZOB. Anielewicz's nickname was "Aniolek," meaning "Little Angel." He was also the publisher of an underground ghetto newspaper, the *Neged Hazerem*, or *Against the Stream*. He believed European Jews needed to protect themselves from the Nazis.

ZOB members in the Warsaw Ghetto fired on thousands of Nazis, using a small supply of pistols, rifles, and Molotov cocktails smuggled into the ghetto. They were able to hold out for approximately 28 days against the overwhelming Nazi force until mid-May 1943. They killed about 50 Germans.

By May 16, 1943, the Germans, under SS Major General Jürgen Stroop, had burned the ghetto to the ground. ZOB fought to the bitter end and Anielewicz was killed during the uprising at age 24.

The Warsaw Ghetto uprising represented the most important organized Jewish battle against the Nazis in World War II. It was also the most significant urban revolt against Nazi occupation in Europe in World War II. The 42,000 Jewish survivors of the uprising were sent to concentration camps. Anielewicz was posthumously awarded Poland's Cross of Valor in July 1944.[18]

It is often asked why Jews didn't do more to resist the Nazis. In part, the answer is they lacked arms and were surrounded by antisemitic populations. Also, there had been years of starvation. Beginning as early as November 1938, in preparation for the Holocaust, the Nazis had enacted regulations making it illegal for

Jews to carry firearms. Another reason was a kind of cultural pacifism practiced by Jews, who historically had to stay quiet to avoid persecution. Many Jews, who were always "strangers in strange lands," practiced the "Golden Rule," as stated in Leviticus: "Thou shalt love thy neighbor as thyself."

Further, the Nazis did their best to hide their true intentions. Based on their militaristic history, folklore, and antisemitism, it is easy to see how the Germans became bullies, the Poles were overrun or co-opted, and the Jews were victimized. Throughout history, no group has been more victimized than the Jewish people. It was not solely the mass murder by the Nazis—the persecution of Jews goes back thousands of years.

It is important to remember that, for all the wisdom hindsight offers now, many Jewish communities in Poland and Germany were blindsided by the speed with which the Nazis launched—and gained traction for—their murderous campaign. Though antisemitism was present in communities across Europe (in some places more strongly and more in the open than others), in many communities, Jews and non-Jews lived side by side in relative peace for as long as anyone could remember. As my father described, his family lived in relative peace in their mixed-religion, mixed-ethnicity community for many years before the start of the Holocaust. Though they experienced antisemitism, it was inconceivable for many Jews, including my father's family, to think their neighbors would turn against them or their countries would fail to protect them. The force and speed behind the Nazi invasion and takeover were a surprise to many Jews.

During World War II, about 1.5 million Jews enlisted and volunteered in Allied armies to fight against the Nazis. This figure included Jews who had earlier escaped from Europe before the start of the war but now returned to fight. Further, some Jews resisted and fought, in addition to in the Warsaw Ghetto Uprising, alongside resistance groups in France, Russia, and Yugoslavia. They resisted the best they could.

Approximately 550,000 Jewish soldiers fought in the U.S. Armed Forces during World War II. They served on all European and Pacific fronts. Some 10,000 were killed in combat, and more than 36,000 received military citations for bravery. Many American Jewish soldiers took part in liberating the concentration camps. About 30,000 Jews served in the British army. 5,000 Palestinian Jews formed the volunteer "Jewish Brigade" in 1944, serving under the Zionist flag. About 500,000 Jewish soldiers fought in the Soviet Union's Red Army during World War II; some 120,000 were killed in fighting, and the Germans murdered 80,000 as prisoners of war. More than 160,000 Jewish Red Army soldiers, at all levels of command, earned military citations for bravery, with over 150 designated "Heroes of the Soviet Union"— the highest honor awarded to soldiers in the Red Army. Approximately 100,000 Jews fought in the Polish army against the German invasion. They made up 10% of the Polish army, commensurate with the percentage of Jews within the general population. Approximately 30,000 Polish Jews died in battle, were taken captive by the Germans, or were declared missing during the battles defending Poland, 11,000 in the defense of Warsaw. Thousands of Jews later served in various Polish armies in the Allied Forces, fighting against the Germans.

Rabbi Menachem Ziemba of Warsaw said, in January 1943, that Halakha [Jewish law] demands that when faced with a ruthless archfoe like the Nazis, Jews must fight to the very end.

Polish Crossroads Between the Holocaust and Horror

One Polish case stands out as the crossroads between the Holocaust and its horror story implications.

The town of Zofiówka was established in 1835 under Czar Nikolai I by Jewish settlers from Belorussia (now Belarus) and Volhynia (the region between southeastern Poland, southwestern Belarus, and western Ukraine). In 1908, the Zofiówka Society for Poor Jews with Nervous and Mental Illnesses opened a sanatorium and hospital in Otwock, a town near Warsaw. Zofiówka was named for its founder, Zofia Endelmanowa, who donated her jewelry toward its establishment. After World War II had started, the Nazis seized the medical facility.

In 1941, patients from other psychiatric hospitals were moved to the town of Otwock; most of them were murdered the following year. This was part of the Nazis' T4 program, which aimed to eliminate people with mental illnesses. That the facility was centered on Jewish mental illness offered the additional benefit to the Nazis of killing two birds with one stone. The Nazis murdered 20,000 mentally ill patients in Poland throughout the Holocaust.

Later in the war, after the Jewish patients were murdered, Zofiówka was turned into the center for the Nazis' Lebensborn initiative. The goal was to care for racially pure Aryan pregnant women carrying racially pure fetuses. The newborns would be placed with racially pure German families to strengthen the "Nordic race of Übermenschen," meaning "superior beings." After the war, Zofiówka continued to function as a hospital until it was closed in 1998. The building is abandoned.

Modern-day believers in the supernatural say the abandoned hospital is one of the most haunted locations in Poland. Believed to be haunted by the spirits of the murdered patients, visitors have reported hearing crying, screaming, and moaning.[19]

AMERICA, THE ALLIES, THE HOLOCAUST, AND SUPERHEROES

"Those above me were killed, I survived."
—Al Kitmacher

America's and the Allies' Attitude Toward the Jews

Before the Nazis' ascent to power in Germany, Jews and other minority group members attempted to emigrate to other countries with little success. With growing right-wing nationalism and isolationism, few countries welcomed them. The vast majority were left in place, awaiting their fates at the hands of the Nazi monsters.

"We heard horrible stories of Jews being persecuted in Europe, but the stories paled in comparison to what we later found out had happened," my mother said. "America, England, France, and others were great countries: why didn't they stop this before it got out of control? We all needed to band together to stop these horrors, not only for those suffering but also for ourselves. No doubt the monsters would be hungry for greater conquests and more victims. None of us would be safe. I always hated war and killing, but something had to be done."

Between 1933 and 1945, more than 340,000 Jews emigrated from Austria and Germany. Tragically, nearly 100,000 of them immigrated to countries that were later overrun by Nazi Germany. German authorities deported and killed most of them.

Following the Nazis' annexation of Austria in March 1938 and Kristallnacht the following November, the United States and Western European countries increasingly feared an influx of Jewish refugees. From March 1938 to September 1939, approximately 85,000 Jewish refugees from Nazi-held territories (out of 120,000 Jewish emigrants) reached America. However, this number of refugees and emigrants was far less than the actual number seeking entrance.

One hundred twenty-five thousand applicants lined up outside U.S. consulates in late 1938, each hoping to obtain one of the 27,000 visas allotted through the American immigration quota system. The number of immigration applicants increased to more than 300,000 by June 1939. Most were unsuccessful. Switzerland, the Shanghai International Settlement, and British Palestine did admit a limited number of Jewish refugees during the 1930s. Also, Bolivia admitted around 30,000 between 1938 and 1941.[1]

Only a few months before Jewish synagogues, businesses, and homes were burned during Kristallnacht, in July 1938, representatives of 32 countries, including the United States, met in France for the Evian Conference to discuss the European refugee crisis. Only one country attending the conference, the Dominican Republic, agreed to accept refugees. Hitler correctly concluded that no other country wanted the Jews.

The Germans took solace in not being the only ones to not want the Jews. According to *Fortune* magazine in April 1939, 83 percent of Americans indicated they were opposed to admitting refugees. This reluctance in part may have been due to the economic impact of the Great Depression. But there's little doubt that antisemitism played a role as well. Fear of those who were different was stoked by Father Charles Edward Coughlin (the "radio priest") and industrialist Henry Ford, known antisemites.

Overall, 200,000 Jews immigrated to the United States between 1933 and 1945, far fewer than tried. This limited success was thanks to First Lady Eleanor Roosevelt, Democratic Senator Robert Wagner (New York), and Republican Congresswoman Edith Nourse Rogers

(Massachusetts), working with American Jewish leaders including Supreme Court Justice Louis Brandeis, and others. It appears most Americans, preoccupied with the war, were unaware of the full extent of European Jewish persecution, until later.

American Super Weapons, and Jews send Captain America, Superman, and Rosie the Riveter to War

The United States developed "superweapons" to help win World War II. The ultimate weapon was the nuclear bomb, which America used on Hiroshima and Nagasaki, Japan, in 1945 to end the war. America relied on the huge amounts of weapons and equipment it produced to help win the war—weapons that overwhelmed and outmatched the Nazis and their allies. Likewise, America, through its Lend-Lease arrangement with Great Britain and Russia, helped those countries implement armament improvements.

Another American secret weapon was the development of cultural icons intended to inspire American pride and solidarity. These creations include superheroes Captain America and Superman. Daily American newspapers in the 1930s and early 1940s did not accept illustrations by Jews, so many of these Jewish artists found work and played a major role in creating comic books and cartoons.

These Jewish artists were concerned about what was happening to their fellow Jews in Europe and concerned that so many were against entering. Americans in support of the war dreamed of creating a "super-soldier" to face off against and defeat the larger-than-life, evil Nazis.

Writer Joe Simon (born Hymie Simon) and artist Jack Kirby (born Jacob Kurzberg), of what would later become Marvel Comics, were both Jewish and determined they had to develop a patriotic superhero who would fill Americans with pride and propel the United States toward entering the war and fighting Nazism. Simon and Kirby were second-generation American Jews whose parents had left Europe before the Holocaust.

Simon and Kirby published *Captain America #1* eight months

before the Japanese attack on Pearl Harbor of December 7, 1941. It was the story of the undersized and sickly Steve Rogers, who was born on the Lower East Side of Manhattan (home to many Jews from the late 1800s through the 1950s). The allegorical Rogers desperately wanted to enlist in the U.S. Army and serve his country. After being repeatedly turned down, Rogers volunteered to receive a top-secret serum developed by Dr. Josef Reinstein (known in the Marvel movies as Dr. Abraham Erskine), a German Jewish scientist (some say modeled after Albert Einstein) who had fled Nazi Germany. Rogers became the superhumanly powerful Captain America after being injected with the serum, dressed in his red, white, and blue uniform and matching stars and stripes shield.[2]

Captain America inspired patriotism in the American public and helped push the United States toward war. In the cartoons, he helped turn the tide of the war and secure victory. He defeated villains such as the evil, demonic, and seemingly invincible Nazi antagonist "The Red Skull," whose face, in true supernatural and horror fashion, was a crimson skull. The Red Skull, like the Nazis, made use of slave labor in achieving his objectives. In the Marvel comics, the Nazi occultist Thule Society was under the guidance and leadership of the Red Skull. Captain America became one of the most widely read comics in the Golden Age of this art form. The character became even more popular with the Marvel movies of the late 2000s through today even though few know of his historical roots.

Captain America and the Golem of Prague share several similarities. Both were designed and intended to protect their communities. Whereas the golem was made of clay and needed a rabbi's prayer to bring it to life, Captain America was frail and needed a secret serum to become powerful. The golem is brought to life by the Hebrew letters spelling out *emet*, the word for "truth." Captain America's mask has the letter "A" for America emblazoned on it, and the Hebrew letter aleph, which is also the first letter in *emet*, is analogous to the English letter "A." Some modern interpretations of the golem place a star on his chest like Captain America has. Captain America also carries a shield with a star on it, in some ways resembling the Biblical hero David who carries a shield with the Jewish Star of David on it.³

Like Captain America, Superman, or as he was also known, "Champion of the Oppressed," was created by two American Jewish teenagers, Jerry Siegel and Joe Shuster, in the 1930s. Superman was created in response to the rise of evil in the forms of Nazis and fascism. Superman had an origin story like that of Moses, with parents saving the baby by setting him adrift in a protected vessel (Moses was set in a reed basket, Superman in an interplanetary spaceship). Superman had the strength of the Biblical Samson. Like the golem, he was virtually indestructible. He had the same type of wisdom and dedication to honesty and fairness as the Biblical King Solomon.⁴

Superman declared war on the Nazis in a February 27, 1940, comic in which he raised Hitler from the ground with his hand around his neck and said, "I'd like to land a strictly non-Aryan sock on your jaw." Superman battled the German *Luftwaffe* (air force) in the air and *Wehrmacht* (Army) on the ground. Later, he took Hitler to Geneva for a war crimes trial.⁵

The Nazis took exception to Superman's apparent Jewish roots when, in an April 25, 1940, SS newspaper, they wrote "Jerry Siegel, an intellectually and physically circumcised chap who has his headquarters in New York ... advertise[s] widely Superman's sense of justice, well-suited for imitation by the American youth ... who live in such a poisoned atmosphere and don't even notice the poison they swallow daily."⁶

The Bund (an American Nazi organization, not to be confused with the Jewish socialist movement called Bundism) sent Superman's creators hate mail and picketed DC Comics' offices.

Siegel and Shuster were undeterred and continued to write of Superman's heroic fight against the Nazis. The U.S. government employed Superman to increase enlistment, secure resources, and raise money needed for the war effort. The American military named bombers, tanks, and other weapons after Superman.

Another American superhero created or co-created by Jews was Batman (created by Bob Kane and Bill Finger in May 1939). Batman battled spies and homegrown bad guys, some of whom were helping the Nazis and their Axis allies.

Stan Lee, a co-creator of superheroes such as Spiderman and others, was born Stanley Martin Lieber and raised by Romanian-born Jewish immigrant parents. Lee and his co-artist Jack Kirby debuted a team of superheroes known as "The Avengers," or "Earth's Mightiest Heroes," in *The Avengers #1* comic in September 1963. The Avengers consisted of Thor, the Hulk, Iron Man, Ant-Man, and the Wasp. Captain America joined the Avengers in issue number 4 and was given "founding member" status. The Avengers spawned a series of highly successful Marvel movies beginning in the 2000s. Interestingly, following the end of World War II, Abba Kovner (1918–1987), a Lithuanian Jew, formed a team of Jewish former ghetto fighters and partisans called "The Avengers." This group sought revenge against SS officers, other Nazis in hiding, and German collaborators.[7]

In addition to Captain America, another American cultural icon and superhero inspired by Jews to encourage American involvement in World War II was "Rosie the Riveter." Rosie was a former housewife who left the kitchen and, through her tireless work and extraordinary efforts, helped build the machinery and weapons necessary to fight and win World War II. Posters emblazoned with her picture, flexing her muscles with a confident and steely look, became a symbol of wartime courage and patriotism. Jewish composer John Jacob Loeb and his collaborator, Redd Evans, created Rosie in music and lyrics in 1942. Loeb and Evans's music was so popular that it motivated women and others to join the war effort against the Nazis. It also motivated American artist Normal Rockwell to create his famous Rosie the Riveter painting.[8]

Loeb and Evans's lyrics included the following:

> *All the day long whether rain or shine*
> *She's a part of the assembly line*
> *She's making history,*
> *working for victory*
> *Rosie the Riveter*

Keeps a sharp lookout for sabotage
Sitting up there on the fuselage
That little frail can do more than a male will do
Rosie the Riveter

Graphic artwork of an American factory worker, 2017. Courtesy of ArtsyBee, Pixabay.

To some degree, America's imaginary superheroes and cultural icons like Captain America, Superman, and Rosie the Riveter serve as part of its folkloric traditions. They tell stories that are passed down from one generation to the next, taking on the characteristics of the time and place in which they were first told.

"Jewish kids then were raised with a belief in moral values," said Captain America's creator Kirby. "In the movies, good always triumphed over evil ... Those are the things I learned from my parents and from the Bible. It's part of my Jewish heritage ... Captain America was me, and I was Captain America ... In the fight scenes, when Cap used to take on seven men at once, and five bodies would fly around the room ... that's how I remember the street fights from my childhood."[9]

In the movie *Captain America: The First Avenger* (2011), these words were said: "... But every army begins with one man. He will be the first in a new breed of super-soldier. We are going to win this war because we have the best men. And they, personally, will escort Adolf Hitler to the gates of Hell."[10]

The Creation of Wonder Woman

In part based on women's achievements and contributions during World War II and to help reshape prevailing views of women, the superhero character Wonder Woman was created in 1941. Wonder Woman was depicted as fighting against the Nazis and their Axis allies.

Psychologist William Moulton Marston created Wonder Woman (with help from wife Elizabeth Holloway Marson), writing in a 1943 issue of *The American Scholar* that his purpose was to: "... create a feminine character with all the strength of Superman plus all the allure of a good and beautiful woman."

Wonder Woman has helped reshape people's views of what women are capable of. In Moulton's words in the 1941 "All Star Comics #8" that introduced Wonder Woman, "At last, in a world torn by the hatred and wars of men, appears a woman to whom the problems and feats of men are mere child's play ... a symbol of integrity and humanity ... to avenge an injustice or right a wrong! ... with the speed of Mercury and the strength of Hercules ..."[11][12]

Others connect the Wonder Woman character to American Jewish suffragette author Miriam Michelson's 1912 creation in the book *The Superwoman*. That character was raised in a matrilineal island society, much like Moulton's creation.

Interestingly, actress Gal Gadot (a former Miss Israel) was cast in the role of Wonder Woman and first appeared in that role in 2016's movie *Batman v. Superman: Dawn of Justice* and continues in it. Gadot's grandfather was a survivor of Auschwitz. She served, as is required, in the Israeli military. In her first standalone *Wonder Woman* movie (2017), she battled the Germans in World War I, with unmistakable similarities to the Germans in World War II. As noted, one of the main antagonists in the movie was Ludendorff, a German general.[13]

German Militarism Before World War II

Germany, unlike most of its European neighbors, has no ancient tradition of self-government, constitution, parliament, or a free press. Whereas ancient Rome brought law and language to France, Spain, and Great Britain, it had a minimal hold over what is now Germany. Over six centuries ago, during the Middle Ages, there were many "Germanys" consisting of duchies, counties, and cities. Each of these entities fought against one another and as mercenaries attached to other European armies.

The Germans had a long, militaristic, and unstable past before World War II, which resulted in their being viewed as brutal and monstrous at several times in their history. This included in the 18th century, when German Hessians served as mercenaries for the British against the American revolutionaries. Great Britain hired approximately 30,000 of these soldiers from the highly militarized northern German state of Hesse-Cassel. They were condemned in the Declaration of Independence in 1776 as: "instruments of death, desolation and tyranny." The best known, if not entirely real, Hessian served as the inspiration for the "Headless Horseman" in author Washington Irving's 1820 story *The Legend of Sleepy Hollow*:

"The dominant spirit ... haunts this enchanted region ... is the apparition of a figure on horseback without a head ... the ghost of a Hessian trooper, whose head had been carried away by a cannonball ... the specter is known, at all the country firesides by the name of the Headless Horseman of Sleepy Hollow."[14]

The Headless Horseman was said to have been the ghost of an actual soldier, possibly killed during the Battle of White Plains (New York) on October 28, 1776. Irving mentioned the battle and a Hessian, writing: "[an] old gentleman ... who, in the battle of White Plains, being an excellent master of defense, parried a musket ball with a small sword."

An American general, William Heath, described the event: "A shot from the American cannon at this place took off the head of a Hessian artilleryman."

America eventually won the Battle of White Plains, and little is remembered of it except the story of the Headless Horseman. As Irving wrote: "Buried in the churchyard, the ghost rides forth to the scene of battle in nightly quest of his head." As the story goes, the Headless Horseman threw a pumpkin at American schoolteacher Ichabod Crane, who was never seen again.

Director Tim Burton's 1999 supernatural horror movie *Sleepy Hollow* loosely retells this story. In it, the Horseman is depicted as a monstrous, ghostly creature who in life filed his teeth to look like fangs to scare his victims and in death murdered many people to acquire heads while searching for his own.[15]

The 18th-century king of Prussia, Frederick the Great, modernized German tactics and strategies. Finally, under Chancellor Otto von Bismarck, Prussia united Germany into one country in 1871, some 45 years before World War I and 68 years before World War II.

In World War I, Great Britain, and later America, began calling the Germans "Huns" to emphasize their brutality. The Huns were a Central Asian nomadic people who, under the leadership of Attila, invaded Rome in the fifth century CE. They were known for their expert horsemanship, mobile tactics, and deadly aim with bow and arrows. The Romans and other Europeans were terrified of this warlike people.

Ironically, it was German Kaiser Wilhelm II who first used the word "Hun" in a July 27, 1900, speech on the topic of his troops going to China to put down the Boxer Rebellion.[16]

In World War I, the Germans were the first country to use chemical and gas weapons to attack their opponents. My great uncle Julius, one of my maternal grandmother Rose's brothers, was horribly injured by German mustard gas in 1917 on the battlefields of Europe. The Germans were seen by many as brutish, bloodthirsty, and monstrous gorilla-like figures.[17]

Following their loss in World War I, many senior German leaders blamed the Jews, among others, for the defeat. Ludendorff in 1922 said that Jews had worked hand in hand with France and England against Germany. This included the imaginary *The Protocols of the Elders of Zion*, a document purported to show that Jews plotted to take over the world. In fact, the document had been written by the Russian secret police in the early 1900s. The Germans used it in part to explain their loss in the war, the economic crises that followed, the Russian Revolution, and other world events. Germany's 500,000 Jews, less than 1 percent of the population, were labeled as an "enemy." Walter Rathenau, a wealthy Jewish businessman, was appointed as Germany's foreign minister, exacerbating hatred toward the Jews. He was murdered on June 24, 1922 by German military veterans who claimed he was an "Elder of Zion."

AMERICA BEFORE WORLD WAR II

"I heard a voice say 'Kitmacher, don't stop here.'"
—Al Kitmacher

The 1920s and 1930s

The Roaring Twenties were an exciting time in America and around the world. It was a time of new styles, freedoms, and innovations. Soon after, the Stock Market Crash of 1929 and the Great Depression struck and people needed to learn to survive with less. Music and movies, many foreshadowing the actions of the monstrous Nazis, were in vogue. Here, my mother describes her life during those periods:

"Our home life was great. I adored my parents and big sister Celia. My dad surprised my mom by buying a small but nice single-family house, and we loved it! It felt like we had a piece of relative wealth, even though at best we were working-class people.

This was a period of excess, freedom, prosperity, and progress. The future looked bright. I was born in 1922, so I was just a kid in the 1920s, but I was aware that women's rights and fashion were growing and becoming more daring; women were cutting their long hair into the short bob cut. Women had gained the right to vote at the beginning of the decade with the Nineteenth Amendment to the Constitution and they felt empowered. Everyone seemed to be taking photographs, listening to jazz music on the radio, talking on the home telephone, buying cars, and flying on airplanes. Formerly only the wealthy could afford a car. Most people now had indoor plumbing and at least one bathroom. They were no longer using a chamber pot and washing weekly in a bathtub filled manually. It was a time of innovation and Pittsfield was thriving!

Then came the Stock Market crash of 1929 and the Great Depression. My father lost everything in the stock market. We were suddenly poor. People had to become more frugal, patching clothes and stretching dollars. A 1930s motto was 'Use it up, wear it out, make do or do without.' The food we ate was simple, with an emphasis on less expensive ingredients, so casseroles, chili, macaroni and cheese, soup, and chipped beef on toast became our average meals. Small kitchen gardens and community 'thrift gardens' became the norm. Potlucks were popular. People spent much of their time at home, and neighbors got together frequently.

We went from the Roaring Twenties, where there was lots of fun and plenty of food, to the Great Depression of the 1930s. We experienced great hardship following the stock market collapse. There wasn't enough work or food. However, we loved each other, neighbors helped neighbors, and we knew we would find a way to survive. Despite it all, I kept a happy and optimistic outlook. We were proud Americans and truly believed we could overcome any obstacles and accomplish anything if we worked together and tried our best.

My nickname was 'Perky Pearl.' I think it was because I always had lots of energy and looked on the bright side! I was usually happy and rarely down; you might call me a 'glass is half full' kind of person. I enjoyed being in high school glee club and part of the chorus in two Gilbert and Sullivan operettas, *The Pirates of Penzance* and *The Mikado*. I graduated high school in June 1941, just before the war. Although the storm clouds of war were visible over the horizon, we had made it through the Great Depression and seemed to be heading in the right direction.

I was always taught that 'If you don't have something nice to say, don't say anything at all.' I was a strong believer in the Golden Rule, too. This is the way I lived my life. I didn't use profanity and tried my best not to say anything mean to or about others. Later, I tried to pass this belief down to my children. While still a high school student, my first job was filling baskets with candy and toys after school before Easter at Kresge's five-and-ten-cent store. I enjoyed the candies and unfortunately, many of them didn't make it into the baskets! I worked next at Newberry's and Grand Silver five-and-ten-cent stores. Jobs were opening at General Electric in Pittsfield due to World War II, so I went to work there for a time.

The U.S. stayed neutral between the world wars, trying to avoid again becoming entangled in a European foreign war. One of our national heroes, aviator Charles Lindbergh, who in May 1927 was the first man to fly solo across the Atlantic, was part of the 'America First' movement and urged neutrality. It was a time of peace and poverty. I didn't know until later that Lindbergh may have been antisemitic.

Despite the difficult times, there were many fun things to do like going to the movies. The movies introduced talking and sound with 1927s *The Jazz Singer*, the story of a Jewish cantor's son who decided to become an entertainer instead of following in his father's footsteps. I especially enjoyed scary movies like *The Wolf Man* of 1941. *King of the Zombies* of 1941 was particularly disturbing. A sinister Nazi doctor and spy, on a Caribbean Island off the American coast, attempted to acquire intelligence using voodoo and zombies against an American admiral whose airplane crashed on the island.

We had heard wild stories about the Nazis' fascination with the occult and the supernatural. In retrospect, I think *King of the Zombies* and its 1943 sequel were preparing us for thinking of the Germans as a sinister, diabolical enemy. The sequel portrayed the Germans as mindless monsters intent on killing us—that may not have been very far from the truth. It was at this time that I started using the terms 'interesting,' 'different,' and 'was it a hit at the movies?' about films which I didn't think were very good. I used this phrase for the rest of my life. I think I liked scary movies in part because I considered myself a Halloween baby, having been born on October 29.

I enjoyed listening to the radio, playing board games like Monopoly and Scrabble, reading, and playing mini-golf. My friends and I loved big band and swing music. Some of the most popular songs offered hope and an escape from the gloom of the Depression, like 'Pennies from Heaven,' 'Happy Days are Here Again,' 'Over the Rainbow,' 'On the Sunny Side of the Street,' and 'Get Happy.'

My entire life, I enjoyed writing cute rhymes and poems. One of these was 'Best Wishes':

>Let things in the future go well for you,
>   Tho' sometimes it seems hard to cope.
>   We have to keep our dreams alive,
>   and never lose our hope.
>   Your life is so busy, with people and pets,
>   from early morning until the sun sets.
>   But people and critters all seem to like you—
>   Maybe because of the good things you do.
>   Take care of yourself—this is good as it gets,
>   Because you are one of my favorite pets."

HOPE, MIRACLES, AND EXTRAORDINARY INTERVENTIONS

"The guards were ordered to kill us, then ran away."
—Al Kitmacher

Despite its tortured history, "hope" is one of Judaism's greatest tenets. Judaism is one of the few cultures whose golden age is in the future. Jews still await an age of peace, termed the "Messianic Age," when "nation will not lift up sword against nation" and "the Lord shall be one and His name One." This future focus and awaiting the messiah is the dividing line between Judaism and Christianity. When asked if the messiah has come, Jews reply, "Not yet." The ancient Greeks believed human destiny lay in the stars or blind fate. This differs from the Jews, whose sense of hope is closely tied to human freedom, free will, and a future yet to be written. We are who we choose to be, the world is what we choose to make it, and there is nothing inevitable except, as American founding father Benjamin Franklin said, death and taxes.[1]

Despite all he endured, my father held on to some amount of hope. His optimism no doubt was in part due to the many miracles and extraordinary interventions he experienced during the Holocaust that saved his life and helped him escape the clutches of the Nazis.

My father experienced the first two of his 11 miracles when, in the spring of 1942, he was able to escape the Warsaw Ghetto with his sister Frieda. He was able to maneuver and negotiate their way through the streets and train stations despite demands for money, not having train tickets, and being pointed out as Jews. His survival skills and ability to blend in with the surrounding Polish community helped him and his family live through the initial stages of the Holocaust.

While there were many good and heroic Poles who risked their lives to save Jews and other persecuted people, many Polish citizens under the yoke of Nazi domination became like the pitchfork- and torch-carrying villagers in horror movies. They pointed out the Jews to the monstrous Nazis, placing them at great risk and often resulting in murder.[2]

My Father's Words: First Miracle: Escape

Typhus is a terrible disease, with victims experiencing chills, fever, headache, stomach pain, vomiting, rash, bleeding into the skin, delirium, stupor, low blood pressure, and shock. While improved hygiene has mostly stopped typhus, it can still happen in places where sanitation is bad or where it's passed on by an infected animal.

"A neighbor got sick with typhus, a disease caused by infection from the bite of infected fleas, lice, ticks, and mites. The smells, sounds, and feelings of disease were thick in the air. We knew we needed to get out of the Warsaw Ghetto.

Life was very hard. We didn't have enough work or food and there were monsters and evil around every corner. No one should have to live like that. However, we strongly believed in God, despite not being traditionally religious and not attending services regularly. We also believed in the power of miracles and had a great sense of hope for the future. I knew God and his angels were watching over me. I could feel it. Repeatedly, some overwhelming force of good intervened on my behalf and saved me. I don't know why I experienced this while so many others didn't.

I was the first one in my family to leave the Warsaw Ghetto. I took my oldest sister, Frieda, along, who was the most responsible and mature among the kids, and bribed a Jewish kapo, who in turn bribed a German, and they let us through. As soon as we got out of the ghetto, a Polish man came over to me and said, 'Give me all of your money.' I told him, 'Come back here tomorrow at five in the morning and take us to the train station without any problem and I'll give you everything I have.' I didn't have anything, he was stupid, and said, 'OK, I'll be here 5:00 o'clock tomorrow morning.'

I had 30 zloty, almost nothing. At four the next morning, it was still dark, Frieda and I left and walked to the Warsaw train station. I never saw the man I'd arranged to meet, and he never saw us again. I wore decent clothes that I made myself. Both Frieda and I had to wear a Jewish star, but we rolled up our sleeves and the star was underneath. We didn't show the star. If I had shown the star, we would have been killed right on the spot. We disappeared and blended in with the Poles and Germans who surrounded us."

Despite Nazi threats against hiding Jews, thousands of ordinary Poles did just that. Israel has honored 7,000 Poles as "Righteous Among the Nations" for risking their lives to save Jews from the Holocaust. Poles are the single largest national group of the 27,000 non-Jews who have been recognized by Yad Vashem: The World Holocaust Remembrance Center in Jerusalem since the award was established in 1963.

"I don't know where I developed these survival skills, to be able to negotiate our way out of the ghetto and through the difficult encounter with the man who demanded money from us. But it wouldn't be the last time that I would need to live by my wits to help my family and survive."

The Nazis required the "Jewish badge" starting in 1939. A similar badge had been used for centuries by Muslim caliphs, medieval bishops, and others before finally disappearing in the late-18th century. The Nazis brought it back to segregate and identify Jews.

My Father's Words: Second Miracle: 'There's a Jew!' and the Invisible Man

"Frieda and I were waiting for a train but didn't have tickets. Suddenly, a Polish girl recognized Frieda and started screaming, 'There's a Jew, there's a Jew!' The inspector from the train came over to us and said we had to go with him. We walked, then I stopped him and said, 'I'll give you 15 zloty if you let us go.' He took the money and let us go. Again, this seemed to be a miracle. What would have possessed me to make a deal with the inspector and what were the chances that he would let us go?

We got on the train and sat still as much as we could, hoping to not draw attention. The conductor, an older Polish man, came to us and asked for tickets, and we said we didn't have any. He was so surprised he almost fainted! He asked how we had traveled with no tickets, and we responded, 'We just took a chance.' He let us go—he probably didn't want to have any problems with the German authorities that would come from reporting us. This wasn't a kindness. But it was a miracle!

My mother's youngest brother Moishe lived in Chelm, near Lublin. Chelm was one of the oldest towns in Poland. Frieda and I wound up at that town's train station, sitting at a table, keeping our heads down. We were scared that we'd be identified as Jews and immediately arrested. We made believe we were sleeping until it was dark out, again disappearing and blending in with the goings-on of the train station. Some years earlier, in 1933, I had seen the horror movie *The Invisible Man*, where a man could literally disappear into his surroundings. I tried to be invisible.

A German Gestapo agent came into the train station and asked a Jewish woman what she was doing there—she said she had papers. They still took her away. I was sure this would be it. We would be spotted and immediately taken into custody, and I prayed to God we be spared, that the Nazis would move on. The Gestapo didn't approach us. It was unfathomable, given the environment, that they didn't approach and ask us what we were doing in the train station. It's as if they didn't see or recognize us as escaping Jews; we were invisible to them. Maybe it was because I looked like them, with blonde hair and blue eyes. Another miracle! We went to Uncle Moishe's. He had a house, was a tailor and worked for the Germans fixing uniforms. He had work for us."

The *Geheime Staatspolizei* (abbreviated Gestapo), or Secret State Police, was the official secret police of Nazi Germany and in German-occupied Europe. The force was created by Hermann Göring in 1933 by combining the various security police agencies of Prussia into one organization. Gestapo police used torture and violence in interrogations, and they coordinated the deportation of Jews to death camps.

AMERICA ENTERS THE WAR

"I weighed only 85 pounds, I recovered."
—Al Kitmacher

My mother's high-school graduation photo

My Mother's Words: Joining the WAVES

Wanting to serve her country and help fellow Jews who were suffering at the hands of the Nazis, my mother decided to join the WAVES. She later said it was the most rewarding experience of her life:

My mother as a U.S. Navy WAVE, 1942

U.S. Navy WAVES and U.S. Army WACS recruitment poster, 1942

"After high school, I attended the Pittsfield Secretarial School and briefly worked at the GE Power Transformer Production Office. I had always wanted to be a teacher, but after high school, I wasn't so sure anymore and lost interest in college. Very few women that I knew of went to college. The world was at war, America had been attacked, rumors swirled of Nazi atrocities, and I wanted to serve my country and help my fellow Jews. Also, the fellows were being drafted into the service. We terribly missed them. My brother-in-law David [Celia's husband] was stationed with the Navy in Great Lakes, Illinois. When I asked him about joining the Navy, he said the WAVES he met seemed very nice and were highly dedicated to the service, so I decided to join the WAVES.

When World War II started in 1941, I was 19 years old and too young to go into the service without my parents' approval. They didn't want me to join and wouldn't give their OK, saying 'Nice girls don't join the Navy!' To enlist in the WAVES, I had to be 20. But I knew it was the right thing for me to do and I told them I would join on my 20th birthday in October 1942, and I did. I was sent to Boston for a physical exam and testing, passing all. I was accepted."[1]

Navy standards were strict and gender-specific for women (in addition to age requirements): high school diploma or equivalent for enlisted, college degree or equivalent for officers, U.S. citizenship, not married to a male service member, and could not marry or become pregnant, or they would face discharge. A new WAVES volunteer had to have a 'minimum of 18 sound teeth, with at least two molars opposing on each side and four opposing front teeth.'

"We felt like we were watching and living history firsthand. I knew I had to do my part to help America in its great war effort. Despite being a shy, quiet girl from a small town, I would join the U.S. Navy and do my best! This was a time for taking chances and accomplishing great things. It was also the time to band together to work for the forces of good against the evil that was the Nazis. I had to decide what I wanted to be: an observer of history, or someone who contributes to the forces of good.

The day I was to leave for basic training at Hunter College in the Bronx, there was a terrific snowstorm in Pittsfield. The snow and wind were blinding and temperatures below freezing. We didn't own a car, and no taxis were working. My dad walked me to the train station, putting his arm around me to shield me from the stinging snow. As we started out, my mother called from the front porch, 'Are you sure you want to go?!' She didn't realize I was already in the Navy! Walking through the snow was a surreal experience. We kept our eyes down and our coats buttoned up high to protect our necks and ears. It was a dramatic sendoff as I headed to a new life with the U.S. Navy. I had waited for so long to join, and it was finally happening! My life would be changed forever."

Women at War and the WAVES

Women fought in the American Revolution, Civil War, Mexican War, Spanish American War, and World War I. At times, they had to disguise themselves as men to join the fight.

It was clear as World War II approached there were not enough men to support the Navy's needs. Women were needed to replace men in critical shore station jobs and responsibilities.

During World War I, U.S. Representative Edith Nourse Rogers of Massachusetts (referenced earlier for helping European Jewish immigrants) had served as a nurse for the Red Cross, inspected field hospitals for the Women's Overseas Service League, and reported on the treatment of veterans. Rogers was determined to ensure that if American women served in the military again, they would be full-service members, with the same benefits as men.

Due in part to Rogers' efforts, Congress passed Public Law 689 to establish the Women's Reserve as an integral part of the Navy. Women volunteers were required to serve for the duration of the war plus six months. As the legislation sat on President Roosevelt's desk awaiting approval, First Lady Eleanor Roosevelt got involved and pushed for his signature. Soon after, he signed the bill into law on July 30, 1942, to: "expedite the war effort by releasing officers and men for duty at sea and their replacement by women in the shore establishment."[2]

There was some reluctance to have women serve in the Navy. As Virginia Gildersleeve, who assisted Rogers, recalled: "Now if the Navy could have used dogs or ducks or monkeys, certain of the older admirals would probably have preferred them." In response to unsavory names being used to refer to women in the Navy (e.g., "Sailorettes"), the name WAVES was created.

The WAVES' numerous and diverse occupations included pharmacist, aircraft mechanic, drafts person, translator, radio person, statistician, aviation machinist, and metalsmith. More than 30 percent of the WAVES worked as naval aviation training pilots, air traffic controllers, and parachute testers. They also excelled as weather specialists, chemists, and lawyers. World War II marked the Navy's first female doctor, lawyer, and bacteriologist.

Twenty thousand officers and 70,000 enlisted women, including my mother, served in the WAVES. They worked at 900 naval commands nationwide, large, and small, as well as overseas. On the WAVES' first anniversary in 1943, President Roosevelt commented: "In their first year, the WAVES have proved that they are capable of accepting the highest responsibility in the service of their country."

NIGHTMARE

"I was bleeding from my eyes, nose, ears, and throat, but survived."
—Al Kitmacher

After escaping with Frieda from the Warsaw Ghetto in spring 1942 and seeing it was possible, my father guided the rest of his family out of that nightmare. He advised them of the steps they needed to take, including what to do on the train and avoiding detection by the Nazis. After their escape, they lived in relative safety before the Nazis arrested them.

Sarah is Taken

"The Warsaw Ghetto had been horrible: starving, suffering, and dying all around us. Little did I know that this was just the beginning and that things would be getting much worse. No imaginary horror story could compare to the horrors we were about to experience. Unless someone escaped before the war started, there seemed to be no way out. Other countries were not accepting Jewish immigrants, and the Nazis were locking things down.

Frieda and I had to get our parents, brother Yitzhak, and sister Sarah out of the ghetto. In the spring of 1942, I went to my mother's cousin, a well-known man who was a tailor in a small eastern Poland town, Krasnik, doing tailoring work for the Germans. He was also known within the family for preparing official-looking papers for people to escape and travel. For lack of a better term, he was a forger, an activity that would be punished by immediate death. I asked him to make some 'official papers' for the rest of our family. He agreed and made out a slip of paper saying the Germans needed my father to do work in Krasnik. I mailed it to my father.[1]

I told my family what to do—roll up their shirt sleeves to hide the mandatory Stars of David they wore and ride the train out of Warsaw to Krasnik. At first, they hesitated out of fear of being caught, but finally made their way out of the ghetto. Our worst fears were almost immediately realized.

The Nazis were searching everyone and abruptly pulled my 25-year-old sister, Sarah, off the train and led her away. There was no time to react—one moment Sarah was there, and the next she was gone. There was nothing we could do. We would never see Sarah again. We were devastated beyond words. We were heartbroken and mourned our loss, the first of many. We never found out why the Germans took Sarah. She did everything right, the same way the rest of the family did. Sarah was such a happy person, always with a smile on her face and a song on her tongue. It was unbelievable—how could this happen? What would make people do this kind of thing to each other? What had Sarah, or any of us, done to deserve this? We didn't know at the time that women and girls were sometimes singled out for contraception and fertility experimentation. Any thoughts that Jews once had of Germans as 'cultured, liberal humanitarians' were destroyed.

I looked for a place for our remaining family to live. I found a farm owned by a Jewish family—a husband, wife, and daughter—and rented a room from them. We all stayed there, mourning the loss of our beloved Sarah until the Nazis issued an order for all farm residents to move to the city. While we lived on the farm, we went from farm to farm to work. Instead of receiving money, the farmers gave us food. We had enough food to live on, and it was pretty good, although there was never any meat. It cost very little for our family to live on the Jewish farm. If we didn't have the money, we'd take milk or cheese as barter to pay the rent."

A Polish farm, 2014. Courtesy of jarmoluk, Pixabay

Yitzhak is Taken

"The Germans opened a forced labor camp, Jenoshov, on the outskirts of Krasnik. There was a lake and prisoners were forced to do irrigation work. Several hundred men were working there. In 1942, a member of the Judenrat came with a Polish policeman with a horse and buggy and forcibly took me from the family farm. I was 22 years old. They took me to Jenoshov, where I worked day and night digging irrigation ditches. It was terrible, with continuous beatings for the slightest perceived transgressions. There wasn't enough food, although it was more than there had been in the Warsaw Ghetto. We slept on bunks with straw on them, three men across and three men stacked above each other. There was a German commander and several Judenrat as foremen who administered the camp. They were cruel. I couldn't believe that fellow Jews were acting like this, like Egyptian overloads whipping us to make mud bricks for the Pharaoh's pyramid.

After six months, I was too weak to stand up anymore and my face and forehead were horribly sunburned. I was blonde and blue-eyed, with a fair complexion, and the sun was particularly hard on my skin. My parents decided to send my brother Yitzhak in my place for a while, as he was a little younger than me at about 20 years old. I went home to the farm.

Suddenly, we didn't know why, the Germans needed someone to do work outside Jenoshov. They picked Yitzhak along with several other people and told him he'd be the foreman for some farm work. Later, Yitzhak tried to smuggle some food, presumably from the farm he was working on, into the camp and the Jewish guards caught him. He was beaten so badly with clubs and whips that he couldn't stand, sit, or work anymore. He was of no value to them, and they took him away. We never found out where they took our youngest sibling, and we never heard from him again. This was our family's second loss, as Sarah was already gone. The feelings of loss, horror, and dread were unbearable. Our sorrow was bone deep. How could this be happening? It was now just my father, mother, Frieda, and me.

While our remaining family members were on the farm, my father became acquainted with a Polish policeman. The policeman found a Jewish man wandering in the woods and told my father that he could save the man's life if my father made him a policeman's coat. To save a Jew's life, my father said he'd make the coat. This man my father saved turned out to be the same man who later beat Yitzhak so badly. I later saw him at the Budzyn concentration camp, and he told me he was forced to do it and didn't know what happened to Yitzhak afterward. He said he was sorry, but I didn't believe him. How could he have done this after what my father did for him? An unspeakable betrayal by a Jew to a fellow Jew. Our own people were doing the monsters' bidding, and evil seemed to be taking control of our world.

When they liquidated Jenoshov, the Judenrat ordered our remaining family members, who were still on the farm, into the train station in Krasnik."

All are Taken

"The Nazis picked me out before I got on the train, along with other young men, and left my parents and Frieda on the train. I didn't know why they separated us or where they were taking my family or me. My father tried to go with me, but a Gestapo officer told me to go and struck my father in the face with his elbow. I can still see and hear the Nazi's blow to my father's face. My father fell to the train's floor. I had never seen my father, the head of our family, hurt before. It was a horrible and unreal feeling. My mother was not coping well, crying hysterically as I was led away, and my father lay bleeding on the floor. I thought the monsters would at least let my sister go, a young woman, but they didn't. Non-Jewish Poles on the train sat and watched all of this in silence or averted their eyes so as not to be involved. I silently said a prayer: 'Please God, please watch over our family and keep them safe.'

I later found out that the Nazis took most of the Jews from that region to their deaths at Treblinka. I had figured that was where they were going. I can't describe the utter feeling of emptiness and loneliness that I felt as my family was taken away. I never saw my parents or Frieda again. It haunted me for the rest of my life. How could this happen? I was alone. We used to have a family of six. How could I go on?

My world fell apart. I felt outrage at the Nazis, Poles, and those Jews that were collaborating with them. I also felt guilt for being the only remaining member of my family. A big part of me was dead."

Hell: Budzyn

Krasnik was the site of the Budzyn camp, a subcamp of the major Majdanek concentration camp near Lublin. It was at Budzyn that 3,000 Jewish prisoners worked for the *Heinkel Flugzeugwerke* (aircraft) factory. Heinkel, established in 1937, was a major user of slave labor from concentration camps. The Jewish workers at Budzyn's Heinkel factory were spared the fate of the other Jewish workers in the Lublin area who had been taken to labor camps that were liquidated. Budzyn remained a Majdanek subcamp until it became its own concentration camp in 1943. Said my father:

"The Nazis took me and the other young men from the Krasnik train station to Budzyn. We didn't know what to expect. I was at Budzyn in 1942 and 1943, for a winter and a summer—I don't know exactly how long. The passage of time meant little to me other than more suffering. Budzyn was the most brutal place I had been imprisoned. It was at Budzyn that I was forced to wear the striped prisoner suit that I would wear for the remainder of the war. I had no other possessions. Everyone was tattooed, branded like animals, like cattle. I had KL tattooed onto my right forearm by the Germans. It stood for *Konzentrationslager*, meaning concentration camp. I had tried to wait until the end to be tattooed, using my 'invisibility' skill when the tattooing was occurring. I hoped we would be, by some miracle, liberated before my turn came. The Germans knew that and gave me the biggest tattoo they could. Others were tattooed with numbers. Tattoos were a way of keeping control, taking stock, and further dehumanizing us."

Holocaust prisoner statue, 2014. Courtesy of EllisaCapelleVaughn, Pixabay

In January 1943, 13 Jewish prisoners escaped from Budzyn. They joined partisan resistance fighters based near Krasnik. It is not likely any survived the war. When Budzyn closed in 1944, the few surviving Jews were transported to Majdanek, which was one of the largest camps, with seven gas chambers and two wooden gallows. An estimated 350 Krasnik Jews survived the Holocaust. Those who survived left Poland after the war.[2]

IN THE NAVY

"I came to the U.S. by myself, not knowing a word of English or anyone."
—Al Kitmacher

My mother enlisted in the WAVES and was stationed in New York City, Iowa, and then Washington, D.C. It was an eye-opening experience for a quiet, small-town girl—an experience that would shape the rest of her life positively.

Boot Camp: Hunter College

Boot camp for the WAVES opened in 1943 at the Bronx campus of Hunter College. WAVES started their days at 5:30 a.m. to learn Navy traditions, customs, courtesy, and discipline. They took classes on radio operations, storekeeping, finance, chemical warfare, aviation ordinance, and administrative support. The WAVES' training and service allowed the U.S. Navy—which grew rapidly after the Japanese attack on Pearl Harbor—to accomplish its central role in the war against Japan as well as assist the British Royal Navy in the naval war against Germany and Italy. At 10:00 p.m., "Taps," the military trumpet or bugle call signifying the end of the day (also traditionally played at military funerals), was played, indicating lights out.

Hunter College opened in 1870 and continues to this day as part of the City University of New York. The United States rented the entire Hunter College campus for WAVES' training activities, at the cost of one million dollars a year. As the school had no dormitories, New York City paid to remove residents from 17 apartment buildings adjacent to the boot camp.

It took two weeks for WAVES to receive tailored uniforms by fashion designer label Mainbocher. Before that, they wore their uniform cover (hat) with blue crown and brim, civilian clothes, and government-issued shoes. It cost $5 more to outfit a WAVE than a sailor. The Navy supplied WAVES recruits with two blue skirts, three long-sleeved navy-blue shirts, two white shirts, two navy ties, two light blue ties, one pair of navy gloves, two pairs of white gloves, one navy topcoat, two hats, and a rain cover. These items were valued at $200, about $3,171 today. Also included were four pairs of stockings, shoes, galoshes (waterproof overshoes), a leather purse, and summer work clothes. Their uniforms were designed to be both functional and stylish.[12]

The cafeteria at Hunter College served 15,000 meals a day for the WAVES. Cafeteria staff found that the women required more than 23 minutes more per meal than their male counterparts at boot camp. The commissary officer noted that while men might eat and grumble about the food, he heard a "gabble of high-pitched voices informing him of women's food preferences." WAVES soon got used to Navy food. In August 1943, a school for Navy cooks and bakers was created. Following the establishment of that school, the WAVES' Hunter College facility became known for its good food, coffee, and freshly baked bread.

"I clearly remember, and often repeat, one of the Navy sayings about food: 'Take all you want but eat all you take!' And we did! In 1943, the WAVES received their own song, *WAVES of the Navy*. It was written to harmonize with *Anchors Aweigh*:

WAVES of the Navy

> WAVES of the Navy,
> There's a ship sailing down the bay
> And she won't slip into port again
> Until that Victory Day.
> Carry on for that gallant ship
> And for every hero brave
> Who will find ashore, his man-sized chore
> Was done by a Navy WAVE.[3]

One of my most vivid memories I have from boot camp relates to the diving and swimming test we all had to complete. Although as a child I played in local lakes in the summers, I had always been afraid of the water, and the swimming pool I was to jump into appeared frighteningly deep. Years later, when writing about this event in my journal, this is what I wrote:

'Hands cold and legs trembling, I looked down into the clear water of the U.S. Navy testing pool. The diving board seemed to extend forever into the distance—I was terrified of the water. The board curved slightly as I approached the edge. I knew this dive was the last step in my becoming a WAVE. If I failed, I would need to return home. My parents were not in favor of my joining the WAVES, saying 'Nice girls don't join the Navy.' Rather, they wanted me to do secretarial work at GE or some other local Pittsfield business. I bounced once on the board, testing its elasticity before I bounced again and jumped determinedly off the board into the water. As I dropped into the pool's water, the sound of the splash resonated off the walls. It was the splash which sent me reeling back to when I first experienced how truly frightening and dangerous something like a pool of water could be. I went back to being a little girl of 12 years old at the YMCA, scared of the water and feeling like I was going to drown. I felt I was never coming back up. That this was just the end.'

How ironic that someone like me, who hated the water, would join the Navy. To repeat the experience I had at age 12 seemed either foolish or heroic! In any case, I was determined to become a U.S. Navy WAVE, water or not!

My mother, in the U.S. Navy WAVES, 1942

My mother, front row, left, 1943

Article in the Berkshire Eagle, *Pittsfield, 1944*

My mother and her friend Betty June in U.S. Navy uniforms, on top of the Empire State Building in New York City, circa 1943

My mother, 1940s

U.S. Navy Waves marching, 1940s

Back home in Pittsfield, articles were written about me in the local newspaper, the *Berkshire Eagle*. Also, when I visited Pittsfield after boot camp, my former GE female coworkers held a dinner in my honor. I was very proud and so was my family. I was serving our great country and making a difference in the world. Not bad for a quiet kid from the Berkshires!"

The Navy in Iowa?

In 1944, after completing basic training at Hunter's College, my mother was sent to Yeoman's School in Cedar Falls, Iowa, for specialized office training at Iowa State Teacher's College. Now known as the University of Northern Iowa, the college hosted WAVES indoctrination and later the Yeomen (naval secretaries) School. The first class of 1,500 WAVES arrived in December 1942, where they went through five to six weeks of intensive introductory training. During its 29 months of operation, the school trained 14,000 WAVES. My mother said:

"Cedar Falls, Iowa was in the middle of farming country; the land was flat with the city, a little smaller than Pittsfield, sitting by a river. There was a big dam that controlled the river currents, and we were cautioned that getting too close to the dam could be dangerous. Crops were grown throughout the area, and farm animals were raised.

Once at Cedar Falls, we were marching down a country road. On the command 'Eyes, right!' we were treated to the sight of a large pig lying down and feeding her piglets. It was an incredible sight!

> We always sang songs while marching, including this one:
> Three worthy gents we all admire,
> Three who saved the day,
> Three who made our lives worthwhile, Dewey, Decatur and Mainbocher."

George Dewey was from the Spanish-American War era [1898]. He became the only person to attain the rank of U.S. Admiral of the Navy. Stephen Decatur was a commodore who played a key role in the early development of the Navy. Mainbocher was the company that designed our uniforms.

"After finishing Yeoman's School in Cedar Falls, I was given three choices of where I'd like to be stationed. I was told by some that no matter where I picked, I'd probably be sent to Washington, D.C. So I chose Washington, D.C., and was sent there!

The WAVES' barracks were in Arlington, Virginia, near Arlington National Cemetery. My first job was at the Bureau of Naval Personnel in Arlington. Later, I was transferred to the Main Navy Building in Washington, D.C. Each day, we walked to and from work, about five miles each way.

I was in the Navy for two and a half years. My experience helped shape my approach to life and thinking. I learned discipline, the importance of teamwork, and how to survive away from home. I met many people from diverse backgrounds and learned that no matter one's background, we're all just people. I experienced other parts of the country too: New York City, Cedar Falls, and Washington, D.C. After the war, I appreciated the comforts in life more than ever. I also developed an even greater love of my country and a desire to serve.

Being in the WAVES was a wonderful experience and one of the happiest times of my life. I made lots of friends and had incredible experiences. I traveled to New York City for training, Iowa for boot camp, and was stationed in Washington, D.C. These were eye-opening experiences for a small-town girl who had stayed close to home for my first 20 years. And I served my country in the fight against the dark forces of evil that were conquering the world and persecuting fellow Jews. I knew the forces of good would overcome evil, as they always do. It would take all of us, working together, and I needed to be part of that great effort."

The role of women in American society changed dramatically in the early to mid-1900s, including their role in the U.S. military and industries supporting the war effort. The issue of race, however, continued to be a difficult one, as military units and society, in general, remained segregated until much later. The United States had a long way to go to realize equality.[4]

Race and Gender

"We knew the traditional role of women was to stay home, get married, have children, and take care of the home. I knew I wanted more; I wanted to contribute to society and make a difference. The Navy was my way to make that difference. Likewise, growing up as a small-town girl, I had few interactions with people of other races. To win this war, people of all races, beliefs, and genders would need to come together in one mighty effort. We were Americans and we knew we could do it!

For all the fun and wonderful times I had in the WAVES, this was still America in the early 1940s. Whites and people of color were largely segregated. Laws were in place in the south, restricting Blacks' opportunities. Despite these conditions and although there were only a few dozen women of color in the WAVES, I made friends with several of them. To me, they were fellow WAVES. One time, while in Washington, D.C., my friend Betty June was going out with friends, and I tagged along. They decided to go out to eat. We walked into a restaurant and all eyes turned to us. I thought to myself, Wow, we must look pretty good in our uniforms! Then I realized I was the only White person there; it was an all-Black restaurant. We had a nice dinner!"

Women's Evolving Role

The first regiment of women in boot camp totaled 1,993. Every two weeks, another 1,600 to 1,700 women began indoctrination. Each recruit was given four sheets, two pillowcases, four towels, a bed pad, and two blankets. The first 6,000 bedspreads came from the passenger liners *Manhattan* and *America,* converted for military use. At their peak in 1945, there were 86,000 WAVE reservists on duty in nearly every type of shore activity. Within three years of their formation, women made up 18 percent of the total U.S. naval force ashore.

World War II permanently changed the role of women. Over 350,000 women volunteered for military service. The U.S. government expected that women's new responsibilities were for the duration of the war only. However, women had other ideas. They seized the opportunity to contribute and did so successfully. Women played a major role in fighting for their country. At home, the world had changed, but not necessarily in a way that benefited them.

While recruitment efforts promised substantial pay, food,

lodging, clothing, and medical and dental care, the Office of War Information wanted recruitment messaging to appeal to "patriotism and the desire to help our fighting men," not on women improving their station in life. In some ways, this is similar to the United States and its allies indicating it was fighting to defeat the Nazis, not necessarily to save the Jews.[5]

The U.S. government's recruitment messaging also emphasized gender, stating things like: "Women in uniform are no less feminine than before they enlisted." To ensure this statement held, the U.S. Navy employed designer fashion in WAVES' uniforms.

Despite their contributions and valiant service, women's military contributions were at times stigmatized and mocked as lesser than men's. Susan B. Anthony II, great-niece of the women's suffrage fighter, worked at the Navy Yard in Washington, D.C. as a grinder in the machine shop. In 1944, she argued women had proven their ability and deserved "equal pay for equal work."

IN HELL
ORDINARY HUMANS TURNED MONSTERS

Budzyn concentration camp, where my father was held captive, was a living hell. Torture and atrocities were carried out daily. Prisoners were not treated as people. Rather, they were treated as materials to be used or as excrement to be wiped away, leaving no trace.

It would be easy to label the Nazis as unintelligent, brutish monsters who murdered at random. Though this description is partially true, the Nazis were also proficient, efficient, and effective in realizing their goals. Some were highly educated.

It took architects, engineers, and experts to design the "decontamination" showers through which cyanide pellets and other poisons were dropped and to create the death camp furnaces optimized for mass cremation. The Nazis built an immensely powerful military, creating and applying tank, airplane, rocket, and other technologies their opponents envied. They cultivated fertile farms and constructed dams to provide irrigation. They created and built a highly efficient rail system as well as Volkswagens and Porsches, allowing personal travel for common people. Most of the German soldiers working at the camps had no criminal record. They were married and had families and children.

How then could these otherwise ordinary or even extraordinary people commit such horrors? Factors supporting this dehumanization include a belief in false realities and antisemitic folklore, a militaristic past, demonization of the enemy to justify violence, deep feelings of humiliation and victimization after World War I, devotion to a cultish leader, radicalization via multimedia, and being drawn to a cause greater than themselves. The impacts of losing World War I, which included a lack of money, food, and a lowered national self-esteem, certainly added to the effect. The Nazis knew how to leverage these deprivations and change the narrative through effective propaganda that communicated the relentless logic of a false premise: that the Aryans were superior, and others were subhuman. The Nazis argued that Jews and other subhumans were to blame for Germany's woes—they had stabbed Germany in the back. Further, Germans seemed to try to think of their victims as anything but fellow human beings. Certainly, they wouldn't have treated their own people in this horrible way.

Nightmares were born from the Nazis' lack of morality, introspection, critical thought, and judgment. The Nazis' utilitarian advantages, evidenced by their technology developed in the Holocaust, reflected their perverse moral standards.

Here again, it's interesting to consider the horror story of *Dr. Jekyll and Mr. Hyde*. Jekyll, a respected professor, chooses to become the brutish, ape-like creature who can commit unspeakable acts that Jekyll could not. Jekyll likes becoming his alter ego because he wants to do all the things Hyde does and enjoys the extra freedom. The question here is: did becoming the brutish, monstrous Nazi—able to murder without hesitation—provide a guilt-free, desired freedom to the otherwise respectable German?[12]

Bad and evil will always hold temptations. Degrees worse than "bad," evil is flashy and seductive but crumbles when opposed. In the case of the Nazis, Hitler and his henchmen killed Jews because they regarded them as a threat to the purity of their "Aryan race." Nazis loved death and annihilation and delighted in destroying human value and meaning. The Nazis were also masters of meticulous organization and propaganda, highly efficient, and orchestrated destruction for destruction's sake. They were history's ultimate nihilists, rejecting life, knowledge, and existence.

Concentration camp prisoner statues, 2013. Courtesy of Bluesnap, Pixabay

Feix the Murderer

"While I was a slave laborer at Budzyn in 1942 and 1943, the Nazis regularly took a number of us to an airplane factory to do hard labor digging ditches. We never saw any airplanes built there. I later found out that it was the Heinkel airplane factory and about 5,000 prisoners [about 3,000 of whom were Jewish] worked there. Ukrainians served as guards at the camp and collaborated with the Nazis in various ways—as part of the *Schutzmannschaft*, or German supervised auxiliary police, in the German military, and as concentration camp guards. Some Ukrainians saw collaboration with the Nazis as a way to gain liberation from the Soviet Union. Many of these Ukrainians were just as brutal as their Nazi masters. Growing up, I heard stories of the brutality of the Cossacks [fierce Russian horse-borne soldiers] toward the Jews. Like in the rest of Eastern Europe, Ukrainian pogroms had been common and brutal. The Holocaust seemed to provide another avenue for these people to exercise their antisemitism.

There was a German camp commandant Adolf Reinhold Feix. He was known for killing Jewish people for no reason or for made-up reasons, like hiding money, being dirty, or being sick. He was a Sudeten German, and formerly a barber. Feix rode a white, pure-bred horse, bought with prisoners' stolen money. Feix proved that he was worthy of his first name, Adolf; his bloodthirsty desire for murder, torture, and sadism were insatiable and widely known. He presided over a regime of torment, torture, terror, and threats. We were helpless in the face of such evil. Feix sadistically always seemed to be smiling and laughing as he carried out his cruelties and atrocities. He spoke quickly and as intelligent people do, knowing what he was doing. It was rumored Feix played the violin and ordered the camp orchestra to play tunes until they dropped from exhaustion. He ordered prisoners to sing and dance while the orchestra played. He was truly a beast."

Nazi Butchers

Nazi guards at the camps were generally from the lower middle class. Their fathers tended to be factory workers, craftsmen, salesmen, or shop workers. Most had finished elementary school, some had finished high school, and a few had finished secondary or vocational school. The German troops working in the camps were called *Totenkopfverbande*, or "Death's Head" detachments. They wore the skull and crossbones insignias on their uniforms, reflecting their unit. It begs the question: how could seemingly ordinary people turn into inhuman butchers?

Torture

"When we first arrived at Budzyn in 1942, to perform slave labor, we resembled human skeletons. We were ordered to leave any suitcases and belongings in the stable; I had none. We were then taken to the showers and our clothes were taken to the *Entlausung* [delousing station] to rid them of supposed lice and other parasites. We were told that holding back money or property was forbidden and would be severely punished. Those with adequate clothing were searched, presumably in search of items of value. Those who were poorly dressed, like me, were not.

We were treated like animals. The Nazis referred to us and other 'undesirables' as Untermenschen. We were seen as subhuman. There was nothing but torture and oppression. The shower was a small room with multiple nozzles. Five to six prisoners were crowded under one nozzle—there was no soap. Even showering was a form of torture. At the time, we were unaware that the Nazis were using other 'showers' to gas victims to death.

We only ate solid food at night. We were given a little piece of bread and 'soup' [if you could call it that] of water, leaves, and maybe a piece of turnip. The daily portion of bread was distributed at night to the heads of prisoner groups by seniority. The prisoner group head then distributed a loaf to groups of ten prisoners, who then divided it up among themselves. This system headed off disputes and arguments. Each stable housed about 600 to 700 people who slept on wooden planks. As the close and crowded conditions made the stables unbearably hot, no blankets were distributed.

In the morning, we were given a coffee-like drink and no food. After drinking the black liquid from the top of the drink, we hungrily consumed the thick substance that remained at the bottom. Although not food, the black sludge filled our stomachs before a day of hard labor. We would then 'fall in' for morning roll call. The camp was divided into work groups called *kompania*, with a *yekke* [German Jew] serving as commander of each group. Each group was then divided into smaller divisions.

We walked just outside the camp and worked digging pits. For what purpose we didn't know. Pits had to be dug to the height of two men. The work was backbreaking! We were burned by the sun. The commander would go from pit to pit, yelling '*Arbeiten! Arbeiten!*' [Work! Work!]" We sang songs and prisoner orchestras played. I think this was forced upon us for the enjoyment of guards—to provide them another opportunity to beat and torture us, and to try to break our will or intimidate us. Orders such as 'In step, march, sing!' and 'Sing a song!' were given, and we were beaten if we didn't immediately comply. Songs were of a military nature and contained obscenities or double meanings, or they were on pleasant topics, to torture us by pointing out the difference between the song and our horrible situation. One particularly despicable song was entitled *Jews' Song*, and went like this:

> For hundreds of years we cheated the people, no swindle was too outrageous, we wangled, we lied, we cheated, we narked, whatever

the currency, the crown, or the mark.

Some music was created by prisoners as a form of distraction from our horrible plight, as an outlet for our emotions, to console ourselves, and in memory of better times.

Lunch consisted of the same soup as was served for dinner. We ate at long wooden tables. Some walked around the tables, after lunch, searching for a leaf or grain of grit that may have been dropped. Many died of starvation. It was all so sad and unreal."

No Life

Budzyn was an SS concentration camp, a fenced-in rectangle flanked by four towers, one at each corner. Looking out from the top of these towers were armed Ukrainian guards manning machine guns. A row of barracks, with a nearby large open square, lay just beyond the barbed wire fence. The area was no bigger than an American football field and was encircled by a belt of open country surrounded by pine trees.

The daily routine at Budzyn began with a 5:00 a.m. parade and counting of prisoners. The prisoners were then left to stand for an hour while the SS ate breakfast. At 6:00 a.m., working parties went out to work in the aircraft factory. At lunchtime, prisoners returned to the camp for soup. In the evening, they returned for a meal consisting of soup and bread. They then went to their bunks, five bunks stacked to the ceiling.

Atrocities

Many atrocities took place at Budzyn. Prisoners described the following:[345]

- Once, when the prisoners came back from work and fell in for roll call, a prisoner was found to have money. The other prisoners were forced to beat him before he was shot and killed by the SS.

- One morning, when the prisoners came out of the barracks, a German Jew was hanged on the roll-call square by the SS. He had been an officer in the German army.
- Two Jews were drowned in the Budzyn latrines because they had bought civilian jackets from Poles.
- Five to seven prisoners were forced to spend the night outside the locked barracks. They were found the next morning dead, having been shot by the SS guards.
- Once, when the prisoners returned from work, they discovered that 100 of the old, sick, and child prisoners were no longer in the camp. They were told the Nazis took them away in a railway wagon and killed them.
- When two prisoners tried to escape into the woods by digging a tunnel under the barracks, the tunnel caved in. One of the escapees was shot and the other was captured. The latter was hung up by his hands for days, leading to the permanent loss of use of his hands. As collective punishment, all prisoners had to stand in the snow for a night.

My father and other prisoners relayed the torture and cruelty displayed by Feix.

On one occasion, Feix saw an old prisoner and said, "You old dog, are you still alive?" He then ordered the Ukrainians (whom the Nazis used as concentration camp guards) to shoot and kill the prisoner. Feix left before the man was killed. The other prisoners surrounded the old man to protect him and the Ukrainians were unable to find him in the crowd. When Feix came back to the camp an hour later and saw the old man still alive, he drew his revolver and shot him. The elderly man was a popular and beloved Warsaw doctor, Dr. Pupko. He had done much as a doctor for poor Jews; he wouldn't take payment.

In another attack, a prisoner was found to have money. Feix beat him and commanded he be hanged. When the hanging rope broke, Feix decided not to hang the prisoner again, but he did not wish to waste a valuable bullet on a Jewish prisoner, either. Feix ordered the prisoner's fellow Jews to beat him to death.

Right out of a horror story, one of Feix's henchmen was called "Otto the Small" or "The Small Monster" due to his stature and cruelty. It was said his appearance was grotesque: he was short and thin, with his eyes frighteningly small and his face filled with pock marks. He was reputed to be a Volga German (ethnic Germans who colonized and lived along the Volga River in southeastern Russia), but instead of wearing SS fatigues, Otto wore the black fatigues of the Ukrainians. He excelled at cruelty, beatings, and torture and was always prepared to execute murderous deeds. While liquidating one small town, Otto was described as brutally murdering dozens of Jewish babies and young children by grabbing them by the legs and chopping off their heads.

My father said, "The sounds of the screaming prisoners being beaten, tortured, and murdered ... I didn't know people could make those sounds. It still haunts me years later. Nazis, barbed wire fences, and dogs—barking, growling, and biting German shepherds—surrounded us. There was always the feeling of suffering and death. Clothes and shoes with no owners were piled all over the camp; they had already been murdered. You could smell the dead bodies being burnt; it was a bit like the smell of bones that people used to boil to make glue. The odor of burning flesh wafted through the air for miles around. We were always being watched when we went to the bathroom, undressed, all the time. We were starving—shrunken from malnutrition, suffering, half-naked and dying.

Living (if you could call it living) conditions were very bad; we were crowded into horse stables to sleep. We lived on top of each other. We were regarded as animals, not people. The beds were several stories high; six men shared a bed. I thought back fondly to our family's little apartments in Lublin and Warsaw. Even our small room in the Warsaw Ghetto seemed luxurious compared to this hell. We were forced to do inhuman manual labor in dirty and crowded conditions, with very little food or drink. No human should have to live like this. In some ways, those that died were the lucky ones."

Concentration camp bunks, 2020. Courtesy of dimitrisvestikas1969, Pixabay

DREAMS AND MORE MIRACLES

After spending his initial time as a prisoner at the nightmarish Budzyn concentration camp, as the Soviets approached, he was moved to the almost-as-horrific Flossenbürg camp. My father continued to experience miracles and extraordinary interventions that saved his life.[1]

Third Miracle: Fighting with the Devil

Dreams are thought to portend events to come. The Talmud says dreams can have prophetic properties. Culturally, bad dreams are often thought to foreshadow evil tidings or negative events to come. In horror films, dreams are sometimes used to foretell an upcoming battle against monsters. My father experienced such a dream.

"I had a dream that saved my life. I was in my father's tailor shop working. Suddenly, the door flew open, and a big black bird flew in and started to fight with me. Finally, I overpowered the bird and threw him out.

I woke up and realized I was sick. Typhus was going around the camp. I couldn't see straight. I couldn't move, I had a fever. I asked my friend—he and his father, who later died in his sleep, slept in the bunk near me—to help me get down from the bunk and get to work.

I had a feeling I needed to move. I didn't want to stay in the barracks. Later, I found out that an order was given and all the people who had remained in the barracks, sick and not sick, were taken out of the buildings, ordered to dig a big ditch, and then shot by the guards. Over 100 people were shot. We had two miles to walk to work and heard guns going off every few minutes. When we got back to the barracks, they told us of the killings. This was not the first time or the last time we heard guns.

When I told the supervisor I was sick and couldn't work outside, he sat me down and I had to pick potatoes. There was an older Jewish man, a religious man, picking potatoes to whom I told my dream. He said in Hebrew, 'You fought the devil and won.' I thanked God for his intervention."

In Judaism, the raven is often viewed as a cruel bird. In fact, according to the Talmud, the raven is too cruel to even care for or feed its young. The Biblical story of Joseph (Genesis 40) also uses birds within a dream to represent harbingers of evil (in the dream, they devour the body of the Pharaoh's chief baker).

Wieliczka Salt Mine

"The Budzyn concentration camp was closed in 1944 as the Soviets reached it. I was then shipped out to Wieliczka, a salt mine near Krakow, which was run by the Polish. They were the worst. The Nazis were monsters—murderers, full of hatred. But the Poles knew us: we were their neighbors, and they turned on us, pointing us out to the Germans to be persecuted and killed. There were about 1,700 Jews forced to work in the mine.

Others, including my friend from Budzyn, were sent to different camps. I wasn't sick anymore as I was at the time of my dream. We did hard labor, digging and carrying salt out of the mine. Not a day went by that someone wasn't killed.

From Wieliczka, I was soon sent to Leichmertz in Germany, about a day's journey by truck from the Wieliczka salt mine. The Germans didn't give us any food for the journey. I was there for months. We slept on bunks in barracks there and again served as slave labor for the Nazis."

Fourth Miracle: Sheet and Metal Worker

"When we arrived in Leichmertz, they asked for each person's trade. I don't know what got in my head, but I said I was a '*Klemperer*,' a sheet-and-metal worker. I thought if they didn't need a tailor, maybe they'll need a sheet and metal worker. Also, when I sit and work, alone, my mind doesn't rest. I thought if I sit and work, I'll go bananas, so I figured if they'd put me to work with a hammer, a chisel, a screwdriver, I'd be better off.

Soon after arriving in Leichmertz, the Nazi guards sounded an alarm, and all the prisoners had to go out and stand in a line. They called my name and several others', and we were loaded on a train. We went west into Germany by open-car cattle train. We sat, but it wasn't comfortable. These trains didn't have water, food, a toilet, or ventilation. I didn't know if I was being taken to be killed or where they were taking me. I also didn't know what was to become of the prisoners whose names weren't called. My mind wandered to my family. Where had they been taken? Were they all dead? Was I truly alone? I ended up in Flossenbürg, a remote concentration camp, at a Messerschmitt airplane manufacturing plant.

Flossenbürg was a big camp with about 15,000 prisoners of all different nationalities. Saying that I was a sheet and metal worker saved my life—we got better food. In the morning, we got a piece of bread with margarine or *Wurst* [sausage], and at night we got soup. I didn't know anyone; I had no friends. If I had said I was a tailor, I would have been killed. I believe God or maybe an angel, watching out for me, put the thought in my brain to say I was a Klemperer. I thanked God for his guidance—another miracle."

Flossenbürg was an important part of the Nazis' Final Solution, although it was not as well-known as the infamous Auschwitz, Dachau, and Treblinka camps.

The SS forcibly relocated prisoners capable of being moved to other German camps in April 1945 as the Allies advanced toward

Flossenbürg. One surviving French prisoner, Marcel Cadet, reported that one man was left for dead roughly every ten yards along the 125-mile route from Flossenbürg south to the German village of Pösing.

Fifth Miracle: "Fritz Wants Your Breakfast"

"I had a very bad experience in Flossenbürg. I was working outside, moving rail tracks. It was cold, freezing. Someone dropped the rail and my hands stuck to the metal. Both of my hands were left bleeding. There was no reason to move the tracks; we just moved them from one place to another—hard labor.

Suddenly, a Jewish man came over and said, 'Fritz wants your breakfast for a week.' Fritz was a German kapo, a concentration camp prisoner assigned to supervise forced labor. At Flossenbürg, there were German, Polish, Russian, and Jewish prisoners—a lot of them. Political prisoners and 'undesirables.'

The Jewish man had already given Fritz his breakfast for a week. I said, 'Anyone can give whatever they want. If I get a breakfast, I'm not going to give it away.'

The man said, 'He's going to kill you.'

I said, 'If he's going to kill me, he's going to kill me, what can I do?'

I prayed to God for his help. Afterward, I heard this Fritz was a murderer, just terrible. I asked people to help me, but no one could help me. On the day Fritz was supposed to kill me, I came out of the barracks. I didn't see him. I asked, 'Where's Fritz?' I was told that Fritz and another kapo were making moonshine, it was poisonous, and several people died from it. They took Fritz and the other kapo away, and we never saw them again. Another miracle. I had miracles right along.

I was at Flossenbürg for many months. We didn't see the SS or other uniformed German soldiers and they didn't single out the Jews there."

Flossenbürg concentration camp was in Bavaria, Germany, near the town of Flossenbürg and the border with Czechoslovakia. The camp was established in May 1938 mainly for political prisoners. Other prisoners and Jews joined them after the war started. By 1944–

1945, the camp held between 5,000 and 18,000 prisoners under the control of Hitler's dreaded SS.

"The horrors continued at Flossenbürg. All around me there was suffering, torture, and death. The miracles that had saved my life many times continued. There were too many close shaves with death. I could sense the end of the ordeal was getting closer. I just needed to survive until then, God willing."

End is Near

By the time my father sensed "the end of the ordeal was getting closer," it was 1944 or 1945. The Germans had short-wave radios and talked among themselves. Some of the prisoners, including my father, understood German and could tell something big was going to happen. The prisoners knew the Americans were coming from the west and the Russians from the east.

The Nazis were more afraid of the Russians than the Americans. My father was sure this was because the Nazis had invaded Russia, costing millions of Russian lives, and the Russians wanted revenge. Little by little, the prisoners also learned just how many Jews had been murdered by the Nazis.

My father was in seven concentration and slave labor camps throughout the Holocaust. He never worked as a tailor during his captivity, and he never heard anything more about his family.

Sixth Miracle: Death on the Train

"In mid-April 1945, the Nazis evacuated Flossenbürg as U.S. forces approached. When the Germans took us out of Flossenbürg, they took us by train. I was in the lower level of a closed-in car, and many prisoners were above me in the upper level, out in the open. It seemed that those above us had it better as they could breathe the open air. But suddenly, English planes came down. I could see them through the slats in the side of the train car—they had circular red, white, and blue markings on their wings and body. They blasted the train with machine guns. A lot of people on the train were killed, especially those who were riding on the upper level. We were showered with the blood of those riding above us. We on the bottom were mostly spared. The Germans saw they couldn't move the trains without being shot at, so they took us out of the trains and on a march to some unknown destination. Another miracle for me. I was sorry for those on the train who had not been as fortunate."

The Nazis used the rail system extensively to transport Jews and other "undesirables" from Germany and German-occupied Europe to concentration and death camps in Poland and elsewhere. Deportations of this scale required expert organization and coordination between German government ministries. The Nazis attempted to hide their true intentions, labeling the deportations as "resettlements." They used both passenger and freight cars for deportations, and there were instances in which Allied airplanes mistakenly believed the trains contained armaments or German troops. This could explain the above-described incident.

Seventh Miracle: a Voice

"We were forced to sleep on the sides of the road. The guards gave us blankets, but the stronger people, those who had eaten more recently —Russians and Poles—took the blankets away from us and we froze. Each day, we received one turnip to eat—that was all. It was terrible. We marched for several weeks, and the rain never stopped. Every few minutes, we saw prisoners who couldn't go on being thrown in the ditch on the side of the road by the butchering Ukrainians (who were serving as guards for the Nazis) and gunned down.

Suddenly, I couldn't go on. My legs just stopped, and I didn't know why. I started to fall behind the rest of the prisoners. I then thought I heard a voice from behind me say, 'Kitmacher, don't stop here.' I didn't have any friends there and didn't know who it was. I somehow found enough strength to keep going. It was God or one of his angels keeping me alive."

Eighth Miracle: Liberation!

"We had the feeling we were going to be saved soon. We were taken to a town in Bavaria called, Stamsried. The Ukrainians were afraid. They put the prisoners in the marketplace and called out the *Bürgermeister* [mayor]. They were all debating what to do with us. The German townspeople stood and watched all this taking place, not lifting a hand to stop this horror or help us. No doubt they would later say they had no idea what was happening.

The Ukrainians' impulse was always to kill us, and they had an order from the Nazis to do just that. Just then, up in the hills, we saw American tanks and troops coming in. We knew they were American because of the white star markings on the tanks. It was the best thing I ever saw in my life! After all I had been through, I knew we were saved!

The Ukrainians ran and disappeared. I later felt bad I didn't grab a gun out of someone's hands and start shooting them. I hope at Judgment Day, all 1,000 angels will vote to punish the Nazis and their Ukrainian lapdogs.

There were about 50 of us left. Many times, that number had died on the march, most of them killed by the monstrous Ukrainians, though some by the English planes.

The U.S. troops took Stamsried without firing a shot—welcomed with a white flag waved by the Germans. Just as the German people had welcomed the monster Hitler and his goosestepping troops, they now welcomed the Americans. This welcome may have been because the Nazis and their Ukrainian allies were absent, having run away. It may have been because most of the Germans were women and children, as men had left to serve in the military. Or it may have been sheer relief for the end of the war being within sight.

I was sick and ended up in a hospital with others who had been liberated. The Americans visited to check on us and started to bring in candy and other things. I was very thankful to the Americans I saw and talked with quite a few American Jewish soldiers. I was so proud that some Jews had been able to fight the Nazis and win! They were not victims They had fought for the forces of good against absolute evil and won. I wish we'd had the strength to fight back."

The Americans, part of the 358th and 359th U.S. Infantry Regiments [90th U.S. Infantry Division], known as the "Tough [H]ombres," told the prisoners they were liberated and free to go wherever they wanted.

American officers and soldiers wrote diaries, logs, and were interviewed about what they found when they liberated Jews and other victims of the Nazis. Below are a few of their thoughts:[2] [3]

"It was as if I had entered hell. ... They were too weak to get up. ... Their eyes were the only indication they were alive. ... The smell was so overpowering I got sick and ran out. ... You couldn't believe it. ... The shock was complete and total. ... Especially when we saw the crematoria—it was still hot, with these piles of bodies, stacked five bodies high."

"There were dead bodies on the left, piles of dead bodies on the right—and their arms and legs looked like broomsticks covered with no flesh. Slowly, the ones who were still alive stumbled toward us like 'the living dead, zombies,' in striped pajamas with a sewn-on Star of David, calling out in German for food, water, and cigarettes."

In the East, Russia's steamrolling Red Army shut down many of the first Nazi death camps in Poland, starting with Majdanek, near Lublin. Yet, surprisingly, many of Russia's Western allies dismissed Russian eyewitness accounts and photos of the camps, skeptical that it was just "Soviet propaganda."

These false beliefs that the accounts and photos were propaganda were shattered with the camps' liberation. The liberating Allies were shocked at the level of human suffering and piles of bodies they discovered left behind by the retreating and surrendering Nazis. There was no longer any question as to the nature of Hitler's Final Solution.

Despite Hitler's prediction in 1941 of a "Thousand-Year Reich," the country crumbled with the Allies' military invasion. German concentration and slave labor camps fell to the advancing Allied armies. Although rumors about the Nazi death camps reached the West via Switzerland as early as 1942, many had found it inconceivable that Nazi Germany, despite all its bluster, would have undertaken a program to exterminate all European Jews.

At approximately 10:30 a.m. on April 23, 1945, the first U.S. troops of the 90th Infantry Division arrived at the Flossenbürg camp. They were horrified at the sight of the estimated 2,000 weak and deathly ill prisoners who remained in the camp. They were also shocked to see that SS guards were still forcibly evacuating those fit to endure the transport south. The SS guards panicked and opened fire on many of the prisoners, killing about 200 in a desperate attempt to create a roadblock of human bodies, leaving 1,800 surviving prisoners. American tanks opened fire on the Germans guards as they fled into the woods, killing over 100 SS troops.

Members of the 90th Division, along with other American units, assisted the sick and dying prisoners, buried the dead, conducted interviews of former prisoners, and sought evidence that would later be used in the post-World War II war crimes trials against Nazi officers and guards. In burying the dead, they directed able-bodied area German men and boys to help.

U.S. Sergeant Harold C. Brandt of the 11th Armored Division took part in the liberating of Flossenbürg, Mauthausen, and Gusen concentration camps. When asked many years after the war about his part in liberating the camps, Brandt stated: "It was just as bad or worse than depicted in the movies and stories about the Holocaust … I cannot describe it adequately. It was sickening. How can other men treat other men like this?"[4]

Said my father: "It was unreal, to go from hell to something that felt like heaven—to liberating angels. Few realized what we had gone through. I felt the same way the Jewish slaves in Egypt must have felt when God, through Moses, forced Pharaoh to let the people go! After the nightmares, the horrors, the monsters, the murders, and the deaths, it was over. But what lay ahead for us?"

PART III
GOOD PREVAILS

BACK TO CIVILIAN LIFE

Back Home

"The war was over, and we won! We took some time to celebrate and rejoice—the forces of good had vanquished those of evil. Good always finds a way! I decided it was time for me to head home, back to a world that, though it resembled the one we had left, was changed forever. The war led to a new sense of confidence and new opportunities. I would need to find new ways to contribute and make a difference. I was excited for what lay ahead!

After being discharged from the WAVES, I returned to Pittsfield. It was home, and my mother, father, and sister still lived there. My sister, Celia, and her husband, Dave—who had given me excellent advice about joining the WAVES—later had two children: Leonard and Susan. They were beautiful children who became wonderful adults. We remained very close.

Serving in the WAVES permanently changed and expanded my perspective on the world around me. I had grown.

In the late 1940s, Pittsfield was a thriving small city of more than 50,000 people. It had four seasons, which I loved! It was a wonderful place to raise a family and the area had so much to offer: Onota and Pontoosuc lakes (where I swam as a young child before I feared the water), Pittsfield State Forest, "Balance Rock," and Mount Greylock. Pittsfield also had so much history: Herman Melville wrote the book *Moby Dick* at Arrowhead [his home in Pittsfield], and it's been said that baseball was invented in Pittsfield in 1791.

Pittsfield seemed to be the exact right place to permanently set down roots, get married, and raise a family. I made so many lifelong friends and unforgettable memories in Pittsfield. I also still loved writing Navy stories and cute little poems, like this one:

I Couldn't Kill a Fly
    A fly was in my kitchen
    Being a real pest.
    I got tired of seeing him—
    Decided to "lay him to rest."
    Did my best to catch him—
    yes, I really tried.
    I would have been quite happy to know that he had died.
    He settled very near to me,
    My hand formed to a cup.
    I reached in his direction
    And picked that black fly up.
    Threw him down the disposal,
    Made the water flow strong.
    Decided to start the machine
    When I gathered more waste—before long.
    Came back to the kitchen—
    What was that spot in the sink?
    The fly had climbed out—all soggy,
    He looked like a blob of ink.
    What a courageous creature,
    Resilient, strong little guy.
    If he could get his strength back,
    I was going to let him try.
    Now he's buzzing round again.
    Seems he's my resident fly.
    I've opened doors so he could leave

> But he stays—guess he feels he's 'my guy.'
> He's here even as I write this
> Seems healthy and strong—oh my.
> I won't try to hurt him again.
> Guess I can't kill a fly.

In fact, I submitted and had published some of my poems and Navy stories in magazines like *Reader's Digest*.

I went back to work at GE. I could have had three years of free college, but I wasn't interested."

Women After the War

Early in his presidency, following FDR's death, President Harry Truman sought to build on the promises of Roosevelt's New Deal. Truman called it the Fair Deal. In addition to demobilizing the armed forces and preparing for the homecoming of servicemen and servicewomen, Truman also had to guide the nation in its return to a peacetime economy.

Women had served bravely in World War II, serving in essential wartime roles, receiving medals and citations for their contributions, and even becoming prisoners of war. But once the war ended, many found themselves jobless and unrecognized. Employers were not legally required to restore former service members to their old jobs or employment. Some employers discriminated against former military women. Some were inexplicably convinced that women's service had been immoral and would subvert gender roles back home in the workplace (for example, the belief men were the "primary bread-winners" and women's focus should be on the home).

Women who had stayed in military auxiliary roles weren't considered veterans or given veteran benefits even though they had served in critical roles during the war. Women's Army Auxiliary Corps service members and WAVES assumed women wouldn't be allowed to serve in such roles in the future.

However, officials in all U.S. military branches were convinced by the toughness and efficiency demonstrated by the military women who served during World War II that it was worth making their roles permanent. In 1948, Truman signed a new law allowing women to serve as permanent, full members of all U.S. military branches.

Further expanding women's rights, in part based on their contributions in World War II, the act required civilian employers to allow women to return to their prewar jobs upon their return to the workforce.[1]

Jews After the War

By 1950, most American Jews had been born in the United States, participated in World Wars I and II, survived the Great Depression, saw the Holocaust and its aftermath, and supported Israel's creation. In the post-World War II years, American Jews became a vital force in the American political process, played a significant role in the cultural life of the nation, and demonstrated on behalf of civil rights at home and oppressed Jews abroad. These transformative events, along with a fully developed network of religious and voluntary organizations, contributed to the Jewish community's perception changing from the United States being a haven to a true home.[2]

FREEDOM

Didn't Recognize Myself—a Ninth Miracle

"Upon being liberated, I weighed only 85 pounds. Before the war, I weighed about 170 pounds. Slave laborers lost about nine to ten pounds a week. I looked in a mirror and didn't recognize myself. I was suffering from malnutrition; my cheekbones were sticking out of my face.

I wound up on a farm in eastern Germany. One day, where I was staying, others killed a pig. A Polish man gave me a piece of it. I cooked and ate it and got very sick—the meat made a mess out of my stomach. It had been a very long time since I had eaten a real meal, let alone meat.

A small hospital was opened for the former prisoners, and I ended up there. I would need to take it slow as I returned to a more normal existence. It took a long time to feel healthy again, to get back to being myself. I knew others who died in similar circumstances. I recovered—a ninth miracle! Following my slow recovery, I anxiously searched for any sign of my immediate family, but there were none to be found.

I was sent to the München Neu Freimann Displaced Persons (DP) camp in Shwabing-Freimann—an American-occupied zone. The DP camp was just outside Munich, and I stayed there for four or five years. I was going to emigrate to Israel, and I wrote to my cousin who had moved there (I located him while searching for surviving family). He responded that I should not come. Palestinians and Jewish refugees were fighting against each other in Israel's War of Independence as the British departed. When my cousin's brother arrived in Israel from a DP camp in Germany, he got off the ship, they put a gun in his hand to fight against the Palestinians, and he was killed within an hour. I survived the horrors of the Holocaust, the only member of my immediate family to still be alive. The last thing I wanted to do was to travel to Palestine, only to be killed shortly after arrival. I had to make other plans. Fortunately, I was sponsored to emigrate to the U.S.

Having experienced the many miracles and extraordinary interventions I did—which allowed me to survive the Holocaust, I again found myself in unfamiliar circumstances. First, as a seriously ill hospital patient, then living in a DP camp with thousands of other survivors. I was truly a person without a home. It was unclear what the next chapter of my life would hold. Either way, I was alone.

My friend from the Budzyn camp and I formed a Jewish community club while at the DP camp. We wrote to the United Jewish Bureau in New York City in search of relatives. It felt good to try and gain control of my life and search for family members who were stolen from me by the Nazis and their allies. I found out that my cousin Rose, the daughter of one of my mother's sisters, was living in Munich, and I contacted her. There was no record to indicate any of my immediate family had survived. A big part of me had died, and I knew I could never be whole again. Why did I survive when all of my loved ones did not?"

In 1945, President Truman's representatives found horrible conditions at the DP camps, including the presence of barbed wire, guards, and prisoners still wearing concentration camp clothing. They observed that prisoners were treated similarly to how the Nazis treated them, minus the killing. Truman asked Eisenhower to oversee the improvement of these conditions. Eisenhower responded by providing Jews better housing, increased rations, and preference in government-related employment over non-Holocaust survivors. Eisenhower also appointed an adviser on Jewish affairs with the rank of major general.

A Displaced Person

At the end of World War II in 1945, the western Allies attempted to repatriate the seven to eight million DPs, including Jews, to their home countries, mostly in Eastern Europe. One and a half to two million of these DPs refused to go back, for good reason. Postwar turmoil and antisemitism were quickly rising again as violent pogroms targeted the few remaining Jews.[1]

"Jewish life was restarting at the Munich DP camp," my father said. "A Talmudic elementary school was established, and matzo was distributed to all Jewish DPs. The DP camp opened in July 1946 and closed in June 1949. I did tailoring for Jewish people who wanted to move to Israel and needed clothes. This was the first time I had done tailoring work since the war started. It felt good to help others as they prepared to start their new lives.

It was strange living and working in Munich, the city where Hitler got his start in 1923 with the Beer Hall Putsch coup," he added. "The Nazis' first concentration camp at Dachau was ten miles northwest of Munich. The Nazis called Munich the *Hauptstadt der Bewegung*, which meant the 'capital of the movement.' It was heavily bombed by Allied bombing raids, and much of it was destroyed by the end of the war."

The Holocaust survivors who were now DPs referred to themselves as *she'erit hapletah* ["the surviving remnant"]. They saw the nightmarish and cursed soil of Germany as a place they wanted to leave as soon as they could. However, the survivors' physical and psychological health made it nearly impossible to move to another location. Further, Palestine and other possible destinations were closed to them.

Increasingly, Jewish refugees fled the growing antisemitism in Poland to Germany and other former Axis (Germany, Italy, and Austria) territories just one year after the Nazis were beaten. Most

DPs lived in the American occupation zone of Germany, which was considered by the survivors to be a steppingstone for emigration to Palestine or the United States. Between 1946 and 1947, DP camps near small German towns became hosts to Jewish cultural and religious life despite never previously having Jewish populations.

The DP camps, though well-intentioned and certainly offering light after the darkness of the Holocaust, were plagued by a lack of medicine, supplies, food, clothing, and professionally trained staff. Particularly difficult for the camp administrators were the psychological effects that persecution had taken on survivors. The medical and psychological communities assisting the survivors were not experienced in dealing with what we now recognize as a mass trauma event. Counseling was conducted but not on a scale that met the residents' needs.

Most DP camps were either former Nazi military barracks or emptied German apartment complexes. Following years of physical and psychological abuse and torture at the hands of the Nazis, it was very difficult for survivors to return to a "normal life." The mere fact of living in former Nazi sleeping and working facilities—recently occupied by monstrous Nazis who had destroyed lives, murdered loved ones, and subjected victims to unimaginable torture—had its own traumatic impact. Survivors were greatly limited in their ability to leave the camps, by the barbed wire and guards, even to search for surviving family members. These conditions existed, in part, to protect DP residents from their German neighbors, some of whom were Nazis and either wittingly or unwittingly participated in the Holocaust. However, to many DPs, this felt like continued incarceration.

Cleanliness (personal and facility hygiene) in DP camps was a major issue during the first months, as was the inability to return to former occupations inside or outside the camps. Occupational opportunities, such as tailoring, were either greatly limited or nonexistent. A line frequently found in Jewish DPs' statements was, "We were liberated, but we are not free."

Holocaust survivors in DP camps created religious and secular forms of culture and expression through Jewish languages—Yiddish and Hebrew—as opposed to using German, which had been the language of the prewar German Jewish culture and religion. They published close to 100 different Jewish newspapers in Europe in the immediate postwar years.

These Jewish DP camp newspapers and journals published lists of survivors and recollections of concentration camp experiences. Theater troupes, musical groups, sports clubs, and schools for the few surviving children and for adults eager to acquire language skills and prepare for new occupations were common in the larger DP camps.

About half of the Jewish DPs in Germany, Austria, and Italy—about 120,000 between 1947 and 1950—emigrated to Palestine/Israel. A smaller number, estimated at 80 to 90,000 emigrated to the United States. This number would have certainly been larger had the United States more widely opened its doors to emigration. About 20,000 Jewish DPs established homes in Canada, and approximately 5,000 went to Australia and South America, respectively. Many other countries welcomed smaller numbers of Jewish DPs.

Many Holocaust survivors who had lost their entire families created new ones at the DP camps. Weddings were a regular occurrence at the larger DP camps. Also, there was a very high birthrate amongst the Jewish survivors, which stood in contrast to the surrounding German population's low birthrate.

Between 1945 and 1952, more than 250,000 lived in DP camps, managed by the Allies and United Nations. Even though some were adjacent to former concentration camps or German army camps, steps were taken to try to achieve a display of normalcy. Just as in the ghetto and concentration camps, music played an important part in restoring this sense of normalcy.

My father found his cousin Rose (as well as others) on one of the rare occasions he was able to leave the camp. She was living in the village of Freimann, near the Neu Freimann DP camp, in a group home. Rose had lost her entire family, too, including her husband and baby.

"I stayed working in Germany for four or five years," my father said. "The DP camp was in some ways like a closed Jewish ghetto, with little contact with Germans or others outside. What little contact I had, I couldn't help but wonder if these Germans I saw, talked to, and interacted with were aware of or supported Hitler and his monsters. They seemed pleasant enough, but I couldn't help but feel they were partly to blame. I made it a rule to trust as few people as possible. Were they just silent, or did they participate in the horror as our Polish neighbors did? As DPs, we had housing, food, health care, work, and help with emigration."

The new state of Israel was created in May 1948. Just prior, there were still 165,000 Jewish DPs living in Germany. Just after Israel's establishment, the number of Jewish DPs in Germany was greatly reduced to some 30,000. Jewish organizations around the world, and official DP publications and statements, called for the remaining Jewish DPs to leave Germany. Most of them did, but a large number stayed behind, unable or unwilling to leave.

Even so, to my father, after suffering through the Holocaust and losing everything, a country created for the Jews sounded like a dream come true.

The last DP camp, in Fohrenwald, closed in February 1957, ending the chapter of displaced persons in postwar Europe.

Purgatory After the War

Life for the Jewish survivors of the Holocaust was anything but normal. Entire Jewish communities had been wiped out of existence. When survivors attempted to return to their homes, they found them destroyed or taken over by others. Generally, Jewish survivors were not welcome in Europe as preexisting antisemitic feelings intensified. It was a dangerous time. Many survivors elected to remain in DP camps due to the dangers outside them, awaiting admission to the United States or another destination. In the postwar years, the United States slowly increased the number of Jewish refugees who could enter the country. This was in part due to the realization of how horrible the Holocaust had been and the continuing danger to Jews in Europe.

Poland after World War II

More than half (3.3 million) of the 6 million Jews murdered during the Holocaust lived in Poland before World War II began. They comprised more than 10 percent of Poland's then population of 24 million, making Poland the European country with the highest percentage of Jews. By the end of the war, approximately 380,000 Polish Jews were still alive. My father's family—mother, father, two sisters, brother, aunts, uncles, almost all cousins and other relatives—were murdered.

Though Lublin—where my father was born—was spared much of the physical destruction Warsaw suffered, the Jewish population in Lublin was decimated. Only about 230 Lublin Jews survived the Holocaust.

Warsaw's population was 1.3 million before the war and its Jewish population was close to 350,000, about one-third of New York City's Jewish population (in 1938, New York City's Jewish population was approximately 1.7 million). Upon liberation in January 1945 by the Russians, it is estimated only 174,000 people remained in Warsaw, and of that number, 11,500 were Jews who had survived the Holocaust.

When the Nazis set their sights on Poland, they sought to destroy everything and rebuild it as an additional homeland for the Germans. In the process, the Nazis situated many of their major killing centers there, organizing a railway that took Jews and other prisoners from their homelands to be murdered in occupied Poland. Before liberation in 1945, nearly five million Polish people had been killed, including more than three million Jews and 1.9 million non-Jewish Polish citizens. The Poland that emerged from the war, as evidenced by postwar attacks on Jewish survivors, lacked the general tolerance that had been essential to Polish culture before World War II. While some Poles were sympathetic to the Jews' and other victims' plight, others seemed unmoved and even hardened by all that occurred.[2]

Polish antisemitism was on the rise after the end of World War II. There were reports that some Poles spread age-old "blood ritual" rumors of Jews killing children and using their blood in religious rituals. Other Poles inexplicably blamed the Jews for the Nazi attack. Whatever the reasons, Poland was not a safe place for Jews.

Emigration to the United States and a Tenth Miracle[3]

After staying in Germany for more than four years after the war, I finally received my emigration papers to the United States! I departed Bremen, Germany, on May 27, 1949.

I came to the U.S. by myself (Rose went to Canada at about the same time) by way of Ellis Island in New York City. I didn't know a word of English and didn't know anyone in the U.S. It was overwhelming. I traveled on the transport ship USS General LeRoy Eltinge (AP-154), which was contracted out and being used in 1949 to transport emigrants from DP camps. Onboard, the Americans made me clean the engine room—it was horribly hot! My blood pressure went too high, and I was bleeding from my eyes, nose, ears, and throat. It was almost like being a slave laborer again. I was taken for medical care onboard the ship and later told that I almost died. To die in this way after all I had been through would have been unthinkable. Miraculously I survived—a tenth miracle! When I later arrived in Erie, Pennsylvania, the people who sponsored my passage told me that they had paid for the entirety of my passage, and I was not supposed to have had to work.

Outside of New York Harbor, I looked at the Statue of Liberty and felt both fortunate to have escaped from Hell and horrible that my family wasn't with me.

Before entering New York Harbor and Ellis Island, our ship had to stop at a quarantine checkpoint, where doctors checked for smallpox, yellow fever, plague, cholera, and leprosy. First- and second-class passengers [there were very few] were interviewed and disembarked once the ship docked. The rest of us had to go through a more in-depth search and security process.

U.S. customs officers checked bags for taxable goods and contraband. I had very few personal items with me. We were then ferried from the USS Eltinge, which was anchored in the New York Harbor, onboard a steamboat and brought to Ellis Island. Women and children were ordered into one line, and men into another. I waited in long lines for medical and legal inspections to determine if I was fit for entry into the U.S. Using chalk, doctors marked some passengers' clothes with an 'H' for suspected heart trouble, 'L' for suspected lameness, and 'X' for suspected feeble-mindedness. Those marked were placed into the 'doctor's pen,' awaiting further inspection. Others were detained if they were suspected of being communists or fascists.

The security process was confusing, especially as I didn't speak or read English. They wanted to know my name, age, occupation, destination, and other information. For me, this process took a day, but I'd heard stories of it taking days, weeks, even months for some people trying to enter. The inspector made a little checkmark by my name, and I was finally free to pass.

I followed the instructions given to me by my sponsors in Erie and set off on the New York City streets to find the train station. Warsaw and Munich were both big cities, but they did not compare to New York. I had never seen skyscrapers, nor so many people and cars. It was an eye-opening experience, and the feeling of freedom I felt at that moment was exhilarating.

In the old country, we had been told that America was the golden land of opportunity where the streets were paved with gold. I didn't see any gold, but I could sense the opportunities. I had heard Erie was a large and active center of Jewish activity and had been since the 1800s. I was eager to see it for myself. Although I tried my best to look ahead, my mind whirled with memories and nightmares of what my family and I had been through."

My Father, after WWII

After all they had endured, Holocaust survivors were filled with hope for the future as they immigrated to the United States and other welcoming countries. They demonstrated remarkable determination and resilience as they traveled to new homes and started new lives. Numerous Jewish organizations sponsored the new immigrants and helped them find employment and housing. Studies in the early 1950s and after found most survivors successfully adjusted to their new lives and to building new families. This was truly a testament to the strength of the human spirit.

AL AND PEARL TOGETHER—HOPE REALIZED

A Chance Meeting

"In early winter 1949, I was walking to Celia's house in Pittsfield when I saw a fellow I knew. He was talking with a young blond man, his friend who was visiting from out of state, about having a New Year's Eve party. The friend, whose name I learned was Al Kitmacher, asked if I would go to the party with him if they went. I told him to let me know if they ended up going, and I'd be happy to join him. Al was visiting from Erie, Pennsylvania, and had been in the U.S. for about six months since immigrating in June 1949. He seemed sweet and thoughtful, speaking in broken English he was clearly trying to master.

Meanwhile, my cousin Annette Harris of Staten Island, a borough of New York with a sizable Jewish population, invited me to visit her for New Year's. She said we would have a nice time—she would set up dates and make plans for us. I hadn't heard from Al, so I accepted Annette's invitation.

The day I was leaving for the train station, there was a knock on my door. There was Al, ready to take me to the party. I apologized and explained that since I hadn't heard from him about going to the party, I accepted an invitation from my cousin and had plans set to go to

New York. Al seemed sad and though I felt bad, I had a feeling this wouldn't be the last time I saw him.

I went to Staten Island for New Year's and had fun with my cousin. Soon after, Al started writing and telephoning me quite often and visited Pittsfield quite a bit, too. I was busy settling back into my civilian life and, at first, I didn't make a lot of time for him. But he was persistent, sweet, and thoughtful. After a while, I became interested.

Al was a new immigrant from Germany and Poland, and I learned that he was the only one of his immediate family in Poland to have survived the Holocaust. He expected to move from Europe to Israel, but at the last minute, he came to the U.S. instead. My dad and his brothers, sister, and father had come to the U.S. from Poland in about 1916. The new Polish Jewish immigrant's story was familiar to me. To me, just like my father and his family, Al was a hero. To come to this country without knowing the language or anyone here; I don't think I could have done it. It struck me that Al was the exact kind of person I had joined the WAVES to help—a European Jew who was suffering at the hands of the evil Nazis. I made time in my life, and Al and I got to know and enjoy each other's company. The rest of my life was unfolding before my very eyes!

Al and I met by chance that winter day in 1949. Al later told me he was immediately attracted to me, though I had been a little more hesitant. We overcame any distance and initial obstacles, fell in love, raised a family, and spent our lives together. We had both been through so much—Al losing his family in the Holocaust, and my serving in the U.S. Navy. Despite it all, and maybe in part because of these experiences, we met and built a happy life together. This was another miracle in itself!"

My parents, 1950s

My mother and father's wedding photo, 1951

Marriage and Raising a Family

My mother: "After dating for about one and a half years, Al asked me to marry him. We were married on August 26, 1951, by Pittsfield Rabbi Morris Fuhrman at the nearby Festival House restaurant in Lenox.

Al felt working in New York City promised a better future than Erie, so he got an apartment in Williamsburg, just outside the Bronx. He fixed it up, and I didn't see it until we went there for our honeymoon. Al worked in New York City at 50 Eldridge Street for Witty Brothers men's fine clothing store, founded in 1888.

After a few months, I got a job with Hotpoint, a small company that was part of GE. The day I started working there, I realized I was pregnant! Al felt it would be better for us to live near my family, so we moved to Pittsfield. He thought my mom would be there to help me, but she let me know she had raised her children herself, and that I could do the same!"

My father: I learned to speak and write English and went to work for Stanley Clarke at the Besse-Clarke clothing store in downtown Pittsfield. Mr. Clarke and I liked each other, and we got along well. I sold clothing, served as the master tailor, and often traveled to New York City as the buyer for Besse-Clark. Every time I went to New York City, I was overwhelmed with the memories of when I first arrived in the U.S. by way of Ellis Island.

I enjoyed my work and was well-liked. I became well known in Pittsfield for the men's clothing I created and repaired. I built up quite a following of customers and clients who wanted only me to help them with their clothing.

In the 1960s, I took a chance and opened my own store in the Miller Building on North Street in Pittsfield and called it 'Albert's Custom Tailor Shop.' I had many clients who brought their work to me instead of going to Besse-Clarke and other competitors. Pearl helped me in the office, and we made a very good team.

Shortly after I opened my business, the owner of the building announced plans for a major renovation, and all businesses had to vacate. Mr. Clarke begged me to come back to Besse-Clarke to work for him again. At the same time, a friend put me in touch with the owner of a clothing store in Beverly Hills, California, and I was offered a tailoring job there! To think: tailor to the stars! Pearl and I talked about moving to California, but it seemed like too much of a change as we were raising a new family. We chose to stay in Pittsfield, which we knew was a wonderful place for our growing family.

Just as my parents had in Europe, Pearl and I had four children, two girls and two boys, whom we named for our parents. Miriam was our first child [the same name as my mother], Gary was next [for my father, Gershon], Lois was third [for Pearl's father, Louis], and then our youngest Ira [for my brother, Yitzhak]. They were great kids! Although one or two of our children were interested in learning to sew, I said no—no more tailors or seamstresses in the family. This was America, and we wanted our kids to go to college and become professionals.

I named our family dog, a German shorthaired pointer, 'Fritz,' after the Flossenbürg kapo who threatened to murder me if I didn't give him my breakfast for a week. I thought it was a just reward for Fritz to be relegated to a dog. He was a very good dog.

Of course, there are some things I wish I had done differently in raising our kids. In the old world from which I came in Europe, boys were often treated as more important than girls. I followed this logic in America."[1]

One United States Holocaust Memorial Museum exhibit is called "Life After—Stories of Holocaust Survivors After the War." It recounts the daunting story of 80,000 Holocaust survivors immigrating to the United States between 1945 and 1952. They lacked financial resources, had few (if any) surviving family members, and made their way to new worlds. Many were able to build new, successful lives and families.

My mother: "I kept busy helping Al with his business, driving the kids around and keeping our home operating and upbeat. I was a positive person by nature, while Al, because of his Holocaust experience, tended to be more negative. We balanced each other out. Al and I often visited my sister, her daughter Susan, and other family who lived close by."

A Move Out West

"After closing his business and returning to Besse-Clarke, Al no longer needed my help with work. The children had grown up, were in school, and no longer needed my full-time attention. In the 1970s, I went to work as a telephone operator for New England Telephone in Pittsfield; they were later taken over by AT&T. It was fun and I made lots of friends, like in the Navy. It gave me something besides family to focus on. At the time, Miriam was also an operator, so we had a chance to work together! Al retired from Besse-Clarke in 1987 and was anxious for me to retire, too. I retired from AT&T that same year.

Al and I had always been very close with Ira, who was working as a manager with the U.S. government in the San Francisco Bay Area. Al and I had always loved California, and we decided to move out West! Later, Miriam also moved to the Bay Area. Al and I first owned a house in Walnut Creek, a very nice town. We then moved to a retirement community there called Rossmoor. We owned a townhouse overlooking the golf course. It was beautiful there, and we enjoyed it very much. I loved going out for long walks around Rossmoor and down to the local five-and-dime store, like the ones I worked in when I was much younger, where they sold very good ice cream.

Ira, his wife, Wendy, and their two beautiful children, David, and Gabi, lived just a few miles away. It was ideal. Al and I enjoyed going with Ira as he traveled for work throughout California, Oregon, and Washington. We joined him whenever we could, including on a trip to Victoria and Vancouver in Canada!

I hadn't learned how to cook while growing up, but after Al and I married, I learned and became very good. I especially liked to cook some of Al's favorite foods from Europe, like kugel, kreplach, chopped chicken liver, cabbage rolls, matzo ball soup, and brisket. On special occasions, I made Al's favorite: cheesecake.[2]

Eleventh Miracle

"My escape from Europe, emigration to America, and meeting Pearl were the best things that ever happened to me. Against all odds, Pearl and I met, fell in love, and built an incredible family together. These together were my eleventh miracle! I asked Ira to look after Pearl when I was gone—she had always done everything for me. I knew he would."[3]

My father experienced 11 miracles during and just after the Holocaust. Odd numbers (like 11 and 13—which some cultures' folklore treats as unlucky) are considered lucky in Judaism, while even numbers are considered bad luck. Also, it is said, "The world was created with ten utterances" (reflecting the Ten Commandments), with 11 referring to the divine—a level above this limited earthly existence. Therefore, 11 is said to represent *Daat Elohim,* the heavenly knowledge needed to extract the hidden light of creation, revealing it to mankind, and causing the great healing referred to as the "final redemption." The final redemption refers to God's liberation of the Jews from exile ahead of the restoration of Israel. The first use in the Bible of the word "redeem" was in Genesis 48:16: "The Angel which redeemed me from all evil." No doubt the 11 miracles my father experienced redeemed and liberated him from the evils of the Holocaust.

In 1988, the West German government began paying reparations to remaining Holocaust survivors of $290 per month for the rest of their lives. In 1990, East Germany admitted, for the first time, its responsibility for the Holocaust. In 1999, a year before my father's death, the German government agreed to compensate Jews and non-Jews for slave and forced labor during the war. These payments continued until 2006.

"The feeling of great loss stayed with me throughout my life, and nothing could replace the family I had lost. I tried many times, through the Red Cross and other organizations, to find my immediate European family, but nothing was ever found. I never lost my grief, but I eventually realized that my grief was more than just grief itself. It was my continuing love for the family I lost. The German government paid me modest 'reparations' for what they put me through in the war, but no amount of money could make up for what was taken from me.

No doubt the hell I experienced in Europe, the monsters, and the torture, made it difficult for me to trust others and I often felt down. I tried my best to shield Pearl and the kids from the stress and horrors I went through, and I rarely talked about it. But sometimes, it seeped through. I did my best. Our family had its ups and downs, as any family does. I always worked hard, holding two or three jobs at a time, and made sure we had all the comforts we could want and that the kids received a good education. All our children finished college. Ira became an attorney, an executive, and had children; Miriam and Lois had successful lives and careers; and Gary had a successful career and children. Like with my family in Europe, we went to synagogue on the high holidays, but not every Sabbath.

I liked to entertain at our house in Pittsfield, and I know I made a positive impact on our community. I became a member of the Freemasons in Pittsfield. Joining gave me a feeling of belonging, and I made lots of friends. The Masons are involved, along with the Shriners, in many humanitarian causes. Membership is open to men of all faiths, and I met several Masons who were also Jewish. The Masons were also one of the groups persecuted by the Nazis.

Pearl and I went to Klezmer concerts, the music I had enjoyed before the war. One of our favorite musicals was 'Fiddler on the Roof,' which told of Eastern European shtetl life and traditions before the Holocaust. I told Ira, who went to see the show with us, that it reminded me of my early years.

We visited my cousin Rose Billerman, who I had found in Munich, her husband Chaim, and their children Jack, Hersh, Nina, and Irwin many times in Montreal. At about the same time I left the Munich DP camp for America, Rose left Munich for Montreal.

We also visited my uncle Moishe Naiman [my mother's youngest brother, who I met in Chelm, Poland], his wife Pearl [also a Holocaust survivor], and their children Tommy and Eli, in Toronto. It was Moishe who took my sister Frieda and me in after we escaped from the Warsaw Ghetto. Pearl and I visited Israel several times and saw friends I made during the war as well as distant relatives. One friend we visited in Tel Aviv was the man who had helped me get out of my bunk in Budzyn after my nightmare about fighting the black bird.

I joined the B'nai B'rith in Walnut Creek in 1994, a Jewish service organization that works to help the community. We traveled quite a bit, including to Hawaii. I loved to take the family on day and longer trips, including Celia and David's kids, Leonard, and Susan. We visited my friends from Erie, the Operchinskys. We went to the Catskill Game Farm, Ghost Town, and Story Town in upstate New York, the Bronx Zoo, Disney World in Florida, and other fun places. I also took great pleasure in taking our family for a quick bite to eat, to a McDonald's or Dairy Queen. It struck me as miraculous, after all those years starving and searching for food, that food was now available immediately, whenever we wanted. What a world!

I always enjoyed the freedom of going places, which was very different from my life in Europe. During the war, when I lied and told the Nazis that I was a sheet and metal worker, it was in part so I could keep busy and stay sane. Now I liked to keep busy, go places, and see things to keep my mind from focusing too long on the horrors of the past. Despite my best efforts, my mind would sometimes go to that dark place, where I was reminded of the monstrous Nazis, the horrors I endured, and the family that was stolen from me.

After retiring in 1987, Pearl and I soon moved to Walnut Creek. We had always loved the idea of living in California and were eager to be near Ira. Retiring helped me lower my stress level. I loved living in California. It was beautiful there. Pearl and I had a very special relationship with Ira. Just as my little brother Yitzhak was the youngest and the tatela shind, Ira, named for him, was our youngest child, and I called him tatela shind. When Ira was a baby, I would sing to him a comforting lullaby my mother sang to me: 'Ah, ah, baby.' Ira was born on my 41st birthday, something which made us even closer. I was so happy when Ira and Wendy had their children David and Gabi. They and my other grandchildren [Gary's children Amy, Sarah, Debbie, and Abbie] gave me hope for the future. I adore all of them."

STEPPING BACK IN TIME—A RETURN TO GERMANY AND END OF LIFE

Back to Germany

My mother: "I frequently entered national write-in contests, hoping to win advertised prizes. I was quite successful in these contests! From one such contest, I won a trip to Europe: 'A Glimpse of Europe' with Trafalgar Tours. I was worried about Al returning to Europe and asked him if he was sure he was OK going back. The tour included stops in Germany, and this would be Al's first time back since the Holocaust. I knew he loved to travel, but I didn't want to do this if it would be too hard for him. He was very brave and said yes, he wanted to go back and see what the countries and people were like now. We made our travel arrangements, planning to spend the first week in the English countryside, the second week in London, and the third week touring several countries, including Germany."

My father: "In October 1992, Pearl, Ira, and I went to Europe and Germany. It was the first time I'd been back in 43 years. It was a wonderful trip but also strange, and it brought back some horrible memories. The Germans we met were very nice, and the country had been rebuilt since the horrors of the war. We took a cruise on the Rhine River, visited the castle in Heidelberg, visited Munich, and stopped in the Black Forest. These sites were so beautiful, and it was such an odd feeling to be a welcomed American tourist as opposed to a hated Jewish slave laborer.

The Black Forest was particularly fascinating. I knew it was named because of the heavy forest canopy which makes the ground practically black, and because of *Waldeinsamkeit*, or forest-loneliness. My father used to tell me haunted stories and folklore of the forest. Werewolves and witches were said to reside in its shadows, as was *der Grossmann*, a tall, horribly disfigured creature with bulging eyes and many arms that was said to be able to hear children's confessions of sin—those with the worst confessions were never seen again. Some of the Brothers Grimm dark stories were also based in the forest.

Europe is truly such an old, and at times dark, world. No wonder they call America 'the new world.' I was struck by just how much had changed since the Holocaust; how Europeans who had once been so consumed with antisemitic folklore, stories, and rhetoric could cast aside such old-world notions and be so welcoming now. I mentioned to Ira that the Black Forest reminded me of the Bavarian Forest near the Flossenbürg concentration camp.

I couldn't help but feel that all the anger, hatred, and antisemitism I'd experienced as a young man lay just below the surface. I didn't want to blame this new generation of Germans for the sins of their parents, but I also couldn't completely forgive. The horrors of the Holocaust, the murder of my family, and the miracles I experienced—I wondered if any of the monsters still lurked in the shadows."[1]

Following World War II, Germany accomplished an amazing metamorphosis with the help of the United States and other countries. That metamorphosis shaped generations of enlightened, liberal, and self-critical citizens. However, as former German Foreign Minister Heiko Maas said, in recent years "[The] culture of remembrance is crumbling." The hard-right Alternative for Germany party is very popular. It rode a shocking rise of German antisemitism and xenophobia in 2017. People wearing Jewish head coverings have been harassed on the streets. In surveys, many Germans have expressed a desire for an authoritarian ruler and a distrust of liberal democracy. Such sentiments serve as a reminder that those who fail to learn from history are bound to repeat it.

Nazis were portrayed in 1980s and 1990s movies and stories as the ultimate harbingers of evil and destruction. A prime example is the 1981 movie *American Werewolf in London*, in which Nazi werewolves appear in Jewish protagonist David Kessler's nightmares. These mutant werewolves light David's menorah-adorned house on fire and murder his family and friends. This moment in the film is jolting and serves as a reminder that even 36 years after the end of World War II, the Nazis wanted to destroy Jews. The character David, a young Jewish man, was unable to help his family before he, too, was killed by Nazis. This was meant to reflect Jews' feeling of helplessness in the face of overwhelming evil, as was the case in the Holocaust.

"The Germans we encountered at restaurants and other places were very nice and many commented that they 'like Americans.' How ironic, I remember thinking. The last time I was there, I was starved and felt fortunate to be given a turnip. It was, of course, completely different now, at least outwardly, compared to during the war. The Nazis were pure evil. They took everything from me. But I always said that in some ways, the Poles were just as bad or worse than the Germans, as they were our family's neighbors and they turned on us. I could handle visiting Germany as a tourist, but I would never want to go back to Poland.

We did not go to any of the concentration or labor camps, as it would have been too much for me. As we made our way across Germany, I saw areas that I had been force-marched through as a prisoner. I could still feel the horror, smell the death, and hear guns, screaming, and war. I wondered how many of the young Germans we encountered knew the extent of these horrors. How could their parents and grandparents have been such monsters? If history were to repeat itself, would they turn into the pursuing villagers, like our Polish neighbors who pointed out Jews and other victims to the Nazis? Would they play an even darker role in this horror?

I could excuse this newer generation of Germans but could never forget or forgive what the generations before had done.

My parents and me on the Rhine River, Germany, 1992

My father on a tour bus, Black Forest, Germany, 1992

Sometime after we returned to the US, Pearl, Ira, Wendy, and I went to see the Holocaust movie *Schindler's List* in San Francisco. The movie was difficult to watch, given its realism. To make matters worse, because of the movie's popularity, we couldn't get seats together. Ira asked me before we went into the theater if we should come back another time when there was more seating, but I said no, I wanted to see the movie. Ira and Wendy sat on the floor at the back of the theater, while Pearl sat in a seat by herself. I was uncomfortable sitting by myself as the horrific images washed over me. Despite its dark story, I knew it was also a movie of hope, as the real-life Oskar Schindler saved the lives of over 1,000 Polish Jews. He was one of many people in Europe who had heroically risked their lives to save Jews. I was glad when the movie ended and I could exit the theater, into the fresh air and the company of my family."[2]

Following the success of 1993's *Schindler's List*, Director Steven Spielberg founded the Survivors of the Shoah Visual History foundation which filmed survivors' testimony. My father participated in an affiliated effort in 1994 and the recording of his interview is housed in the United States Holocaust Memorial Museum.

Several years before his passing, at his request, my father, mother, and I visited the museum.

"Visiting the Holocaust Museum was a very emotional experience for me," my father said. "Much like the trip to Europe two years before, the museum brought back horrific memories. Nevertheless, I felt it was very important for me to visit. I appreciate that this permanent reminder of the horrors I experienced was created; maybe that will help future generations avoid similar actions and fates. I'm afraid that if such reminders aren't etched in stone, future generations will be unable or unwilling to believe that people—not all that long ago—could have done such unspeakable things to their fellow human."

My Father's Death

My father's health declined through the late 1990s. He often said that his life had been great since arriving in the United States. He loved his family and, as he told me, owed everything to my mother. His life in Europe was, for the most part, a nightmare. He hoped that no one else would ever have to experience such a nightmare. My father was physically and psychologically damaged by the Holocaust. He fully trusted very few people after the war. His ability to demonstrate love to his children, especially to my sisters, was stunted. He would have been a very different person but for what he went through. In my eyes, my father was an incredible man who survived and persevered despite enduring unimaginable horrors. My father hoped to be reunited in heaven with the family he lost in Europe.

My father passed away peacefully in 2000 at the age of 79, just a few days before his and my shared birthday. My mother said he had an expression on his face that she could only describe as "peaceful." He had a slight smile, and my mother believed he had reunited with his beloved family from Poland. She always wished we had taken a picture of his expression.

My father's obituary was printed in the *Berkshire Eagle* and is included below.

> Albert Leon Kitmacher
>
> Berkshire Eagle, Wednesday, February 23, 2000
>
> PITTSFIELD – Albert Leon Kitmacher, 79, of Walnut Creek, Calif., formerly of Pittsfield, died Monday at home. Born in Lublin, Poland, on Feb. 23, 1920, he was a Holocaust concentration camp survivor who lost all of his family in the concentration camps.
>
> He resided in Erie, Pa., and New York for a short time before moving to Pittsfield in the 1950s. He was employed as a tailor at Besse-Clarke on North Street in Pittsfield until his retirement in the late 1980s. He also owned Albert's Custom Tailoring.
>
> He leaves his wife, Pearl Harris; two sons, Ira Kitmacher of Danville, Calif., and Gary Kitmacher of Webster, Texas; two daughters, Miriam Kitmacher of Danville and Lois Karhinen of Niagara Falls, N.Y., and six grandchildren.

My Mother's Death

My mother relayed her story through writings, conversations, and interviews with the Women's War Memorial, located adjacent to Arlington National Cemetery in Virginia.

Wendy and I thought it best for my mother and father to move in with us, and we began building a cottage for them to live in on our property in Danville. My father passed away just before they could move in, and my mother moved in alone. My mother helped watch over David and Gabi.

Always wanting to keep busy, my mother went to work for Costco as a "sample person" in the late 2000s. She had always expressed love through food and figured what better way to help people than to hand out food samples! She said it was fun.

My mother also sang with a local senior group's choir. She loved to play word games and bingo and seemed to frequently win at write-in contests. In addition to winning the trip to Europe in the 1990s, she was the national "7-Up" winner one year (while my father was still alive) and rewarded with tickets to the Super Bowl in Tampa, Florida!

At her request, several years before my mother's passing, we visited the newly opened World War II Memorial in Washington as well as some of the U.S. Navy sites where she worked.

"I was always filled with pride for serving in the WAVES during World War II," my mother said. "I contributed to stopping the evil spreading across the world and I helped save our fellow Jews in Europe. I even married one of the survivors of that horror. I often looked back fondly on the many friendships I made. I looked for my old friend Betty June but discovered she had died some years before. I never thought I would live such a long life; I think I did because I always kept a positive and cheerful attitude! I had a wonderful life and family and wouldn't exchange it for anything!"

My mother lived to be almost 94. She felt strongly that she did not want her or my father's bodies to be buried, though that is the traditional form of Jewish burial. Per their wishes, both my father's and mother's bodies were cremated (a controversial choice for Jews, particularly for those who survived the Holocaust), and I have their ashes.

My mother's obituary was printed in the *Glens Falls* (N.Y.) *Post Star* and is included below.

Pearl Harris Kitmacher
October 29, 1922–June 22, 2016
GLENS FALLS—Pearl Harris Kitmacher, beloved Mother,

dedicated wife and retired Navy Veteran, formerly of Pittsfield, Massachusetts, California and Virginia—passed away peacefully June 22, 2016, of natural causes at The Pines of Glens Falls, NY with her loving family by her side.

Born in Schenectady, NY on October 29, 1922, she was the second daughter of Louis and Rose Harris and grew up on Bradford Street in Pittsfield. She was granddaughter of Sam and Celia Shapiro who settled in Glens Falls, NY, at the turn of the century.

Pearl was a 1941 graduate of Pittsfield High School, where she participated in musicals such as the *Mikado* and the *Pirates of Penzance* and was on the staff of the *Student Pen*. She enjoyed English and was an avid reader and wrote cute poems for most of her life. She was an enthusiastic and active walker until just a few years ago.

Pearl worked at the local 5 and Dime stores and then worked at GE until she joined the United States Navy as a WAVE in 1944. She also completed her education at Iowa State Teacher's College. After her children were older, she took a job with Bell Telephone as a Telephone Operator in Pittsfield and retired from AT&T in the late 1980s.

In 1950 Pearl married Albert L. Kitmacher, a Holocaust Survivor who retired from Besse-Clarke and had his own business, Albert's Custom Tailoring in Pittsfield. She devoted herself to him until his passing in 2000.

In addition to her husband Albert, Pearl was predeceased by her sister Celia Cohen.

She is survived by her four children, Miriam Kitmacher of Queensbury, NY, Gary Kitmacher (Susan) of Webster, TX, Lois Kitmacher Karhinen (John) of Queensbury, NY, and Ira Kitmacher (Wendy) of Fairfax, VA; grandchildren Amy, Sarah, Debbie and Abby (Gary) and David and Gabi (Ira); as well as 4 great-grandchildren and her beloved cat "DD." She also leaves her nephew Leonard Cohen and niece Susan Cohen Wilansky.

She will be cremated and there will be no funeral or calling hours.

Pearl loved animals and donations may be made in her memory to Berkshire Humane Society, 214 Barker Rd, Pittsfield, MA 01201.

We'd like to thank the caregivers on the 2nd floor of the Pine's, especially Jose, for their compassion and kindness.

To paraphrase Proverbs 10:7: May the memory of my father and my mother, and all victims of the Holocaust, antisemitism, and other hatred—righteous people, be a blessing.

WHY IT HAPPENED: GRIM REALITY, BLACK HOLES, AND HOPE SURVIVES

Black Holes

As with all horrible events, we try to make sense of the Holocaust. How and why could this have happened? How should we remember it and honor the millions of innocent victims?

Various perspectives have been offered in the years since World War II. One such postwar example involves views on what should become of Auschwitz.

Auschwitz was the largest and deadliest of the concentration camps. Of the estimated 1.3 million imprisoned at Auschwitz, approximately 1.1 million were Jewish—960,000 of whom did not live to see the camp's liberation. For most Jews, Auschwitz remains a place of great horror, an aberration in world history, and an ethical and moral black hole from which little seemed to escape. Auschwitz has such a dark and horrific history that many believe all it should be is a place for silent prayer.[1,2]

However, in the 1980s, the Jewish community near Auschwitz faced pressure to place religious symbols at the camp to reclaim it in some way. The local Jewish population did not act on this pressure, believing the camp was beyond redemption, symbolic or otherwise.

But in 1984, Polish Cardinal Franciszek Macharski, the Archbishop of Krakow, allowed a Carmelite (Roman Catholic) nunnery to move into Auschwitz and stay in the building where poison gas was once kept. Local Catholics filled what they saw as a spiritual void with their own religious symbols. Under pressure, the nunnery eventually moved out.

It can be said that every concentration and forced labor camp, and each location that hosted Nazis' terror, is a black hole of cosmic nothingness. Though this phrase sounds like a concept out of the paranormal television series *The Twilight Zone*, it's nevertheless a phrase that comes close to encompassing the sheer nonsensical insanity that was the Holocaust. The 1983 *Twilight Zone* movie includes a segment highlighting this point. In it, a white man is passed over for a promotion given to his Jewish coworker. The white man hurls slurs toward Jews, Blacks, and Asians, then inexplicably finds himself in Nazi-occupied France during World War II. He is interrogated and shot to death by SS officers.[3]

It isn't clear what the correct approach is for addressing a place such as Auschwitz, and to this day, there isn't agreement on why and how the Holocaust occurred.

Free Will and the Holocaust

A central tenet of Jewish belief is that nothing happens in a vacuum. History, oppression, suffering, and the Holocaust must therefore hold some meaning. With every Holocaust victim, an entire world was lost. A new lesson must be learned, although the meaning of the Holocaust is as varied as the victims. The Holocaust is the story of absolute hatred and war intended to destroy Jewish and "subhuman" people.

For many Jews, the Holocaust is a reminder of the importance of demonstrating the gift of life through justice and mercy. The Biblical text makes it clear that God gave humans free will to choose good, bad, or something in between. Just as people have free will to choose love, they can also choose indifference and hatred. God deliberately does not interfere in such decisions out of respect for free will. Humans must therefore make good choices and rise above baser instincts.[45]

Many Holocaust survivors, including my father, maintained their faith and hope despite all they lost and the evil they endured at the hands of the Nazis. As survivor Elie Wiesel once said, "After the Holocaust I did not lose faith in God ... I lost faith in mankind." For some Jews, the Holocaust contributed to a loss of faith; they became agnostics or atheists, doubting the existence of God. Though it is certainly understandable how the horrors of the Holocaust could have this effect, I can't help but believe that the Holocaust calls for a stronger belief and faith.

Historical Factors Giving Rise to the Holocaust

World War I ushered in instability and extremist movements, including communism, fascism, and National Socialism. Monarchies, including Russia's, collapsed. Germany felt humiliated by the harsh economic, military, and territorial terms outlined in the Treaty of Versailles that ended the war, which held the Germans solely responsible for initiating it. In truth, several disparate elements led to the war

It was France and Great Britain that dictated the treaty's terms as they sought vengeance for the war and to minimize the chance Germany would again launch conflict. The peace terms forced Germany to surrender about 10% of its territory, all its overseas possessions, and called for its demilitarization. It included crushing economic reparations for Germany (more than 132 billion gold Reichsmarks, equivalent to $33 billion today). The Germans who negotiated the agreement were later labeled the "November Criminals." The humiliating treaty and the Depression contributed to the rise of Hitler and World War II.

The Germans blamed Jews in part for their loss in World War I. Germans labeled Jews and communists as "internal traitors" who had stabbed Germany in the back even though Jews had loyally served in large numbers in the military. Some Germans believed that, as in *The Elders of Zion*, Jews sought worldwide domination (in part through Germany's loss). They also were seen as enriching themselves at Germany's expense and as orchestrating the treaty's terms.

The blame soon fell as well on the Weimar Republic, which replaced the German monarchy, for failing to push back on the terms of the treaty. Street violence erupted, coup attempts occurred, the economic crisis took hold, and political instability ensued. The people of Germany were scared, hungry, and unemployed. They were vulnerable to the authoritarian promises of strong leadership put forth by Hitler and the Nazis, so much so that they accepted the suspension of Germany's constitution, which had protected equal rights for all, including Jews.

Folklore also played a role in the atmosphere that allowed the Holocaust to occur. It had long held an important role in German culture. German children were told such tales from an early age, including ones that were unapologetically racist and antisemitic. Such antisemitism simmered just under the surface of German society.

Though in retrospect we may scoff at the image of Hitler—small in stature with a mustache mocked by comedian Charlie Chaplin in *The Great Dictator*—people accepted his dictatorship and bought into the idea of the superiority of the German people—the "master race"—and the inferiority and danger of the "subhumans." They agreed with the murder of mentally and physically disabled people, whom they viewed as a drain on resources and not worthy of life, and the Jews themselves. The Nazis employed propaganda, technology, Hitler Youth training, military, police, and other means to achieve their ends.

Hitler blamed Jews, whom he said ruled the entertainment and banking industries, for a wide range of issues. He said Jews intended to destroy national states, like Germany, by flooding them with immigrants, empowering minorities, and forming an international government ruled by Jews.

There is little doubt that being raised in a militaristic culture and on a historically steady diet of antisemitism, brutal folklore, supernatural beliefs, and conspiracy theories encouraged extreme views. The impact of losing World War I certainly exacerbated matters. The Nazis knew how to leverage these deprivations into action. Nightmares were born from the Nazis' lack of morality, introspection, critical thought, and judgment. The Nazis' utilitarian advantages, evidenced by the technology they used, reflected their perverse moral standards.

Initially, the Nazis wanted Jews and other "undesirables" to leave Germany. Some Jews looked for safe havens outside of Germany but found that other countries, including the United States, did not welcome them. Other Jews who identified as German couldn't bring themselves to believe what was happening. The Nazis then turned to genocide. Hitler persuaded the country that genocide was necessary to ensure the survival of the motherland. At the beginning of World War II, fewer than 300,000 Jews were living in Germany. The six million Jews murdered by the Nazis lived primarily in territories the Germans conquered, such as in Poland.

Though the circumstances that gave rise to the Holocaust have been examined for more than 80 years, there is still not one easy answer for why it occurred. From my point of view, there are a few primary circumstances that led to the Holocaust: scapegoating, eugenics, and historical conspiracy-laden antisemitism.

Scapegoating is an all-too-common human trait. When things go awry, humans tend to want to blame others. For centuries, Jews have been blamed for a wide range of issues such as the killing of Jesus, plagues, bad harvests, and economic downturns. Jews were treated as the "stranger" and minority in their community and have frequently been targeted for blame. The persecution of Jews goes back thousands of years. It is important to note, however, that about one and a half million Jews enlisted and volunteered in the Allied armies during World War II. Some Jews did resist and fight—in the Warsaw

Ghetto uprising and alongside resistance groups in France, Russia, and Yugoslavia.

Eugenics provided Hitler with a defense for mass murder. German writer Hans Gunther was an outspoken advocate of eugenics in Nazi Germany. He coined the term *Herrenvolk*, or master race, for Aryans. He preached the superiority of Nordic people, including Germans, and the inferiority of Jews and others. To the Nazis, Jews and other "subhumans" restricted the Aryans' expansion and success. The Aryans needed *Lebensraum* ["living space"]. Gunther represented the worst in German society of the late-19th and early-20th centuries —the son of a musician and a student of linguistics at the Sorbonne in Paris who devolved into the inspiration for mass murder. Gunther lived well into the 20th century, dying in 1968. He never renounced his hateful views.[67]

For centuries, antisemites have preached that Jews have their sights set on world domination. This invariably reflected the theme seen in many other stereotypical tales, such as Jews being in supposed control over monetary resources. There is no doubt that some Jews have made a career in finance. But the demonized usurer or moneylender had its beginnings in the Middle Ages when the Church sought to end the practice of Christians collecting interest from other Christians while permitting Jews to lend to Christians with interest. At the same time, Jews in Central and Eastern Europe were barred from landholding and handicrafts guilds, leaving few other ways of making a living.

The United States, Great Britain, and other powerful countries, while waging war to defeat the Germans and the Axis powers, did little to help Jewish (and other) refugees desperately trying to escape the Holocaust. At a minimum, their hands-off attitude further emboldened Hitler, who believed Germany would suffer no consequences for their elimination.

If one believes the story of Creation—Genesis—and Adam and Eve, humans have always had free will and the ability to choose good or evil. Throughout history, just as people have chosen to be good and kind, people have also chosen to do mind-boggling, horrible things to their fellow humans. Many German figures were highly cultured humanitarians, liberals, poets, philosophers, and composers. Unfathomably, that same country gave life to the monstrous Nazis.

Aging Survivors and the Second Generation

Those who survived the Holocaust are now in their eighties, nineties, and older; my father, if he were still alive, would be over 100. Many feel a responsibility to share their wartime experiences while they still can: with dignity despite the trauma, suffering, and loss they endured. The passage of time hasn't diminished their stories.

Psychological experts believe survivors repressed traumatic memories in the immediate aftermath of the war, instead focusing on rebuilding their lives and creating new opportunities. Though survivors demonstrate remarkable resilience, they also suffer posttraumatic stress and other psychological harm.

The children of Holocaust survivors, like me, may be thought of as the second generation of survivors. They carry the burden of passing on their parents' stories, and they must deal with the horror of the Holocaust more intimately than others. They are a diverse group who have inherited a complicated set of emotions impacting their lives in different ways. At a young age, many experienced great confusion as they watched their parents struggle with lingering trauma and survivor's guilt.

Research into "generational trauma" suggests extreme stress or starvation can leave a chemical mark on a person's genes. This mark can be biologically passed from one generation to the next. This passing down is referred to as epigenetics and is the body's way of biologically preparing the next generation to deal with similar trauma. Second-generation Holocaust survivors may not demonstrate direct symptoms of posttraumatic stress disorder, but experts say they are at risk of high levels of psychological distress. Generational trauma can be addressed through various means, including therapy.

For the children of Holocaust survivors, the past is a treacherous place fractured by a tragedy both unknown but familiar and shared.

Their connection to events they were not alive to witness has shaped them in interdependent ways. These horrors could not help but affect their mothers' and fathers' parenting. It is difficult for the children of survivors to imagine their parents without the shadow cast by this trauma. Dysfunction frequently rules the relationships of second-generation survivors, for whom the Holocaust was their families' creation story.

Many, having "inherited" the knowledge of their parents' experiences, think of themselves as the guardians of this knowledge. Although lacking firsthand experience, they understand the effects of state-sponsored torture, oppression, and genocide. They are weighed down by feelings of guilt and the need to ensure this knowledge lives on after the survivors are gone. There is great anxiety that the world otherwise will forget the Holocaust happened and that if the world forgets, genocide will inevitably reoccur. To prevent that fate, many try to make sense of their connection to the Holocaust and navigate how they will share their knowledge. As the survivor population continues to rapidly disappear, the need to bear witness has become even more pressing.[8][9][10]

Antisemitism and Other Hatred Since World War II

Since World War II, antisemitism has persisted in Western Europe and elsewhere, although governments have tried to dissuade and punish those espousing such views. The increase in contemporary Western Europe's antisemitism has created a dangerous environment for Jews and their human rights, freedom, and safety.[11]

Due to economic turmoil, including the recession of 2008, incidents of antisemitism in Europe have increased and given rise to hateful political parties and policies. In one example, in France, 614 antisemitic acts, including physical and verbal attacks, were recorded in 2012, a 58% increase from the previous year.

The Roma and Jews have been perceived as unwanted outsiders, and both were targets of Nazi persecution during the Holocaust. Jewish persecution hit its height in Europe in the 1930s and 1940s, while the Roma continue to experience such persecution. In 2010, the

German government repatriated Roma back to Kosovo, an area they had fled due to persecution.

Antisemitism is not just a European phenomenon. It hit an all-time high in the United States in 2019 with 2,100 acts of assault, vandalism, and harassment reported, a 12% increase from the prior year. The Anti-Defamation League (ADL) reported a doubling of antisemitic incidents between 2015 and 2019. In 2018, the Tree of Life Synagogue in Pittsburgh was attacked by an antisemitic gunman—11 were murdered and six injured in the deadliest attack ever on the American Jewish community. In 2019, ADL CEO Jonathan A. Greenblatt stated:

"It's clear we must remain vigilant ... to counter the threat of violent antisemitism and denounce it in all forms ... ensure that synagogues and community centers have the right security measures ... to prevent the next potential attack ... to ensure that funding is in place and that all states mandate Holocaust education, which can serve as an effective deterrent for future acts of hate."[12][13]

The 2020s echo the 1920s–1940s

After World War I and the Great Depression, there was great hope for an economic golden age. Yet the 2020s, like the 1920s, have seen increases in economic turmoil, right-wing extremism, mistrust of "outsiders," divisiveness, and a heavy-handed approach to immigration. The turmoil is, in part, due to the impact of the COVID-19 pandemic that started at the end of 2019 and in many ways mirrors that of the 1918–1920 Spanish flu.

We have also witnessed the dehumanization of those perceived to be "different" by people who believe in false realities, have been radicalized via multimedia, and support demonizing "the enemy" to justify violence.

Times of crisis and uncertainty have always allowed conspiracy theories to thrive. Today's unprecedented combination of a global pandemic, racial injustice, and economic uncertainty provides fertile ground for the resurgence of dangerous folk beliefs that have persisted for millennia. Recognizing the folkloric roots of today's conspiracy theories, including antisemitic ones may allow us to better understand both its appeal and danger.

Germans are rightly proud of the music, art, and folklore their people brought the world. One only needs to visit a Disney theme park to witness many of the Brothers Grimm and other folk stories brought to life. However, Germany has not fully come to terms with the underlying antisemitic elements of some of its folklore, as represented by the Judensau sculptures.

Chillingly, Nazi Propaganda Minister Josef Goebbels' 105-year-old secretary Brunhilde Pomsel, before she died in 2017, said: "I just cling to the hope that the world doesn't turn upside down again as it did then, though there have been some ghastly developments, haven't there? I'm relieved I never had any children that I have to worry about."[14]

How Do We Stop Another Holocaust?

Is another Holocaust probable? I believe the answer is no. Just as there is evil, there is good. Whether one believes in God or some other source of good, history has shown time and again that good wins—eventually. However, one needs only look at present-day Holocaust deniers, antisemitism, and conspiracy theories to fear the possibility.

It became painfully and personally clear to me that antisemitism and Nazism were alive and well one Fourth of July in 2005. I was working in Washington and took a weekend trip to southern Virginia. I hoped to visit Yorktown, where George Washington and French General Marquis de Lafayette defeated the British in 1781, ending the Revolutionary War. However, when I arrived, I discovered about 100 American neo-Nazis and other white supremacists, in full Nazi uniform, staging rallies at the site of the battlefield. They were outnumbered by about 500 counter protesters.

Rabbi Eric Carlson, of Congregation Zion, blew a shofar and shouted over a megaphone: "As you can see, the face of love is greater than the face of hate! Hallelujah!" Other counter protesters carried signs reading "Die Nazi Scum!"

The neo-Nazi protestors said immigrants from non-European countries were threatening the United States. "We're here to reclaim the nation! ... This nation was formed by proud white men," they said.

Once more, I was forced to face the reality some people hate me simply because of my heritage.

The events in Yorktown were eerily like the antisemitic, white supremacist "Unite the Right" rally that took place in Charlottesville, Virginia, in August 2017. It was at that rally that protesters marched and chanted "Jews will not replace us."[15]

The primary way to combat conspiracy theories is to maintain an open society where many sources of reliable information are available and government sources are known to be credible rather than propaganda. Public and civic leaders should speak out against antisemitism and extremism, and independent nongovernmental organizations must correct misinformation. Law enforcement must be provided the tools and training they need to prevent and effectively respond to hate crimes.

Approaches to combat the appeal of conspiracy theories may be based on combating their emotional and social nature. Interventions promoting analytical thinking are likely to combat conspiracy theories. In addition, presenting people with factual corrections, or highlighting the logical contradictions in conspiracy theories, has been effective in dissuading 9/11 conspiracy theories. Schools should promote anti-bias and conflict resolution training, bullying prevention, and Holocaust education programs.

Jews and other "outsiders" must be included within countries' socioeconomic and political fabric. The media must studiously avoid antisemitic rhetoric, including messages of hate spread by far right-wing parties.

While there is a tradition in Judaism of pursuing the "middle way," and the Talmud says compromise (*p'sharah*) and mediation (*bitzua*) are good deeds, we must guard against surrender and appeasement. In the Holocaust, this approach proved disastrous with Chamberlain attempting to appease Hitler.

I believe we can overcome evil and avoid another Holocaust by practicing the Golden Rule and simply being good to each other. Though it takes work and sometimes conscious effort, it is well worth it.

Earlier, I paraphrased Proverbs 10:7 in saying may the memory of my father and mother and all victims of the Holocaust, antisemitism, and other hatred—righteous people—be a blessing. Again, paraphrasing Proverbs 10:7, may the names of Adolf Hitler, his henchmen, and others who traffic in antisemitism and other forms of hatred—all wicked people—perish and be blotted out.[16]

Family Legacies

Much research has been conducted on the impact of the Holocaust on the families of survivors. *Scientific American* reported that children of survivors have altered stress hormones, predisposing them to anxiety disorders. This generational trauma has devastating and lasting effects.[17]

Second-generation survivors may find themselves attempting to make sense of their family's traumatic history, which can be especially challenging as many survivors find it difficult to speak about their experiences. Research has also shown that second-generation survivors, often named (as I was) for relatives murdered in the Holocaust, feel stress due to their perceived roles as living "memorial candles" who embody hope for the future. Second-generation survivors may also feel an obligation to bear witness on behalf of their relatives who perished in the Holocaust.[18][19][20]

Though I will not attempt to speak for others, the Holocaust impacted me in several ways, many of which I've been forced to reexamine while researching and writing this book.

Throughout my life, I have been keenly aware of and taken great pride in my Jewish heritage. This pride is one of the reasons I chose to write this book. At the same time, I have always been purposely guarded, viewing my religion as a personal matter and one that I do not ordinarily share except with those with whom I am close. No doubt this is an inherited fear of how strangers and acquaintances may react to my heritage. I have chosen not to be as free about it, in part based on knowing my Judaism has at times colored how others think. I am also cognizant of stereotypical views toward Jewish people in upper-level or government positions. During most of my adult life, I served in management and executive positions, leading hundreds of employees. I never wanted someone to say, "Oh, he's doing this or that because he's Jewish."

Perhaps because I was the youngest child in my family and the tatela shind, I felt absolute love from my parents. My siblings, particularly my sisters, didn't enjoy this status, something that has become painfully clear to me as we have aged. I believe this was because of a combination of the extreme psychological damage and trauma my father experienced from the Holocaust and because of his old-world views on the roles of men and women that he either experienced, had passed on to him, or both. My father treated my sisters negatively. Verbally and through his actions, they experienced some of the trauma and drama he experienced by having it passed on to them. I won't speak for them, but I believe they felt a lack of love and nurturing, had heightened expectations placed upon them, and were subject to criticism about their appearance and relationships. They have battled to overcome the drama and negativities of their childhoods.

My mother, a loving and angelic person, struggled at times to shield my sisters from him. I believe this response was due to my mother's secondary role to my father in raising children, her natural timidity, and her desire to avoid conflict. Her essential goodness was tested by my father's demons. She sacrificed some of her sense of self and ironically her connections with her own family to help ensure my father's happiness. To this day, I struggle to reconcile my childhood experience with my sisters'. Although I love my family dearly, we have strained relationships (to varying degrees) with each other and those outside the immediate family.

As he aged, my father experienced significant insomnia, anxiety, difficulty trusting others, and a more negative outlook. As I am only one generation away from the terrors my father faced, there is no doubt—whether through generational trauma or because these terrors were taught to me at an early age—I also suffer from anxiety, have difficulty trusting others, and, at times overreact to negative experiences. I sometimes find myself reverting to "very old scripts," words I heard my father use that reflected his lack of trust. As I have aged, I also find myself disliking "downtime" and being alone, both issues my father faced.

I have always been aware that I am named after my father's brother, Yitzhak, who was murdered in the Holocaust. In my youth, I was painfully shy, withdrawn, and experienced bullying at school. In part I believe this was because I was "big for my age," and refused to fight back. I believe another reason was my sensitivity regarding my Jewish first name and that I was Jewish in a mostly Christian area.

I have always felt the need to "achieve." I continuously climbed the ladder, moving from location to location to achieve promotions. I earned my master's degree while working full time and teaching college courses. I earned my law degree and passed the California bar while working full time and helping raise our two children. I worked my way up to becoming a senior federal executive in Washington, university professor, author, consultant, conference speaker, and expert witness. I have decided that I never want to fully retire—I have more to contribute. I believe this need to achieve is in part related to the need to make a mark and not be forgotten, which many Jews—particularly second-generation survivors—feel. This need, along with, in my case, a desire to make my Holocaust-surviving father proud, is just one more reason I wrote this book. As American founding father Benjamin Franklin said: "Either write something worth reading or do something worth writing about."

In 2010, I self-published a book titled *Solomon's Steps* partly based on my father's experiences. It is a guide to resolving differences and disagreements before they become worse. Based on the book, I taught workshops in the San Francisco area, and established a mediation/conflict resolution program at a Virginia synagogue. I have also written and published books focusing on U.S. Pacific Northwest history and folklore.

Much has been written about "Jewish guilt." I have experienced this feeling throughout my life, with my father's experiences a contributing cause. This Jewish guilt has shown itself at the most unfortunate times, like in 1999 when I was scheduled to take the California bar exam. Throughout law school, I had not been able to spend as much time with my parents as I would have liked, and my father had been in declining health. The day before the bar exam, my father passed away. I debated whether to take the exam. All those around me encouraged me to do so—even the police officer present to transport my father's body. I did so largely because I believed my father would have wanted me to. But during the exam, I experienced chest pain and shortness of breath and had to leave the test room several times. I did not pass on that first try. Looking back, I believe I was experiencing a panic attack brought on by my father's death. I have felt guilt over it for years.

I know my father's and mother's experiences played a major role in shaping who I am today. That said, I am a strong believer in free will, that we each control our own destiny. Though this knowledge has helped me achieve many things in my life, it has also presented obstacles, emotionally and personally.

Next Steps

In 2021, my sister Miriam and I commissioned Joshua Grayson, PhD, head of the Lost Roots genealogy company (and our distant cousin), to trace our family's roots as far back as possible. I greatly appreciate Joshua's excellent work and research, as we continue to trace our family's history.

In April 2021, my sisters and I held a Zoom video call with many of the extended relatives from my father's mother's side. One thing that struck me during our call was the long-lasting impact the Holocaust had on the extended families of survivors. The descendants have been scattered to all parts of the world. This pattern is related to which countries allowed survivors to immigrate. I was also struck by how desperate we, as second-generation survivors, are to reconnect with family members with whom we've had minimal or no contact due to this diaspora. We, the second generation, want to be a whole, unified people.

As of this writing, my wife and I are planning a trip to Poland and

Germany to retrace my father's footsteps and to further explore my Jewish European heritage.

Thank you for joining me on this difficult journey. I firmly believe that by reexamining the Holocaust, and through our joint humanity and hope, we can prevent a similar nightmare.

ABOUT THE AUTHOR

Ira Wesley Kitmacher is a professor, attorney, and retired senior U.S. government executive. In addition to this book, he is a published author of books on American Pacific Northwest history and folklore. He is also a member of The History Writers Association.

In this book, he combines his interests in Jewish history, his family's story, folklore, the supernatural, horror and superhero stories, and movies. In researching, he was greatly affected by the brutality, outright inhumanity, raw courage, and hope that took place. It has caused him to examine his own Jewishness.

In his career, he rose to the highest levels of the U.S. government and academia and brings the skills he developed in research, organization, and storytelling to this book.

KIND REQUEST

Dear Reader,

If you have enjoyed reading my book,
please do leave a review on Amazon or Goodreads. A few kind words would be enough. This would be greatly appreciated.

Alternatively, if you have read my book as Kindle eBook you could leave a rating.
That is just one simple click, indicating how many stars of five you think this book deserves.

This will only cost you a split second.
Thank you very much in advance!

Ira Wesley Kitmacher

BIBLIOGRAPHY AND FILMOGRAPHY

A Day in Warsaw—The Spirit of Jewish Life in Warsaw, Poland, before World War II. Jewish Film Festival.

America and the Holocaust. Facinghistory.org. 2020.

American Response to the Holocaust. History Channel. October 29, 2009.

Angebert, Jean. *The Occult and the Third Reich: The Mystical Origins of Nazism and the Search for the Holy Grail.* Macmillan, 1974.

"Antisemitic Incidents Hit All-Time High in 2019." 2019 American Defense League Annual Report.

A Polish Nightmare: 8 Horrific Creatures from Poland, CrazypolishgGuy.com. October 15, 2016.

Bailey, Ronald. "Victor Frankenstein Is the Real Monster." *Reason,* April 2018.

Barron, Melody. "I Bet You Didn't Know Captain America was a Golem!" *Librarians,* June 11, 2017.

Beck, Pearl., Miller, Ron., and Torr, Berna. Jewish Survivors of the Holocaust Residing in the United States, Estimates and Projections: 2010–2030. October 23, 2009.

Bell, David. "History's Black Hole: The Holocaust in Eastern Europe." The National Interest. August 21, 2015.

Belzec Perpetrators—An Overview of the German and Austrian SS and Police Staff. ARC. September 23, 2006.

Ben David, Rabbi Dr. Hillel. H. *The Significance of the Number 12*. Betemunah.org.

Bennett-Smith, Michael. "Vampire Graveyard Unearthed in Poland." *Huffington Post,* July 12, 2013.

Berkovits, Rabbi Yitzchak. "Understanding the Holocaust." Aish.com. December 31, 1969.

Blakemore, Erin. "How Women Fought Their Way into the U.S. Armed Forces." History.com. June 2018.

Boteach, Shmuley. "The Haunting Spirits of Auschwitz." *Jerusalem Post*. January 27, 2020.

Bohr, Felix, Cordula, Meyer, and Klaus, Wiegrefe. *I Do Not Feel Like a Criminal*. Spiegel International. August 28, 2014.

Brenner, Michael. "Displaced Persons After the Holocaust." MyJewishLearning.com. December 2021.

Browning, Tod. *Dracula*. Universal Pictures. 1931.

Budzyn Labour Camp. Holocaust Education & Archive Research Team, HolocaustResearchProject.org. 2007.

Bund. JewishvirtuallLibrary.org. 2008.

Burke, Michael. "Antisemitic Incidents U.S. Have Doubled Since 2015, Anti-Defamation League says." *Hill.* 2019.

Burstein, Nathan. "The Werewolf's Jewish Roots." *Forward.* February 10, 2010.

Burton, Tim. "Sleepy Hollow." Paramount Pictures. 1999.

Chaplin, Charlie. *The Great Dictator.* United Artists. 1940.

Connolly, Kate. "Joseph Goebbels' 105-Year-Old Secretary: "No One Believes Me Now, But I Knew Nothing," *Guardian.*

Cooper, Merian C. *King Kong.* RKO Radio Pictures. 1933.

Cymer, Anna. "Old Haunts: Exploring Poland's Spookiest Spots." *Culture.pl.* October 30, 2018.

Dabrowski, Colonel John R. "U.S. Army Liberates Flossenburg Concentration Camp," U.S. Army Heritage and Education Center. April 11, 2008.

Datner, Szymon. "Genocide, 1939-1945." United States Holocaust Museum.

Disorganizing Experiences in Second and Third Generation Holocaust Survivors. SAGE Journals. 2011.

"Do Jews Believe in Angels?" Myjewishlearning.com. February 17, 2012.

Eagleton, Terry. "So Bad It's Good: Why Do We Find Evil So Much More Fascinating Than Goodness?" *Independent.* October 22, 2011.

Eftink, Johnathan. *The Rise of Antisemitism in Post-Cold War Western Europe: The Effect on Current Jewish Populations in Europe, Jewish Human Rights, and the Role of the Jewish Religion Within Western Europe.* Washington University in St. Louis. 2014.

Eisenberg, Ronald. "8 Popular Jewish Superstitions." Myjewishlearning.com.

Elder, Simon. "We Can Still Believe in Miracles—Jewish Views on Miracles." Thejc.com. April 5, 2018.

"Ellis Island." History.com. June 2018.

Ender, Elizabeth., and St. Clair, Betty. *WAVES of the Navy.* 1943.

Erdelac, Edward. "Monstrumfuhrer." Comet Press. 2017

Evans, Redd., and Joeb, John Jacob. *Rosie the Riveter.* 1942.

The Evolution of Mastectomy Surgical Technique: From Mutilation to Medicine. U.S. National Library of Medicine Nation Institutes of Health. June 2018.

Fackler, Guido. *Music in Concentration Camps 1933-1945.* University of Michigan, 2007.

Fendley, Caitlin. "Eugenics is Trending. That's a Problem." *Washington Post.* February 17, 2020.

Finger, Bill, and Kane, Bob. *Batman.* Detective Comics. 1939.

Fleming, Victor. The Wonderful Wizard of Oz. Metro-Goldwyn-Mayer. 1939.

Foy, Henry. "*The Lost Faces of Lublin.*" *Financial Times.* November 20, 2015.

"Franklin Delano Roosevelt." United States Holocaust Memorial Museum.

Freiberg, D. *The Holocaust and Resistance.* Jewishgen.org.

"From Citizens to Outcasts, 1933-1938." United States Holocaust Memorial Museum.

From Haven to Home: 350 Years of Jewish Life in America, A of Immigration, 1820- 1924. Library of Congress.

"Germans Introduce Poison Gas." History.com. February 9, 2010.
    Gilbert, Martin. *The Holocaust.* London: William Collins, 1986.

Golden, Jonathan, and Sarna, Jonathan. *The American Jewish Experience in the Twentieth : Antisemitism and Assimilation.* Brandeis University, 2000.

Golinkin, Lev. "It's Time to Confront the Dark Postscript to America's Role in Defeating the Nazis." CNN.com. February 24, 2021.

Goode, E. "Insane or Just Evil? A Psychiatrist Takes a New Look at Hitler." *New York Times.* Nov. 17, 1998.

Green, David. "Why Did Adolf Hitler Hate the Jews?" *Haaretz.* November 4, 2016.

Greenspan, Jesse. "The Dark Side of the Grimm Fairy Tales." History.com. September 17, 2013.

Grimm, Jacob, and Grimm, Wilhelm. *Grimms Complete Fairy Tales.* Canterbury Classics, 2011.

Harrison-Kahan, Lori. *The Jewish Roots of Wonder Woman's Pop Feminism.* Jewish Book Council. 2020.

Hartmann, Corinna, and Goudarzi, Sara. "Does Birth Order Affect Personality?" *Scientific American.* August 8, 2019.

Hilberg, Raul. *The Destruction of the European Jews.* New Haven, CT: Yale University Press, 2003.

Hitler, Adolf. *Mein Kampf.* 1925.

Hockenos, Paul. "Has Germany Forgotten the Lessons of the Nazis?" *New York Times.* April 15, 2019.

Holocaust Education & Archive Research Team. *Budzyn Labour Camp.* Holocaustresearchproject.org.

Holocaust Resistance: The Warsaw Ghetto Uprising. How Did Germans Get That Way? American Historical Association. 2021.

"Holocaust Survivors Remember the Foods They Ate." *South Florida Sun-Sentinel.* April 19, 2012.

How WWI Transformed the American Jewish Community. Jewish Genealogical Society of Greater Boston. November 4, 2018.

Idelson-Schein, Iris, and Wiese, Christian. Monsters and Monstrosity in Jewish History. Bloomsbury. 2019.

Irving, Washington. *The Legend of Sleepy Hollow.* Tribeca Books. 2011.

Jacobs, Joela. *Of Monsters and Menschen: A Typology of Jewish Monsters.* Jewish Book Council. 2019.

Jarniewski, S. "A Jewish Prisoner of War-SS Labour Camp Budzyn." Holocaust Historical Society, Jewishgen.org. 2012.

Jazowska, Marta. "9 Supernatural Beings & Places of Polish Folklore." Culture.pl. October 30, 2014.

Jenkins, Patty. *Wonder Woman*. Warner Brothers. 2017.

"Jewish Badge: During the Nazi Era." United States Holocaust Memorial Museum.

"Jewish Communities of Prewar Germany." United States Holocaust Memorial Museum.

"Jewish Life in Poland Before the Holocaust." Facinghistory.org. 2020.

"Jews Have Too Much Power." Anti-Defamation League.

"Jews in the American Military." Museum of American Jewish Military History.

Johnson, Robert, and Sterbenz, Christina. "11 Shockingly Accurate Predictions from Nostradamus." Businessinsider.in. May 30, 2014.

Johnston, Joe. *Captain America: The First Avenger*. Marvel Studios. July 19, 2011.

Jpost.com staff. "No Truth in Claim That Walt Disney Was an Anti-Semite." *Jerusalem Post*. February 25, 2020

"Judenrat: Introductory History." Jewish Virtual Library-A Project of the American-Israeli Cooperative Enterprise (AICE).

Kasprzyk-Chevriaux, Magdalena. "The Taste of Tradition: The Lasting Influence of Jewish Cuisine in Poland." Culture.pl, January 22, 2015.

Kevles. Daniel J. *Eugenics and Human Rights*. U.S. National Library of Medicine, National Institutes of Health. 1999.

King, Susan. "'Wolf Man' writer reflected wartime Jewish Experience." L.A. Times. February 3, 2010.

Kirby, Jack., and Lee, Stan. *The Avengers #1*. Marvel Comics. September 1, 1963.

Kirby, Jack, and Simon, Joe. *Captain America #1*. Timely Comics. March 1, 1941.

Kopstein, J., and J. Wittenberg. *Intimate Violence: Anti-Jewish Pogroms on the Eve of the Holocaust*. Ithaca, NY: Cornell University Press, June 15, 2018.

Kopstein, Jeffrey, and Wittenberg, Jason. "Nazi Guards Weren't the Only Ones Killing Jews During the Holocaust. Some—But Not All—Communities Did It Themselves First. Why." *Washington Post*. August 22, 2018.

Krasner, Jonathan. "American Jews Between the Wars: The Character of the American Jewish Community Changed, As a Nation of Immigrants Americanized." MyJewishLearning.com.

Kripke, Eric. *Supernatural*. Warner Bros. Television. 2005-2020.

Kurlander, Eric. "A Supernatural History of the Third Reich" Yale University Press. July 18, 2017.

Landis, John. *American Werewolf in London*. PolyGram Pictures. August 21, 1981.

Landis, John. *Twilight Zone: The Movie*. Warner Brothers. 1983.

Learning—Voices of the Holocaust. British Library Board.

Leman, Kevin. "The Birth Order Book: Why You Are the Way You Are." *Revell*. October 1, 2009.

Levi, Primo. "The Black Hole of Auschwitz." Polity. 2005.

Levinson, L. "Concentration Camp Liberators Reveal Their Silent Trauma. Liberators' Testimonies." Remember.org.

Levinson, Leila. "Concentration Camp Liberators Reveal Their Silent Trauma." Warfare History Network.

"Life in the Ghettos." United States Holocaust Memorial Museum.

Lurie, Rabbi Alan. "How Could God Have Allowed the Holocaust?" *Huffington Post*. January 17, 2012.

Mamoulian, Rouben. *Dr. Jekyll and Mr. Hyde*. Paramount Pictures. 1931.

Markusz, Katarzyna. "University of Warsaw Students Remember Pre-WWII Segregation of Jews." *Jerusalem Post*. October 8, 2019.

Marston, William Marston. *Wonder Woman*. 1941.

Marvel Studios movies. Various directors. 2008—present.

McCormack, J.W. "Hitler Used Werewolves, Vampires, and Astrology to Brainwash Germany." *Vice*. June 29, 2017.

Mill, Olivia Erin. "Stepping Out of the Shadows: Second Generation Holocaust Representation." Trinity University. April 2017.

Muller, Sanan. "German Mythological Creatures from German Folklore." Germany Daily, May 24, 2021.

Muraskin, Bennett. "Jewish Surnames Explained." Slate. January 8, 2014.

"Murder of the Jews of Poland." Yad Vashem, World Holocaust Remembrance Center.

Murnau, F. W. *Nosferatu*. 1922.

"Musique Et Shoah." World ORT. Jewish Virtual Library-A Project of AICE.

Navigating the WAVES in World War II. Naval History and Heritage Command.

Noack, Rick. "Long-Lost Film That Predicted Rise of Antisemitism Has Ominous Message for Today's World." *Washington Post*. March 30, 2018.

Nostredame, Michel de. *Les Prophéties*. 1555.

Onion, Rebecca. "The Nazis were Obsessed With Magic." Slate. August 24, 2017.

Padnick, Steven. "What Everybody Gets Wrong About Jekyll and Hyde. Files.schudio.com.

Padre Steve. "To Forget a Holocaust Is to Kill Twice, The Liberation of Auschwitz at 76." The Inglorious Padre Steve's World. January 27, 2021.

Parker, Clifton. "Jewish Émigrés Who Fled Nazi Germany Revolutionized U.S. Science and Technology." Stanford University news release. August 11, 2014

Phillips, Gervase. "Antisemitism: how the origins of history's hatred still hold sway today." The Conversation. February 27, 2018.

"Psychological Pain of Holocaust Still Haunts Survivors." American Psychological Association. 2010.

Ramirez, Rachelle. "Secrets of the Horror Genre." *Story Grid*. 2018.

Remember Jewish Krasnik. Genealogy Group.

"The Rise and Fall of GE's Empire." *Berkshire Eagle*. July 1, 2011.

Rodriguez, Toni. "Descendants of Holocaust Survivors Have Altered Stress Hormones." *Scientific American*. March 1, 2015.

Rosenfeld, David. "Judaism and Dreams." Aish.com.

Sacks, Rabbi Jonathan. "How the Jewish People Invented Hope." MyJewishLearning.com.

Schaffner, Franklin. *The Boys from Brazil*. 20th Fox. 1978.

Schertel, Ernst. *Magic: History, Theory, Practice*. Cotum, 2009.

Schulson, Michael. "The Supernatural Pseudoscience of Nazi Germany." *Religion & Politics*. October 24, 2017.

Schwartz, Roy. "Superman vs. the Nazis." Aish.com. June 5, 2021.

Schwartz, Teresa. P. "The Holocaust: Non-Jewish Victims." Jewish Virtual Library.

Scott, Carol. "Neo-Nazi Group Rallies in Yorktown." *Daily Press*. June 26, 2005.

Shelley, Mary. Frankenstein; or, The Modern Prometheus. Lackington, Hughes, Harding, Mavor & Jones. 1818.

Serling, Rod. "The Twilight Zone." ViacomCBS. 1959-1964.

Shakespeare, William. "The Merchant of Venice." Simon & Schuster. 2009.

The Second Generation—The Effects of the Holocaust on the Children of Survivors. Georgetown University.

The Secrets of War— The Holocaust Secret. Directed by K. Burns and L. Novick. Narrated by Charlton Heston. 1998.

Sekely, Steve. *Revenge of the Zombies.* 1943.

Shelley, Mary. *Frankenstein or the Modern Prometheus.* Simon & Brown. 2012.

Sholem, A. *Tevye the Dairyman and Motl the Cantor's Son.* Penguin Classics, 2009.

Siegel, Jerry, and Shuster, Joe. *Superman.* Action Comics. 1938.

Snyder, Zack. *Batman v. Superman: Dawn of Justice.* Warner Bros. March 25, 2016.

"Songs of the Ghettos, Concentration Camps, and World War II Partisan Outposts." United States Holocaust Museum.

Spielberg, Steven. *Raiders of the Lost Ark.* Lucasfilm Ltd. 1981.

Spielberg, Steven. *Schindler's List.* Universal Pictures. 1993.

Spitzer, Yannay. *Pogroms, Networks, and Migration, The Jewish Migration from the Russian Empire to the United States 1881–1914.* Maurice Falk Institute for Economic Research in Israel. September 17, 2013.

Stanley, Jason. "Movie at the Ellipse: A Study in Fascist Propaganda." *Just Security*. February 4, 2021.

Stevenson, Robert Lewis. *Strange Case of Dr. Jekyll and Mr. Hyde*. Chump Change. 1886.

Stoker, Bram. *Dracula*. Archibald Constable and Company. 1897.

"The Story of Ernst Bornstein 1939—They Can't Be Killing Jews, Surely?" Holocaust Matters.

Stolen Youth. Yad Vashem. 2005.

"The Survivors." United States Holocaust Memorial Museum.

Tarantino, Quentin. *Inglourious Basterds*. Universal Pictures. 2009.

Taylor, Alan. "American Nazis in the 1930s—The German American Bund." *The Atlantic*. June 5, 2017.

"The Truth about Poland's Role in the Holocaust." *Atlantic*. February 6, 2018.

Waggner, George. *The Wolf Man*. Universal Pictures. 1941.

"War of Words—Hun." *Military-history*.org. May 11, 2020.

The WAVES' 75th Birthday. Naval History and Heritage Command.

Waxman, Olivia. "We Weren't Prepared for This: Inside the Accidental Liberation of a Concentration Camp." *Time*. January 26, 2018.

Wegener, Paul. and Henrik, Galeen. *The Golem*. 1915.

Weikart, Richard. *Hitler's Ethic: The Nazi Pursuit of Evolutionary Progress.* Palgrave Macmillan. 2009.

Wells, H. G. *The Invisible Man—A Grotesque Romance.* Bantam Classics, 1983.

Whale, James. *Frankenstein.* Universal Pictures. 1931.

Whale, James. *The Invisible Man.* Universal Pictures Corp. 1933.

"Wilhelm II: 'Hun Speech.'" (1900). GHDI-dc.org.

Winkler, A. *The Medieval Holocaust: The Approach of the Plague and the Destruction of Jews in Germany, 1348-1349.* Brigham Young University. 2005.

Wood, Angela Gluck. *Holocaust.* Penguin. 2007.

Yarbrough, Jean. *King of the Zombie.* Monogram Pictures Corporation. 1941.

Zitter, Emmy. "Anti-Semitism in Chaucer's 'Prioress's Tale.'" Jstor.org. Volume 25, No. 4.

NOTES

Introduction

1. Jack Kirby, and Joe Simon. *Captain America #1*. Timely Comics. March 1, 1941.
2. Jerry Siegel, and Joe Shuster. *Superman*. Action Comics. 1938.
3. Redd Evans, and John Jacob Loeb. *Rosie the Riveter*. 1942.
4. William Marston. *Wonder Woman*. 1941.
5. Patty Jenkins. *Wonder Woman*. Warner Brothers. 2017.
6. Primo Levi. "The Black Hole of Auschwitz." Polity. 2005.
7. David Bell. "History's Black Hole: The Holocaust in Eastern Europe." The National Interest. August 21, 2015.
8. Serling, Rod. *The Twilight Zone*. ViacomCBS. 1959-1964.
9. Robert Lewis Stevenson. *Strange Case of Dr. Jekyll and Mr. Hyde*. Chump Change. 1886.
10. Rouben Mamoulian. *Dr. Jekyll and Mr. Hyde*. Paramount Pictures. 1931.
11. H. G. Wells. *The Invisible Man—A Grotesque Romance*. Bantam Classics, 1983.
12. James Whale. *The Invisible Man*. Universal Pictures Corp. 1933.
13. Tod Browning. *Dracula*. Universal Pictures. 1931.
14. James Whale. Frankenstein. Universal Pictures. 1931.
15. Paul Wegener, and Galeen Henrik. *The Golem. 1915*.
16. F. W. Murnau. *Nosferatu*. 1922.
17. Bram Stoker. *Dracula*. Archibald Constable and Company. 1897.
18. Tod Browning. *Dracula*. Universal Pictures. 1931.
19. Mary Shelley. *Frankenstein or The Modern Prometheus*. Lackington, Hughes, Harding, Mavor & Jones. 1818.
20. James Whale. *Frankenstein*. Universal Pictures. 1931.
21. James Whale. *The Invisible Man*. Universal Pictures Corp. 1933.
22. George Waggner. *The Wolf Man*. Universal Pictures. 1941.
23. Jean Yarbrough. *King of the Zombies*. Monogram Pictures Corporation. 1941.
24. Steve Sekely. *Revenge of the Zombies*. Monogram Pictures. 1943.
25. Tod Browning. *Dracula*. Universal Pictures. 1931.
26. Paul Wegener, and Galeen Henrik. *The Golem. 1915*.
27. F. W. Murnau. *Nosferatu*. 1922.
28. Steven Spielberg. *Raiders of the Lost Ark*. Lucasfilm Ltd. 1981.
29. Quentin Tarantino. *Inglourious Basterds*. The Weinstein Company. 2009.
30. Robert Lewis Stevenson. *Strange Case of Dr. Jekyll and Mr. Hyde*. Chump Change. 1886.
31. Washington Irving. *The Legend of Sleepy Hollow*. Tribeca Books. 2011.
32. Mary Shelley. *Frankenstein or The Modern Prometheus*. Lackington, Hughes, Harding, Mavor & Jones. 1818.

33. Steven Spielberg. *Schindler's List*. Universal Pictures. 1993.

Bustling, Simple Life before the Torches and Pitchforks

1. "Jewish Life in Poland Before the Holocaust." Facinghistory.org. 2020.
2. Henry Foy. "*The Lost Faces of Lublin.*" *Financial Times.* November 20, 2015.
3. *A Day in Warsaw—The Spirit of Jewish Life in Warsaw, Poland, before World War II.* Jewish Film Festival.
4. "Holocaust Survivors Remember the Foods They Ate." *South Florida Sun-Sentinel.* April 19, 2012.
5. Sholem Aleichem. *Tevye the Dairyman and Motl the Cantor's Son.* Penguin Classics, 2009.
6. H.K. Breslauer. "The City Without Jews." Walterskirchen und Bittner, 1924.
7. Rick Noack. "Long-Lost Film That Predicted Rise of Antisemitism Has Ominous Message for Today's World." *Washington Post.* March 30, 2018.

Jewish, Polish, and German Folklore, Monsters, and Miracles

1. Ronald Eisenberg. "8 Popular Jewish Superstitions." Myjewishlearning.com.
2. Iris Idelson-Schein, and Christian Wiese. *Monsters and Monstrosity in Jewish History.* Bloomsbury. 2019.
3. Joela Jacobs. *Of Monsters and Menschen: A Typology of Jewish Monsters.* Jewish Book Council. 2019.
4. *A Polish Nightmare: 8 Horrific Creatures from Poland,* CrazypolishgGuy.com. October 15, 2016.
5. Marta Jazowska. "9 Supernatural Beings & Places of Polish Folklore." Culture.pl. October 30, 2014.
6. Michael Bennett-Smith. "Vampire Graveyard Unearthed in Poland." *Huffington Post,* July 12, 2013.
7. Sanan Muller. "German Mythological Creatures from German Folklore." Germany Daily, May 24, 2021.
8. David Rosenfeld. "Judaism and Dreams." Aish.com.
9. Simon Elder. "We Can Still Believe in Miracles—Jewish Views on Miracles." Thejc.com. April 5, 2018.
10. "Do Jews Believe in Angels?" Myjewishlearning.com. February 17, 2012.

Early Christian and German Views of Jews. Dr. Jekyll and Mr. Hyde (Good or Evil)

1. Susan King. "'Wolf Man' writer reflected wartime Jewish Experience." L.A. Times. February 3, 2010.
2. Gervase Phillips. "Antisemitism: how the origins of history's hatred still hold sway today." The Conversation. February 27, 2018.
3. Emmy Zitter. "Anti-Semitism in Chaucer's 'Prioress's Tale.'" Jstor.org. Volume 25, No. 4.
4. "Jews Have Too Much Power." Anti-Defamation League.
5. A. Winkler. *The Medieval Holocaust: The Approach of the Plague and the Destruction of Jews in Germany, 1348-1349*. Brigham Young University. 2005.
6. Paul Wegener, and Galeen Henrik. *The Golem. 1915*.
7. F. W. Murnau. *Nosferatu*. 1922.
8. Ronald Bailey. "Victor Frankenstein Is the Real Monster." *Reason*, April 2018.
9. Michael Schulson. "The Supernatural Pseudoscience of Nazi Germany." *Religion & Politics*. October 24, 2017.
10. Jean Angebert. *The Occult and the Third Reich: The Mystical Origins of Nazism and the Search for the Holy Grail*. Macmillan, 1974.
11. Bram Stoker. *Dracula*. Archibald Constable and Company. 1897.
12. Rebecca Onion. "The Nazis were Obsessed With Magic." Slate. August 24, 2017.
13. Michael Schulson. "The Supernatural Pseudoscience of Nazi Germany." Religion & Politics. October 24, 2017.
14. Jesse Greenspan. "The Dark Side of the Grimm Fairy Tales." History.com. September 17, 2013.
15. Jpost.com staff. "No Truth in Claim That Walt Disney Was an Anti-Semite." *Jerusalem Post*. February 25, 2020.
16. Jesse Greenspan. "The Dark Side of the Grimm Fairy Tales." History.com. September 17, 2013.
17. Steven Spielberg. *Raiders of the Lost Ark*. Lucasfilm Ltd. 1981.

The Kitmachers

1. Bennett Muraskin. "Jewish Surnames Explained." Slate. January 8, 2014.
2. Kevin Leman. "The Birth Order Book: Why You Are the Way You Are." *Revell*. October 1, 2009.

The Harris Family

1. Jonathan Krasner. "American Jews Between the Wars: The Character of the American Jewish Community Changed, As a Nation of Immigrants Americanized." MyJewishLearning.com.
2. "Ellis Island." History.com. June 2018.
3. "Germans Introduce Poison Gas." History.com. February 9, 2010.

Nazis Invade and the Holocaust Begins

1. David Green. "Why Did Adolf Hitler Hate the Jews?" *Haaretz*. November 4, 2016.
2. J.W. McCormack. "Hitler Used Werewolves, Vampires, and Astrology to Brainwash Germany." *Vice*. June 29, 2017.
3. Jason Stanley. "Movie at the Ellipse: A Study in Fascist Propaganda." *Just Security*. February 4, 2021.
4. Robert Johnson, and Christina Sterbenz. "11 Shockingly Accurate Predictions from Nostradamus." Businessinsider.in. May 30, 2014.
5. Patty Jenkins. *Wonder Woman*. Warner Brothers. 2017.
6. Richard Weikart. *Hitler's Ethic: The Nazi Pursuit of Evolutionary Progress*. Palgrave Macmillan. 2009.
7. Franklin Schaffner. *The Boys from Brazil*. 20th Century Fox. 1978.
8. Caitlin Fendley. "Eugenics is Trending. That's a Problem." *Washington Post*. February 17, 2020.
9. Daniel J. Kevles. *Eugenics and Human Rights*. U.S. National Library of Medicine, National Institutes of Health. 1999.
10. E. Goode. "Insane or Just Evil? A Psychiatrist Takes a New Look at Hitler." *New York Times*. Nov. 17, 1998.
11. Martin Gilbert. *The Holocaust*. London: William Collins, 1986.
12. "Jewish Badge: During the Nazi Era." United States Holocaust Memorial Museum.
13. "From Citizens to Outcasts, 1933-1938." United States Holocaust Memorial Museum.
14. Szymon Datner, "Genocide, 1939-1945." United States Holocaust Memorial Museum.
15. "Life in the Ghettos." United States Holocaust Memorial Museum.
16. "Songs of the Ghettos, Concentration Camps, and World War II Partisan Outposts." United States Holocaust Museum.
17. "Judenrat: Introductory History." Jewish Virtual Library-A Project of the American-Israeli Cooperative Enterprise (AICE).
18. *Holocaust Resistance: The Warsaw Ghetto Uprising. How Did Germans Get That Way?* American Historical Association. 2021.
19. Anna Cymer. "Old Haunts: Exploring Poland's Spookiest Spots." *Culture.pl*. October 30, 2018.

America, the Allies, the Holocaust, and Superheroes

1. *From Haven to Home: 350 Years of Jewish Life in America, A Century of Immigration, 1820- 1924*. Library of Congress.
2. Jack Kirby, and Joe Simon. *Captain America #1*. Timely Comics. March 1, 1941.
3. Melody Barron. "I Bet You Didn't Know Captain America was a Golem!" *Librarians*, June 11, 2017.
4. Roy Schwartz. "Superman vs. the Nazis." Aish.com. June 5, 2021.
5. Jerry Siegel, and Joe Shuster. *Superman*. Action Comics. 1938.

6. Roy Schwartz. "Superman vs. the Nazis." Aish.com. June 5, 2021.
7. Jack Kirby, Stan Lee. *The Avengers #1*. Marvel Comics. September 1, 1963.
8. Redd Evans, and John Jacob Loeb. *Rosie the Riveter*. 1942.
9. Melody Barron. "I Bet You Didn't Know Captain America was a Golem!" *Librarians*, June 11, 2017.
10. Joe Johnston. *Captain America: The First Avenger*. Marvel Studios. July 19, 2011.
11. William Marston. *Wonder Woman*. 1941.
12. Lori Harrison-Kahan. *The Jewish Roots of Wonder Woman's Pop Feminism*. Jewish Book Council. 2020.
13. Patty Jenkins. *Wonder Woman*. Warner Brothers. 2017.
14. Washington Irving. *The Legend of Sleepy Hollow*. Tribeca Books. 2011.
15. Tim Burton. *Sleepy Hollow*. Paramount Pictures. 1999.
16. "Wilhelm II: 'Hun Speech.'" (1900). GHDI-dc.org.
17. "Germans Introduce Poison Gas." History.com. February 9, 2010.

Hope, Miracles, and Extraordinary Interventions

1. Rabbi Jonathan Sacks. "How the Jewish People Invented Hope." MyJewishLearning.com.
2. "Life in the Ghettos." United States Holocaust Memorial Museum.

America Enters the War

1. *Navigating the WAVES in World War II*. Naval History and Heritage Command.
2. *The WAVES' 75th Birthday*. Naval History and Heritage Command.

Nightmare

1. *Remember Jewish Krasnik*. Genealogy Group.
2. *Budzyn Labour Camp*. Holocaust Education & Archive Research Team, HolocaustResearchProject.org. 2007.

In the Navy

1. *Navigating the WAVES in World War II*. Naval History and Heritage Command.
2. *The WAVES' 75th Birthday*. Naval History and Heritage Command.
3. Elizabeth Ender, and Betty St. Clair. *WAVES of the Navy*. 1943.
4. Erin Blakemore. "How Women Fought Their Way into the U.S. Armed Forces." History.com. June 2018.
5. Erin Blakemore. "How Women Fought Their Way into the U.S. Armed Forces." History.com. June 2018.

In Hell

1. Robert Lewis Stevenson. *Strange Case of Dr. Jekyll and Mr. Hyde.* Chump Change. 1886.
2. Steven Padnick. "What Everybody Gets Wrong About Jekyll and Hyde. Files.schudio.com.
3. S. Janiewski. "A Jewish Prisoner of War-SS Labour Camp Budzyn." Holocaust Historical Society, Jewishgen.org. 2012.
4. *Budzyn Labour Camp.* Holocaust Education & Archive Research Team, HolocaustResearchProject.org. 2007.
5. Holocaust Education & Archive Research Team. *Budzyn Labour Camp.* Holocaustresearchproject.org.

Dreams and More Miracles

1. Colonel John R. Dabrowski. "U.S. Army Liberates Flossenburg Concentration Camp," U.S. Army Heritage and Education Center. April 11, 2008.
2. Olivia Waxman. "We Weren't Prepared for This: Inside the Accidental Liberation of a Concentration Camp." *Time.* January 26, 2018.
3. Steve Padre. "To Forget a Holocaust Is to Kill Twice, The Liberation of Auschwitz at 76." The Inglorious Padre Steve's World. January 27, 2021.
4. Colonel John R. Dabrowski. "U.S. Army Liberates Flossenburg Concentration Camp," U.S. Army Heritage and Education Center. April 11, 2008.

Back to Civilian Life

1. Erin Blakemore. "How Women Fought Their Way into the U.S. Armed Forces." History.com. June 2018.
2. Jonathan Krasner. "American Jews Between the Wars: The Character of the American Jewish Community Changed, As a Nation of Immigrants Americanized." MyJewishLearning.com.

Freedom

1. Michael Brenner. "Displaced Persons After the Holocaust." MyJewishLearning.com. December 2021.
2. "The Truth about Poland's Role in the Holocaust." *Atlantic.* February 6, 2018.
3. "Ellis Island." History.com. June 2018.

Al and Pearl Together—Hope Realized

1. "The Survivors." United States Holocaust Memorial Museum
2. This was my favorite recipe for cheesecake.
    Crust:
    4 tablespoons butter
    1 egg
    half teaspoon baking power
    1 cup flour
    Pinch of salt
    18 crumbled graham crackers
    2 tablespoons margarine or butter
    2 tablespoons sugar
    Blend ingredients together, then press into the bottom of a springform pan.
    Pineapple layer:
    one-third cup sugar
    1 tablespoon cornstarch
    9 oz. crushed pineapple (not drained)
   Heat sugar, cornstarch, and pineapple on the stove. Stir constantly until thick, then allow to cool. When cool, pour on top of crust.
    Filling:
    1 teaspoon vanilla
    half cup sugar
    2 tablespoons flour
    one-quarter teaspoon salt
    1 pound cream cheese, softened
    4 eggs, separated
    1 cup cream or canned milk
   Blend sugar, flour, salt, and cream cheese. Add vanilla. Add egg yolks, one at a time, mixing well after each. Add cream/milk and blend thoroughly. Beat egg whites until stiff, then fold into mixture. Pour mixture into springform pan on top of crust and pineapple layer. Bake at 325 degrees (F) for one hour, or until set in the center. Cool before removing springform pan. Do not invert."
3. Rabbi Dr. Hillel Ben David. H. *The Significance of the Number Eleven*. Betemunah.org.

Stepping Back in Time—a Return to Germany and End of Life

1. John Landis. *American Werewolf in London*. PolyGram Pictures. August 21, 1981.
2. Steven Spielberg. *Schindler's List*. Universal Pictures. 1993.

Why It Happened: Grim Reality, Black Holes, and Hope Survives

1. Primo Levi. "The Black Hole of Auschwitz." Polity. 2005.
2. David Bell. "History's Black Hole: The Holocaust in Eastern Europe." The National Interest. August 21, 2015.
3. John Landis. *Twilight Zone: The Movie.* Warner Brothers. 1983.
4. Rabbi Yitzchak Berkovits. "Understanding the Holocaust." Aish.com. December 31, 1969.
5. Rabbi Alan Lurie. "How Could God Have Allowed the Holocaust?" *Huffington Post.* January 17, 2012.
6. Caitlin Fendley. "Eugenics is Trending. That's a Problem." *Washington Post.* February 17, 2020.
7. Daniel J. Kevles. *Eugenics and Human Rights.* U.S. National Library of Medicine, National Institutes of Health. 1999.
8. *Disorganizing Experiences in Second and Third Generation Holocaust Survivors.* SAGE Journals. 2011.
9. Olivia Erin Mill. "Stepping Out of the Shadows: Second Generation Holocaust Representation." Trinity University. April 2017.
10. *The Second Generation—The Effects of the Holocaust on the Children of Survivors.* Georgetown University.
11. Johnathan Eftink. *The Rise of Antisemitism in Post-Cold War Western Europe: The Effect on Current Jewish Populations in Europe, Jewish Human Rights, and the Role of the Jewish Religion Within Western Europe.* Washington University in St. Louis. 2014.
12. "Antisemitic Incidents Hit All-Time High in 2019." 2019 American Defense League Annual Report.
13. Michael Burke. "Antisemitic Incidents U.S. Have Doubled Since 2015, Anti-Defamation League says." *Hill.* 2019.
14. Kate Connolly. "Joseph Goebbels' 105-Year-Old Secretary: "No One Believes Me Now, But I Knew Nothing," *Guardian.*
15. Carol Scott. "Neo-Nazi Group Rallies in Yorktown." *Daily Press.* June 26, 2005.
16. Gervase Phillips. "Antisemitism: how the origins of history's hatred still hold sway today." The Conversation. February 27, 2018.
17. Toni Rodriguez. "Descendants of Holocaust Survivors Have Altered Stress Hormones." *Scientific American.* March 1, 2015.
18. *Disorganizing Experiences in Second and Third Generation Holocaust Survivors.* SAGE Journals. 2011.
19. Olivia Erin Mill. "Stepping Out of the Shadows: Second Generation Holocaust Representation." Trinity University. April 2017.
20. *The Second Generation—The Effects of the Holocaust on the Children of Survivors.* Georgetown University.

AMSTERDAM PUBLISHERS HOLOCAUST LIBRARY

The series **Holocaust Survivor Memoirs World War II** consists of the following autobiographies of survivors:

Outcry. Holocaust Memoirs, by Manny Steinberg

Hank Brodt Holocaust Memoirs. A Candle and a Promise, by Deborah Donnelly

The Dead Years. Holocaust Memoirs, by Joseph Schupack

Rescued from the Ashes. The Diary of Leokadia Schmidt, Survivor of the Warsaw Ghetto, by Leokadia Schmidt

My Lvov. Holocaust Memoir of a twelve-year-old Girl, by Janina Hescheles

Remembering Ravensbrück. From Holocaust to Healing, by Natalie Hess

Wolf. A Story of Hate, by Zeev Scheinwald with Ella Scheinwald

Save my Children. An Astonishing Tale of Survival and its Unlikely Hero, by Leon Kleiner with Edwin Stepp

Holocaust Memoirs of a Bergen-Belsen Survivor & Classmate of Anne Frank, by Nanette Blitz Konig

Defiant German - Defiant Jew. A Holocaust Memoir from inside the Third Reich, by Walter Leopold with Les Leopold

In a Land of Forest and Darkness. The Holocaust Story of two Jewish Partisans, by Sara Lustigman Omelinski

Holocaust Memories. Annihilation and Survival in Slovakia, by Paul Davidovits

From Auschwitz with Love. The Inspiring Memoir of Two Sisters' Survival, Devotion and Triumph Told by Manci Grunberger Beran & Ruth Grunberger Mermelstein, by Daniel Seymour

Remetz. Resistance Fighter and Survivor of the Warsaw Ghetto, by Jan Yohay Remetz

My March Through Hell. A Young Girl's Terrifying Journey to Survival, by Halina Kleiner with Edwin Stepp

---

The series **Holocaust Survivor True Stories WWII** consists of the following biographies:

Among the Reeds. The true story of how a family survived the Holocaust, by Tammy Bottner

A Holocaust Memoir of Love & Resilience. Mama's Survival from Lithuania to America, by Ettie Zilber

Living among the Dead. My Grandmother's Holocaust Survival Story of Love and Strength, by Adena Bernstein Astrowsky

Heart Songs. A Holocaust Memoir, by Barbara Gilford

Shoes of the Shoah. The Tomorrow of Yesterday, by Dorothy Pierce

Hidden in Berlin. A Holocaust Memoir, by Evelyn Joseph Grossman

Separated Together. The Incredible True WWII Story of Soulmates Stranded an Ocean Apart, by Kenneth P. Price, Ph.D.

The Man Across the River. The incredible story of one man's will to survive the Holocaust, by Zvi Wiesenfeld

If Anyone Calls, Tell Them I Died. A Memoir, by Emanuel (Manu) Rosen

The House on Thrömerstrasse. A Story of Rebirth and Renewal in the Wake of the Holocaust, by Ron Vincent

Dancing with my Father. His hidden past. Her quest for truth. How Nazi Vienna shaped a family's identity, by Jo Sorochinsky

The Story Keeper. Weaving the Threads of Time and Memory - A Memoir, by Fred Feldman

Krisia's Silence. The Girl who was not on Schindler's List, by Ronny Hein

Defying Death on the Danube. A Holocaust Survival Story, by Debbie J. Callahan with Henry Stern

A Doorway to Heroism. A decorated German-Jewish Soldier who became an American Hero, by Rabbi W. Jack Romberg

The Shoemaker's Son. The Life of a Holocaust Resister, by Laura Beth Bakst

The Redhead of Auschwitz. A True Story, by Nechama Birnbaum

Land of Many Bridges. My Father's Story, by Bela Ruth Samuel Tenenholtz

Creating Beauty from the Abyss. The Amazing Story of Sam Herciger, Auschwitz Survivor and Artist, by Lesley Ann Richardson

On Sunny Days We Sang. A Holocaust Story of Survival and Resilience, by Jeannette Grunhaus de Gelman

Painful Joy. A Holocaust Family Memoir, by Max J. Friedman

I Give You My Heart. A True Story of Courage and Survival, by Wendy Holden

In the Time of Madmen, by Mark A. Prelas

Aftermath: Coming-of-Age on Three Continents. A Memoir, by Annette Libeskind Berkovits

Monsters and Miracles. Horror, Heroes and the Holocaust, by Ira Wesley Kitmacher

The Glassmaker's Son. Looking for the World my Father left behind in Nazi Germany, by Peter Kupfer

Flower of Vlora. Growing up Jewish in Communist Albania, by Anna Kohen

Zaidy's War, by Martin Bodek

The series **Jewish Children in the Holocaust** consists of the following autobiographies of Jewish children hidden during WWII in the Netherlands:

Searching for Home. The Impact of WWII on a Hidden Child, by Joseph Gosler

See You Tonight and Promise to be a Good Boy! War memories, by Salo Muller

Sounds from Silence. Reflections of a Child Holocaust Survivor, Psychiatrist and Teacher, by Robert Krell

Sabine's Odyssey. A Hidden Child and her Dutch Rescuers, by Agnes Schipper

The Journey of a Hidden Child, by Harry Pila with Robin Black

The series **New Jewish Fiction** consists of the following novels, written by Jewish authors. All novels are set in the time during or after the Holocaust.

The Corset Maker. A Novel, by Annette Libeskind Berkovits

Escaping the Whale. The Holocaust is over. But is it ever over for the next generation? by Ruth Rotkowitz

When the Music Stopped. Willy Rosen's Holocaust, by Casey Hayes

Hands of Gold. One Man's Quest to Find the Silver Lining in Misfortune, by Roni Robbins

There was a garden in Nuremberg. A Novel, by Navina Michal Clemerson

The Girl Who Counted Numbers. A Novel, by Roslyn Bernstein

The Butterfly and the Axe, by Omer Bartov

The series **Holocaust Books for Young Adults** consists of the following novels, based on true stories:

The Boy behind the Door. How Salomon Kool Escaped the Nazis, by David Tabatsky

Running for Shelter. A True Story, by Suzette Sheft

The Precious Few. An Inspirational Saga of Courage based on True Stories, by David Twain with Art Twain

Want to be an AP book reviewer?

Reviews are very important in a world dominated by the social media and social proof. Please drop us a line if you want to join the *AP review team*. We will then add you to our list of advance reviewers. No strings attached, and we promise that we will not be spamming you.

info@amsterdampublishers.com

www.ingramcontent.com/pod-product-compliance
Lightning Source LLC
LaVergne TN
LVHW041907070526
838199LV00051BA/2536